"Had 'Em All the Way"

ALSO BY THAD MUMAU

An Indian Summer: The 1957 Milwaukee Braves, Champions of Baseball (McFarland, 2007)

"Had 'Em All the Way"
The 1960 Pittsburgh Pirates

Thad Mumau

McFarland & Company, Inc., Publishers
Jefferson, North Carolina

All photographs in this book are property of, and used with the permission of, the National Baseball Hall of Fame, Cooperstown, New York.

LIBRARY OF CONGRESS CATALOGUING-IN-PUBLICATION DATA

Mumau, Thad.
    Had 'em all the way : the 1960 Pittsburgh Pirates / Thad Mumau.
       p.   cm.
    Includes bibliographical references and index.

    ISBN 978-0-7864-9711-9 (softcover : acid free paper) ∞
    ISBN 978-1-4766-1937-8 (ebook)

    1. Pittsburgh Pirates (Baseball team)—History—20th century.
I. Title.
GV875.P5M85 2015
796.357'640974886—dc23   2015020599

BRITISH LIBRARY CATALOGUING DATA ARE AVAILABLE

© 2015 Thad Mumau. All rights reserved

No part of this book may be reproduced or transmitted in any form or by any means, electronic or mechanical, including photocopying or recording, or by any information storage and retrieval system, without permission in writing from the publisher.

Front cover: Pittsburgh Pirates second baseman Bill Mazeroski (National Baseball Hall of Fame Library, Cooperstown, New York)

Printed in the United States of America

McFarland & Company, Inc., Publishers
  Box 611, Jefferson, North Carolina 28640
    www.mcfarlandpub.com

For Dahlia, as always

Acknowledgments

I want to thank five people for making this book possible.

First, I remember my dad and his love for baseball. He passed that—as well as the knowledge of how to play the game the right way—along to me. He was a wonderful dad. For all of that, I am most grateful.

I am thankful to my family for love and support in whatever I attempt. I am a huge baseball fan, and an even greater fan of Dahlia and our daughters, Laura and Erika.

Malcolm Kittrell is my cousin and my friend. He was the best youth league baseball player I have ever seen, and I have seen many, many of them. It's a shame a career in the sport did not work out for him. Malcolm was a tremendous help in getting this book written. He knows baseball and he knows grammar, which made him a fantastic proofreader. Making him even more valuable were his knowledge of the game and his following of the Pittsburgh Pirates. I appreciate his time and interest.

Baseball-Reference.com was a vast source for statistics and box scores. The archives of the *Pittsburgh Post-Gazette* and the *New York Times* were superb resources.

Table of Contents

Acknowledgments vi
Preface 1
Introduction 5

ONE. Unlikely Champions 11
TWO. Baseball's Landscape in 1960 20
THREE. Building the Roster 28
FOUR. Making Spring Count 36
FIVE. A Fast Start 43
SIX. The Little Irishman 49
SEVEN. Invasion of the Giants 58
EIGHT. Heart of the Pirates 69
NINE. Staying in Front 81
TEN. A Friend, a Face and the Law 91
ELEVEN. The Great One, Billy and Bob 104
TWELVE. The Road Through Milwaukee 112
THIRTEEN. Dog Days and Doubleheaders 125
FOURTEEN. Bucs' Bench Just Ducky 145
FIFTEEN. Character and Characters 153

Table of Contents

SIXTEEN. World Series Mismatch	162
SEVENTEEN. Six Games of Sparring	170
EIGHTEEN. *The* Game	192
NINETEEN. How It All Happened	201
TWENTY. What Next?	210
Chapter Notes	219
Bibliography	224
Index	225

Preface

It was 1955 when my dad took me to Forbes Field to see my first major league baseball game. I was nine years old.

Our family lived in North Carolina, and every year during Dad's vacation week, we visited Indiana, Pennsylvania, which is about sixty miles to the east of Pittsburgh. Indiana was my dad's hometown and was where his mother and sister lived. It was also the town where I was born.

Baseball had entered my life a couple years earlier when my dad came home from work one day and handed me a paper bag from the Western Auto store. In it was a hunk of dark brown leather that was flat as a pancake and appeared to have five stubby fingers. The Johnny Sain model fielder's glove ignited a romance that is still blazing.

Initially, it was fueled by sessions of throw and catch with Dad almost every evening in our yard. No matter how hard he had worked—and it was always hard because he made a living changing tires the old-fashioned way—when he got home, he would go in the house, put down his lunch pail, have a drink of water, and return with his battered old catcher's mitt that he had from his high school days. I was waiting with my glove and a baseball.

While tossing the ball back and forth, my dad taught me fundamentals of the game of baseball. After supper, from the spring through the fall, we listened to Pittsburgh Pirates baseball games on the radio. There was more static than anything else as we strained to hear the action over station KDKA.

More often than not, Dad was disappointed with the game's outcome. He wasn't surprised, though, because the Pirates were terrible. No matter. My dad loved them and he loved baseball even more. Just hearing those games seemed to trigger a certain energy from him.

Preface

What I remember about that first trip to Forbes was that, after batting practice, the batting cage was rolled out to deep center field, where it remained—inside the fence—during the game. I remember that the Pirates took infield, and that their young right fielder made throws to third base and home plate that took my breath away. I can still remember my dad, a smile on his lips, telling me to notice how fast the Pittsburgh second baseman got rid of the ball when practicing double plays.

So it was that five years later, the once downtrodden Pirates were taking the National League by storm. Once again, my dad and I listened to their games on the radio. We had only done that occasionally the past couple years, but this battling bunch of Buccos had grabbed our attention.

The colorful accounts of the games came from Bob Prince and his sidekick, Jim Woods, known to Pirates fans as the Gunner and Possum. Prince's excitement over a big Pittsburgh hit or defensive play was always evident, and it sparked our excitement as well.

When the season stretched into late August and early September, and the Pirates were still leading the National League standings, every game grew more intense. Could they hold on? Could they really do it? Could they win the pennant?

Dad and I wondered those things every night, and when the score was close, we would slide to the edge of our seats in anticipation, trying to help Law or Friend or Face get one more key out or pleading for Clemente or Groat or Skinner to come through with one more clutch hit.

There were times that we almost felt we were there—Forbes Field, County Stadium, Candlestick Park—wherever the Pirates were playing. We even applauded outstanding plays described by Prince and stood a few times when the great Clemente gunned down an adventurous base runner or when Maz somehow completed a double play that had not seemed possible.

We experienced many thrilling moments as our beloved Bucs rallied in the late innings to pull out one victory after another. When that happened, we loved hearing Prince, in that gravelly voice of his, say, "We had 'em all the way."

A few times, when the radio crackled with interference, Dad would

Preface

drive us a little ways to the top of a hill a few miles from our house so we could get a clear signal over the car radio.

It was fun listening to the Pirates come from behind to win again and again. And watching my dad finally get pleasure, and not pain, from being a Pirates fan. I would go to sleep smiling about that.

Those are great memories.

Maz's historic home run was the perfect ending, of course, not just for a very unusual World Series, but for a very wonderful summer for my dad and me.

Which is one of the reasons for this book. The other is that the 1960 Pittsburgh Pirates are simply a downright fabulous story.

Introduction

Pittsburgh's major league baseball franchise dates back to 1882 with a team called the Alleghenies. They played in the American Association until moving to the National League for the 1887 season.

A 23–113 record in 1890 brought a housecleaning and new players such as Peek-A-Boo Veach and Phenomenal Smith. They were so inexperienced that they were officially dubbed the Innocents, but that nickname lasted just one year.[1]

A second baseman named Lou Bierbauer was signed by Pittsburgh following the 1890 season even though he had been playing for the Philadelphia A's, who had left him off of their printed reserve list. Philadelphia protested, claiming the Innocents had "pirated" Bierbauer. Pittsburgh was granted the right to keep him and was tagged with a new nickname in the process. The Pirates moniker stuck.[2]

Pittsburgh played in the first World Series in baseball history, losing to the Boston Pilgrims in 1903. The Pirates returned to the Fall Classic six years later to defeat the Detroit Tigers. Honus Wagner, rated by many as the greatest Pirate of all time, played his first season with the team in 1900 and won the National League batting title with a .381 average.

The Pirates were National League champions from 1901 to 1903 and again in 1909. They did not win another pennant until 1925, when future Hall of Famers Kiki Cuyler, Pie Traynor and Max Carey led a Pittsburgh club that defeated the Washington Senators in the World Series. The Pirates hit .307 as a team, with seven of eight players in the starting lineup batting over .300 and the eighth .298.

After dropping to third place the next season, the Pirates returned to the World Series in 1927 and were massacred. Brothers Paul and Lloyd

Introduction

Waner, eventual Cooperstown inductees called "Big Poison" and "Little Poison," were Pittsburgh's main weapons.

Their opponent had a complete arsenal. The 1927 Yankees are believed by many to be the greatest team in baseball history. Featuring the famous Murderers' Row of Earle Combs, Mark Koenig, Babe Ruth, Lou Gehrig, Bob Meusel and Tony Lazzeri, the Yanks batted .307 as a team and clubbed 158 home runs in winning 110 games. Ruth hit .356 with 60 homers and 165 RBI. Gehrig had a .373 batting average with 47 home runs and 173 RBI. Lazzeri hit .309 with 18 homers and 102 RBI. They finished one-two-three in home runs in the American League.

The Pirates were swept in four games. It would be more than three decades before they made it back into the October spotlight. Following a handful of second-place finishes and mostly mediocrity, things really got bad starting with the 1946 season. Pittsburgh finished seventh or eighth in the eight-team National League ten times in twelve years, placing last seven times from 1946 to 1957. The Bucs' worst year was 1952, when their record was 42–112, 54½ games back of first-place Brooklyn.

Former big league catcher and broadcaster Joe Garagiola felt the 1952 Pirates, for whom he played, deserved the distinction of being the major leagues' worst team ever. "It's not fair to compare us to expansion clubs," he said. "They are bad because they're new. Pittsburgh had been in the National League 65 years when we came along. We finished 22½ games behind Boston, and Boston finished next to last."[3]

"Last-place clubs sometimes have one area where they do better than other clubs," Garagiola said. "Not us. As Branch Rickey said, 'This team finished last on merit.' We clinched last place on opening day ... during the singing of the National Anthem."[4]

But at least the fans had a new hero. Wagner, Cuyler, Traynor, the Waners, Max Carey, Arky Vaughan, and Bob Elliott had been outstanding hitters for the Pirates from their early days through the mid–1940s. But none of them possessed the raw power of Ralph Kiner, a young slugger who arrived on the Bucs' scene in 1946.

Kiner belted 23 home runs as a rookie to lead the National League. It was the first of seven consecutive home run titles he would either win or share. He hit 51 homers in 1947 and a career-high 54 in 1949. During

Introduction

Kiner's reign as home run king, the Pirates played .500 baseball only once, going 83–71 for a fourth-place finish in 1948. Pittsburgh bought slugging first baseman Hank Greenberg from the Detroit Tigers for $75,000 in January of 1947 and made the two-time American League MVP the first National League player to be paid $100,000 for a season. The Forbes Field left field fence was moved thirty feet closer to home plate, creating what came to be known as Greenberg Gardens.

Greenberg had clouted 306 homers in the American League, 58 in 1938. Thirty-six years old and struggling with back problems, he hit 25 home runs in the 1947 season and was released by the Pirates in September.

A 30-year-old second baseman named Danny Murtaugh played his first season in a Pirates uniform in 1948, having come to Pittsburgh in a trade with the Boston Braves the previous November. He had played parts of four seasons with the Phillies, two as a regular, and his best batting average was .273. Murtaugh played 146 games for the Bucs, hitting .290 and knocking in 71 runs. He finished out his career with Pittsburgh, leaving after the 1951 season with a .254 lifetime average and eight career home runs. Six years later, he would again be wearing a black cap with a yellow "P" on it and would play a major role in lifting the Pirates out of their doldrums.

Prior to the 1951 season, Bucs majority owner and president John Galbreath brought in Branch Rickey to run the Pirates. Rickey was well respected in baseball, having organized the farm system that helped make the St. Louis Cardinals a powerhouse and having signed Jackie Robinson and promoted him to play for the Brooklyn Dodgers.

Upon his arrival in Pittsburgh, Rickey told sportswriters that the Pirates had less talent than any team with which he had worked. Still, he was brash enough to predict a pennant by 1954.

That didn't happen, but at least there were some key pieces in place by then. Dick Groat had led the team in hitting as a rookie shortstop in 1952, and Bob Friend was already in his second year in Pittsburgh's pitching rotation. Elroy Face debuted in 1953, starting 13 games, and Bob Skinner was in the lineup almost every day in 1954. Vernon Law returned from the military and to the rotation.

Roberto Clemente was a rookie center fielder the next year, and

Introduction

19-year-old Bill Mazeroski was called up from the minors to play second base in 1956. Things were definitely shaping up for a brighter future. It took a while. Pittsburgh stayed in last place from 1953 to 1955, crawling up a spot to seventh in 1956 and falling back into the basement in 1957.

When Rickey, who was 73, retired to become the Pirates' chairman of the board and team vice-president after the 1955 season, Joe L. Brown, his assistant, was a unanimous choice of the board to take over as general manager. Brown gradually made moves which strengthened the team considerably, and it was his influence, much more than Rickey's, that finally turned the Pirates into a solid ball club. Pittsburgh's 26–26 record over the final two months of the 1957 season gave fans cause to be anxious for the next season to start. There was hope that the Bucs could not only escape the National League basement, but be contenders in 1958.

And they were, despite a sluggish start. The Pirates survived losing streaks of five and seven games in June, evened their record in July, then rode two winning streaks for a 21-12 August. A six-game win streak in September put Pittsburgh 19 games over .500 and within five games of the National League-leading Milwaukee Braves with five games left in the 1958 season.

But the Pirates dropped all five to finish eight games back of the pennant-winning Braves and in second place. Despite the disappointment of falling flat down the stretch, there was hope in Pittsburgh.

The young Bucs, after going from 30 games under .500 to fourteen over in 1958, were picked by some prognosticators to win the National League pennant in 1959. But they fell far short. Their final record was just two games above .500, leaving them in fourth place, eight games out of first. Pittsburgh never made a serious run at contention. In many ways, the 1959 season was exactly what Pittsburgh fans had come to expect of their Pirates. Finishing second the previous year and then being picked to win a pennant was like fool's gold. Hopefulness turned into simply more disappointment following a long string of haplessness.

Two years of better but not good enough painted the Pittsburgh Pirates as a mystery team heading into the 1960 season. They had become a first-division team all right; the question was whether the Bucs could be any more than that.

Introduction

They had potential, but was it first-place potential? Did the Pirates have what it took to play with the defending World Series champion Dodgers, and the Giants and Braves for 154 games? Could they be a legitimate pennant contender? Could the men in black be really good?

The Pirates' answers to those questions made for an exciting 1960 season for them and their fans. As outfielder Gino Cimoli said, "It was just one of those times in baseball when it was our turn. It was a magical season."[5]

ONE

Unlikely Champions

The 1960 Pittsburgh Pirates were a fascinating baseball team, one that seemed to squeeze just about everything possible from its personnel. Men, pretty much nondescript as big league ballplayers to that point, did what good teams do. They picked one another up, took turns on the hero's platform, and collectively and methodically marched through 155 regular-season games and seven more in a tension-charged World Series to win baseball's grandest prize.

The 1960 Pirates did not steamroll anybody; they won by decision, not knockout. They didn't dazzle folks along the way. They shocked almost everyone in the end. Many could not believe what happened. Some still don't believe it.

They were men named Clemente and Groat and Mazeroski, Law and Friend and Face, Smith and Skinner, Virdon and Hoak, Burgess and Mizell, Stuart and Schofield, Nelson and Haddix, Cimoli and Green. With a squat little man named Murtaugh in charge. They wore vest-type baseball jerseys, black undershirt sleeves providing a nice contrast, the black cap with the gold "P" neatly finishing off a simple, smart look. Perfect for baseball men going to work every day. And those Pirates of 1960 were workmanlike.

When analyzing the franchise's meager accomplishments of the immediate past and future, there was little, if any, justification for expecting the emergence of the Battlin' Bucs who quietly ruled that special 1960 season. It truly was a quiet dominance as they spent almost the entire summer atop the National League standings, doing it more with precision than power.

The easy explanation for what the 1960 Pittsburgh baseball team accomplished, a ready-made one-word explanation in the opinion of

"Had 'Em All the Way"

many baseball followers, would seem to be overachievement, but that would be unfair. Maximizing talent is what this club did. Was the Pirates' world championship a surprise? For sure, but then surprises happen all the time in sports. That, as they say, is why they play the games.

Going back to spring training in 1960, Pittsburgh was viewed at best as a fringe contender for the National League pennant, a team that might slip in the back door if injuries and bad seasons did in opponents that were more talented. Opponents like the defending World Series champion Dodgers, the Braves, and the Giants.

There were far too many ifs and shortcomings for the Pirates to be viewed as a consensus pick to capture the flag. Bucs publicity man Jack Berger wrote a story for the *Pittsburgh Post-Gazette* in early April that detailed some of those ifs. "Last year," Berger said, "the Pirates had a lot of injuries, and six of our key players had what we considered 'off' seasons—Bob Friend, Bob Skinner, Dick Groat, Bill Mazeroski, Bill Virdon, and George Witt. If those six players can play up to what they played before, we have as much chance for the 1960 pennant as any other club."[1]

In addition to the ifs, there was the matter of pay cuts. Elroy Face, coming off a famously astonishing 18–1 year out of the bullpen, was the highest-paid Pirate at $35,000 a year after a $10,000 raise. Roberto Clemente saw his salary remain at $17,500 and was not happy. Neither was Bill Mazeroski, whose pay was decreased. Also cut was Dick Groat, who reportedly was bitter.[2]

Not the best way to be starting a season. On the other hand, those players who were upset over what they were paid were more likely to be motivated than discouraged. Motivated to have good years and earn more money the following season. It was the day of one-year contracts in the major leagues, with every negotiation based on "what have you done for me lately?"

The disposition of the Pirates' front office was not particularly happy, either. The ball club was in the tenth year of Branch Rickey's original "five-year plan" for winning a pennant. The disappointment (collapse) of 1959 was on the minds of the men running the team, and they put some of the blame on guys like Mazeroski and Bob Friend being overweight.[3] The Bucs' brass took out its irritation on players in the

ONE. Unlikely Champions

form of pay cuts and also with some new rules, deemed silly "off the record" by those affected. Pirates wives would not be allowed to travel with their husbands on the road. The *Pittsburgh Post-Gazette* reported that manager Danny Murtaugh alleged that there had been "too much sightseeing" in the afternoons before night games.[4]

Perhaps no World Series champion has ever received less respect than the 1960 Pittsburgh Pirates. Although Bill Mazeroski's Series-ending home run is frequently replayed and is arguably the most dramatic finish to a postseason in any sport, the Pirates' triumph itself has, in a way, been treated with disrespect. It is almost as if an invisible asterisk of apology has been placed next to the Pittsburgh title. Kind of like the team is without pedigree.

The word "fluke" has been used so often in discussing the Bucs' triumph that it is practically a reflex. Many accounts leave the impression that their 1960 World Series win over the New York Yankees was almost accidental, that Pittsburgh lucked into the championship. As a matter of fact, many of the Yankees said that was exactly the way they felt; they didn't even bother mincing words. Mickey Mantle sat in the locker room and wept following the seventh game, saying that the best team did not win. He wasn't the only Yankee to voice that opinion.

While there are a great many sports fans who love to see the underdog win, there are probably just as many, if not more, who feel there is something wrong when the mighty don't prevail, when the best team on paper does not prove it in the arena. When Goliath wears pinstripes, plays in the House That Ruth Built, and is loaded with a lion's share of the brightest stars, he is supposed to be the conqueror. Which leads to the assumption that David and his slingshot—in this case, the Pittsburgh Pirates—just got lucky.

Look at New York's winning scores—16–3, 10–0, and 12–0—and it appears that is the case. Sure, the Pirates won the necessary four games, but 6–4, 3–2, 5–2, and 10–9 scores are so comparatively unconvincing. The composite box score would make one think the Yanks ran away with the Series. They outscored the Bucs, 55–27, and outhit them, 91–60, batting a collective .338 to Pittsburgh's .256, and slugging 10 home runs to the Pirates' four.

Maybe it gets down to the individuals, the Yankees strutting a cast of stars while the Pirates' low-budget version was comprised strictly of supporting actors. The 1960 Yankees roster, like so many Yankees rosters down through history, was loaded with big names. They included Mantle, Maris, Berra, Howard, Skowron, Ford, Richardson, and Kubek. The 1960 Pirates had a nice collection of fine players, none of whom were steady headliners, none who had etched a household name among those who religiously followed the National Pastime. They were not exactly marquee material, since Clemente had not yet become "The Great One."

The pages of baseball history are filled with famous lineups. The 1927 New York Yankees featured Murderer's Row, named mostly for the first six hitters who included Combs, Koenig, Ruth, Gehrig, Meusel, and Lazzeri. The Brooklyn Dodgers' Boys of Summer in the 1950s boasted names like Robinson, Reese, Campanella, Hodges, and Snider.

The 1975 Cincinnati Reds possessed what might have been the best balanced one-through-eight group of all time. Among the everyday regulars were guys who hit for power and average, and there were speed guys, too. Rose, Griffey, Morgan, Bench, Perez, Foster, Concepcion, and Geronimo were the "Big Red Machine."

The 1960 Pittsburgh Pirates lineup was not viewed as lethal, dangerous, or famous. None of its members had basked in the summer spotlight. They lacked a big basher and a stolen base threat. There was no superstar to carry the team on his shoulders. The Pirates did not strike fear into the hearts of anyone.

So when Mazeroski's blast cleared the left-center field wall of Forbes Field to defeat the New York Yankees and win Game Seven of the World Series, baseball analysts were left shaking their heads. The baseball world was in shock. When numbers and personnel were compared, the Bucs indeed were not the best team—not even in their own league.

The Pirates, unlike the Dodgers of Brooklyn and Los Angeles, or the St. Louis Cardinals, or the Braves of Milwaukee and Atlanta, have never been darlings of the National League. For much of the past three decades, the Bucs had been cast as buffoons, ne'r-do-wells who frequently occupied the basement. One season, they even wore helmets while playing in the field. It was said by some they did it for their own protection. By the end of the 1950s, they had gained some respectability, but the Pittsburgh Pirates were nobody's pick to win the 1960 pennant.

ONE. Unlikely Champions

When they did, so-called experts believed the Pirates would be laughed right out of the World Series by the mighty New York Yankees.

Instead, the Bucs took the Yankees' best punches, three of them, and pushed the Series to the deciding game. Then, displaying the never-say-die spirit that had been a season-long trademark and getting heroics from a couple of castoffs, the Pirates set the stage for a Hollywood ending. That was provided by Mazeroski, a second baseman who would bronze a Hall of Fame plaque with his glove and quick-draw release on the double play, not with his bat.

Almost anyone who has heard or read anything about World Series lore knows the rest. Mazeroski delivered the home run that wrote the most dramatic Series conclusion of all time and is generally regarded as the most exciting finish to a championship game in any sport.

It broke the Yankees' muscular backs.

There were no good reasons for thinking Pittsburgh would be a candidate to win the 1960 National League pennant. The Pirates had finished fourth in 1959, with not one .300 hitter. No Pirate scored or drove in as many as 80 runs. Only three hit 13 or more home runs. Vernon Law, an 18-game winner, was the only starting pitcher whose winning percentage was above .500. Bob Friend, who led the team in starts, was a 19-game loser. Pittsburgh gave up 29 more runs than it scored.

The Pirates of 1960 did not feature a headline performer. Maury Wills represented a new offensive approach for the world champion Dodgers, who turned to speed as the power faded from Old Time Bums like Gil Hodges and Duke Snider. Hank Aaron and Eddie Mathews gave the Braves the most potent home run duo of all time. The Giants had Orlando Cepeda and the Willies—McCovey, Kirkland, and, of course, the most fabulous all-around player ever in Mays, the "Say Hey Kid." The Cardinals leaned on an old Stan "The Man" Musial and a young Kenny Boyer.

Roberto Clemente was the only member of the 1960 Pirates to achieve superstar status, but that was still in the future. The right fielder was already wowing folks with his rifle arm, but he was just starting to blossom as a hitter—one who would become one of the best of all time.

The rest of the team was comprised of solid, unspectacular types who filled out a roster built more through front office deals than from a farm system that churned out home-grown talent. Mazeroski and double-play partner Dick Groat were emblematic of a blue-collar Pittsburgh team that personified Western Pennsylvania with its coal miners and steel workers. They worked hard for what they got, and so did the Bucs. Groat, Mazeroski, and left fielder Bob Skinner were the only Pirates regulars originally signed by the team. The mainstays of the pitching staff, Law and Friend, were both lifetime Pirates, but the other two starting hurlers and the two top relievers were not. Of the 25 Bucs who played in the 1960 World Series, 16 had initially been signed by other teams.

There were characters on that Pittsburgh club, especially at the infield corners where a tiger and a doctor resided. And there was character, exemplified by a battery comprised of a Mormon pitcher called Deacon and a stubby Southern catcher who neither drank alcohol nor used tobacco. The pitching staff included a left-handed Kitten, a southpaw future Congressman known as Vinegar Bend, and a minuscule relief ace with the swagger of Clint Eastwood. Quail and Doggie were in the outfield, Rocky and Ducky provided help off the bench, and a leather-faced Irishman sat at master control in the dugout. In the press box, broadcasters called Gunner and Possum were as much a part of the team persona as the players.

The 1960 Pirates were unlikely champions.

There are two worthwhile points to make in this regard. First is that intangibles always factor into athletic success. "Heart" is the word most often used to explain lofty achievements by the proverbial underdog. "Desire" is a close second. The Pittsburgh Pirates of 1960 possessed plenty of heart and desire. Don Hoak, their fearless third baseman, set the example, but there were other quieter teammates who played with the same inner drive, the same penchant for winning, no matter the odds—and in the case of the 1960 Bucs, no matter the score late in ball games. Groat, Virdon, Clemente, Skinner, Mazeroski—that year, they all had a propensity to produce in the clutch which translated into a tremendous passion to win.

To imply that their passion was greater in 1960 would not be accurate. To do so would suggest they didn't want to win every year. It's just that—and players understand this explanation better than fans—it is difficult to reproduce the same collective measures of desire, execution,

One. *Unlikely Champions*

and focus every year. It is rare when 25 players maximize all three over a full baseball season that is so long and demanding.

The second point important in analyzing the 1960 Pirates is that they relied upon, and exhibited, terrific teamwork. This is not to be confused with five guys playing together in basketball—sharing the ball, throwing it to the man who is open for a better shot. We all know baseball is an individual sport. The ultimate team concept is when everyone on the roster contributes, consistently does his part. That was the 1960 Pittsburgh Pirates. The perfect example was when the National League MVP went down with an injury for several games, and his replacement played like an All-Star.

Other bench players came through for the Pirates as well, and the starters picked each other up too. They took turns carrying the club for a game or two. Winning streaks featured several players getting the big hit or driving in the big run.

"What we accomplished in 1960," Groat said, "was a total team effort. You hear people saying that, and sometimes there are a couple of guys who have real big years and carry the club practically the entire season. With us, it was literally a different guy every day."[5]

In baseball, teamwork translates to everyone on the team doing his job and well. All 25 guys may not have big statistical years, but they may lay down a sacrifice bunt or hit a ground ball to second to move over a base runner who eventually scores a tying or winning run in a close game. It may mean pitching some seemingly meaningless innings in a long-lost game and giving a worn-out bullpen a much-needed rest. It may mean driving in a crucial run only a few times, but those times proved the difference in critical games. Teamwork in baseball is exhibited more over a season than one game.

The 1960 Pirates' world championship has not always been draped with the same illustrious prose as most World Series winners. Many sportswriters and fans viewed it as an aberration because of the New York Yankees' three lopsided wins over the Bucs and because Pittsburgh's recent baseball history at that time was so dismal.

However, close examination of the team reveals that the Bucs were the cream of the National League crop almost the entire 1960 season. Unexpected, yes. A lucky league title, no. That they out-battled the fabled

"Had 'Em All the Way"

Yankees in all four closely contested Series games was further testament of Pittsburgh's ability to come through when it counted, a quality far more important than a fact sheet full of flashy individual numbers.

"We had 'em all the way" is how Bob Prince, the immensely popular Pirates radio broadcaster, signed off on Maz's heroics and Pittsburgh's world championship. It had been Prince's signature goodbye after Pirates victories of a narrow margin throughout the mystical 1960 season. And the Bucs really did have National League opponents practically all the way. From May 30 on, they sat on top of the league standings every day but one.

Dick Groat put together a 1960 season baseball purists have to love. In addition to earning the National League MVP award and winning the league batting championship, the captain was the ultimate team leader. He executed the hit-and-run in textbook fashion, consistently made the plays at shortstop, and did all the little things that help a team win. Groat led, not with talk, but by example.

One reason some fans may consider the 1960 Pittsburgh success a fluke is that Pirates titles of any kind were few and far between. The Bucs' NL flag was a bit of a surprise for the 1960 season, and when looking back, an even bigger surprise. Their futility was long and legendary.

The Milwaukee Braves had won National League pennants in 1957 and 1958, and they just missed making it three in a row. Los Angeles defeated the Braves in a 1959 playoff, giving the Dodgers their fifth National League flag of the decade. The St. Louis Cardinals, who were in the thick of the 1960 pennant race, won four league championships in the 1940s and are the National League's answer to the New York Yankees in

One. Unlikely Champions

terms of most pennants and World Series titles, with 18 and 10, respectively.

The Pirates, meanwhile, languished at or near the bottom of the National League standings for the better part of a decade.

Prior to 1960, the Bucs had not played in a World Series since 1927. During their 33-year drought, every other National League team, with the exception of Philadelphia, had won at least two pennants. And the Phillies had managed one.

The truth was that the pieces were in place for the Pittsburgh Pirates to make 1960 a very special year. The Bucs would become one of numerous big stories in the dawning of a new decade.

Two
Baseball's Landscape in 1960

Following televised debates that received as much attention as the election itself, John F. Kennedy defeated Richard Nixon in November of 1960 to become the 44th President of the United States.

Cassius Clay, who would earn universal icon status as Muhammad Ali, won his first professional fight. Harper Lee's novel, *To Kill a Mockingbird*, was published; the Beatles debuted in Hamburg, Germany; and people were raving about the movie *Psycho* directed by Alfred Hitchcock.

Baseball in 1960 was equally eventful. Forty-two-year-old Ted Williams socked his 500th home run early in the season and homered in the final at-bat of his career in the fall. The Fenway Park blast on September 28 was the perfect ending for "the greatest hitter who ever lived," a knighthood accorded the Splendid Splinter by many knowledgeable baseball people. At the age of 39, Warren Spahn pitched the first of his two career no-hitters, striking out a career-high 15, for his 20th win of the season.

It was one of three no-hitters in the majors in 1960 and was the second time that year the Phillies had been no-hit victims of Milwaukee pitchers. Lew Burdette threw a gem at Philadelphia, and the Cubs' Don Cardwell, a former Phillie, no-hit the St. Louis Cardinals.

July 19, 1960, marked the big league debut of Juan Marichal, a stylish right-handed pitcher from the Dominican Republic and a future Hall of Famer with flair to match his ability. Pitching for the San Francisco Giants, Marichal provided a preview of what was to come as he threw a complete-game one-hitter in shutting out the Philadelphia Phillies. He struck out 12 and set down the first 19 batters he faced in notching the first of his 243 career victories.

Two. Baseball's Landscape in 1960

It was the final year of the majors having two eight-team leagues. Expansion was inevitable, and it began in 1961 with the addition of the Los Angeles Angels and the Washington Senators in the American League. The Senators of 1960 moved to Minnesota and became the Twins. The 10 American League teams played 162 games apiece, eight more than the previous year.

National League teams still played 154 games, moving to 162-game schedules in 1962 when the New York Mets and Houston Colt .45s joined the league. Post-season in the majors had always been synonymous with the World Series. It would not be long before that changed, as expansion was the precursor to the playoffs, used since 1969 to decide league champions.

Today, there are 30 big league teams—nearly twice as many as in 1960—and 10 of them participate in post-season play every year. More teams in the post-season equals more money, with television paying the freight and being given the privilege of helping set dates and times for playoff and World Series games.

Kerry Keene conveyed the feelings of many baseball fans with the title of his book, *1960: The Last Pure Season*. It was the beginning of the end of a wonderful era. Williams was going out, and over the next 10 years, Musial, Mantle, Snider, Spahn, Yogi Berra, Robin Roberts, Nellie Fox, Sandy Koufax, and Don Drysdale would follow.

Baseball would never be the same without them. And it would never be the same with the additional teams. Adding more teams to the major leagues meant more fans could see the grand game. It also meant pitching would be diluted, and that one factor produced a domino effect.

The obvious result was, and still is, that pitchers who are not major league–ready pitch in the major leagues. Some are rushed to the big leagues and either fail or get hurt. Some continue to fill rotation spots because somebody has to do it. Every year, there seems to be a great many job openings for number-five slots.

Before expansion, there was always the opposite in baseball: pitchers who were Triple-A aces sometimes endured excessively long waits for a call-up. It did, however, make for better overall pitching in the majors. With 30 teams, the pitching suffers.

Dick Groat pointed that out. "There are just too many teams today.

"Had 'Em All the Way"

You watch the pitchers and can't believe how many hanging curveballs and hanging sliders they're throwing. These are kids who should sill be in the minor leagues learning how to pitch. But because teams are so short of major-league talent, you have Double-A– and Triple-A–quality players in the big leagues."[1]

The same is true, to a lesser degree, of position players. Simply do the math to see how many additional players have big-league jobs now as opposed to the 16-team days, then check some of the marginal players' minor league stats, and you might wonder what they are doing in The Show. The answer is: filling out 25-man rosters.

Modern-day fans may disagree, but baseball's pre-expansion post-season was more fair than today's in that it rewarded success over the long haul of the regular season. It was clear-cut in terms of deciding a champion. The teams with the best regular-season record in each league met in the World Series. No wild cards, no strung-out playoff schedules, just the ultimate best-of-seven series for the championship.

Of course, teams that finished one game out of first place might feel differently.

Dick Groat wrote the foreword for Keene's book, and said,

> I am very proud to have played back in that era—one that I truly consider a "Golden Age of Baseball." It was so much more of a team game, as opposed to playing for individual glory.[2]
>
> We had a very nice relationship with the fans, with virtually none of the hostilities that seem to exist today. We actually knew a lot of the steady fans who sat in the box seats on a first-name basis. There appears to be a noticeable dilution of talent in the majors today, with players spread throughout thirty teams. If there were sixteen, or even twenty teams, as there were back in my era, no doubt the quality of play would be far better.

Keene wrote,

> How easy it was to follow the game, and to know the teams and their players back in the pre-expansion era. Eight teams in the American, eight in the National. A full schedule of action in the major leagues would yield only eight box scores to examine in the newspaper the following morning! Committing to memory the starting lineups in the [entire] league of one's hometown team was not a particularly daunting task. To attempt the equivalent today would seem to require nearly full-time study.[3]

Two. Baseball's Landscape in 1960

Baseball in the 1960s paralleled a series of tumultuous events that shook the American civilization. The game's rules were altered, first to tame hitters and then to neutralize pitchers. The number of major league teams increased by 50 percent, bringing about a drastic re-structuring of post-season play.

Players gained bargaining strength, allowing them to loosen the club owners' vice-like grip, and by the end of the decade, there was a hint of what would become free agency. Highlighting the dramatic 10-year period was an explosion of African American stars who brought a new level of excitement to baseball. Jackie Robinson integrated the game in 1947, and the next year, his teammate, Roy Campanella, became the second African American to stand out in the major leagues. The following decade saw a parade of African American players who quickly achieved star status: first Don Newcombe, then Willie Mays, Ernie Banks, Henry Aaron, and Frank Robinson. A larger wave of African American stars emerged in the 1960s.

As a result, glossy pictures of Mays, Aaron, Clemente, and Banks were tacked onto kids' bedroom walls, walls that previously had been filled solely with photos of Williams, DiMaggio, Musial, and Mantle, and other white players.

Just two decades earlier, an African American man playing in a big league game for the first time had made headlines. As one African American player after another excelled in the major leagues, people stopped keeping count. Although they were clearly in the minority on big league rosters, African American players comprised a very high percentage of the stars in the 1960s. The rosters for the two 1959 All-Star Games included a total of 13 African American players for the American and National Leagues. In 1969, 23 African Americans were among 59 players selected for one All-Star Game. The difference in those numbers is indicative of the overall increase in African American stars in the majors over that 10-year period.

Memories of the 1960s are filled with unforgettable images: Carl Yastrzemski playing a drive off of the Green Monster perfectly, Sandy Koufax delivering another unhittable pitch, and Brooks Robinson making a backhand stab behind third base. There was electricity in Roberto Clemente unleashing one of his rocket throws, Hank Aaron flicking his famous wrists to send a blast over the fence, Maury Wills swiping one more base, Bob Gibson defiantly daring a batter to dig in, and Willie Mays making a difficult catch look easy.

Aaron, Mays, and Newcombe each won an MVP award, Ernie Banks took two, and Roy Campanella won three of them in the 1950s. Frank Robinson also established himself among baseball's elite players, while Clemente, Wills, Orlando Cepeda, and Willie McCovey began paving their roads to stardom.

Seven of the 10 National League Most Valuable Players in the 1960s were African American, and they were seven different players: Frank Robinson, Wills, Mays, Clemente, Cepeda, Gibson, and McCovey. African American players captured the top four spots in the MVP voting two of those years and comprised four of the top five two other times. Listing the top five players in each year's National League MVP voting to compile a total of 50 for the entire decade (even though some of the names were repeated), 29 of the names belonged to African American players.

The impressive thing about that is that more than 80 percent of the major league players during the decade were white. Almost every pennant-winning effort during the 1960s was fueled by spectacular exploits from African American players, many of whom were just beginning to flirt with greatness. As the decade progressed, names like Marichal, Brock, Stargell, Morgan, and Gibson grew to be recognized. By 1969, a large number of baseball's so-called household names—those of the biggest stars—belonged to African American players.

George Altman, a two-time National League All-Star, offered an opinion as to why so many African American players were standouts in the 1960s. "To tell you the truth, I believe we were just hungry," he said. "African Americans did not have the opportunity to play major league baseball for a long time. When we did, we wanted to be exceptional. I'm not saying the African American players were hungrier than the white ones; it's just that we really wanted to take advantage of the chance we had."

Altman said it was obvious at first glance that Mays, Aaron, Banks, Clemente, and Frank Robinson were great ballplayers, noting that they played exceptionally year-in and year-out, which is what makes a superstar. Pointing to the number of African Americans from the 1960s who went on to Hall of Fame induction, Altman called it "a gold mine," explaining that is why he thinks that era was such a special time. He feels it is amazing that so many of the major league stars and superstars from the 1960s were African American players.[4]

During the 1960s, African American players won seven batting championships, all 10 home run crowns, and eight RBI titles in the National League. Clemente won each of his four batting titles and led all big league hitters with a .328 average for the decade. Aaron, Mays, and McCovey led or shared the lead in homers three times apiece. Aaron led the entire major leagues with 1,107 RBI during the 1960s, while driving in the most runs in the National League in three seasons. Aaron slammed 375 home runs in the decade, second in the majors behind Harmon Killebrew's 393.

African American pitchers were one-two in big league wins for the 10-year period, Juan Marichal recording 191 and Gibson 164. American League African American players won four batting titles, one home run crown, and one RBI title during the decade.

The 1960s were a special time for big league baseball, with the fun launched by *Home Run Derby*, which aired in 1960. The predecessor of the current home run contest that takes place during All-Star Game festivities every year, the original was created for television. Former Cincinnati Reds broadcaster Mark Scott came up with the idea, which proved very popular. Sluggers were pitted against one another in nine-inning games which were home run or nothing. A batted ball that did not go over the fence in fair territory was an out. After three outs, the other hitter took his turn. The winner of each game advanced in what amounted to a tournament.

Games were filmed during winter months at Wrigley Field in Los Angeles. Hank Aaron, Mickey Mantle, Willie Mays, Harmon Killebrew, Ernie Banks, and most of the other slugging stars participated. The money they won was a nice supplement to pay checks that were not huge in those days. Aaron was the overall winner, coming out on top in six of seven games and banking more than $13,000. There was a winner's and loser's share for each game. *Home Run Derby* lasted only one season as Scott passed away and no one else kept it going.[5]

"Had 'Em All the Way"

With the dawning of a new decade, big league baseball had already moved to the west coast. The Dodgers were in Los Angeles and the Giants in San Francisco for the 1958 season. While there was general celebration of the National Pastime spreading from coast to coast, there was sadness in seeing New York City lose two of its three teams. The Mets have since joined the Yankees to provide the city with a team from each league, but there will never be anything to match the days of having the Bums, Yanks, and Giants together.

In February of 1960, the melancholy grew worse. A wrecking ball cranked up in Brooklyn for the purpose of leveling Ebbets Field, a baseball shrine. Roy Campanella watched from his wheelchair. Former Dodgers pitcher Preacher Roe chose not to show up. "I couldn't have taken it," he said.[6]

There have been numerous changes in baseball in the last five-plus decades, several making tremendously greater impact over the long haul than the loss of a ball park. The biggest change is financial. No one could have envisioned the fantasyland figures attached to the payrolls of teams and the salaries of players. With both ballooning out of sight, salaries have become a hot topic, one that never used to be discussed. In 1960, sports pages did not run stories about pay checks, and players didn't talk about them, either. Dick Groat said he and Bill Virdon roomed together for nearly eight years and never discussed salaries. The same was true with Jerry Lynch, another old teammate of Groat's. "I have no idea what either Bill or Jerry ever made," Groat said. "You signed your contract and that was it, a closed chapter."[7]

There are no closed chapters in the lives of pro athletes of the 21st century. Everything is out there. The drama is constant. That is so different from the 1950s and 1960s. Back then, players' values, in the fans' eyes, were based on batting averages and earned run averages, not price tags.

Players today get caught up with the hype and with themselves. While winning remains the goal in any game or sport, that sometimes seems to take a back seat to all of the individual-driven antics, the late-night television highlights, and online-generated conversations.

The 1960 Pittsburgh Pirates, and the other teams of that era, were not sucked down by the obsession for personal glory. Money is a big reason that is now the case. So is a "me" mentality that, while it is most apparent in sports and entertainment, has permeated the country's general population. It wasn't true in 1960, not in society and not in sports. Especially not with the Bucs.

"Nobody in our locker room cared anything about headlines," Pittsburgh utility infielder Dick Schofield said. "We pulled for each other, and we pulled together. We were a real team."[8]

Extensive change was on the way in baseball. Free agency that opened new doors for opportunities to instantly escalate salaries and teams' talent levels; an emphasis on pitching that turned into incredible dominance from the mound; followed by an effort to re-emphasize hitting and run-scoring; and a refreshing offensive approach that was predicated on speed instead of power. All would have visible effects on the game.

On the immediate horizon was parity, at least in the National League, slower to come in the American. After the Dodgers won half of the 1950s pennants, the 1960s awakened with five different NL pennant winners in the first five years. The Yankees continued to roll through the opening five years of the 1960s before losing their American League foothold. When that did happen, a team south of New York sat atop the AL for a while before a drastic shift of power moved all the way across the country to the west coast.

The major league landscape was definitely changing, and the men wearing the black hats—all without fame and fortune—were the good guys, the players who helped start a new era of baseball in a very exciting way.

Three

Building the Roster

Frank Lane traded baseball players like they were baseball cards. As the general manager for six major league teams—the Cleveland Indians, St. Louis Cardinals, Cincinnati Reds, Kansas City Athletics, Chicago White Sox, and Milwaukee Brewers—he made more than 400 trades during his career. He was called "Trader Frank" for good reason; he sometimes made a deal just for the sake of making one.

Two days before Cleveland's 1960 season opener, Lane sent popular Indians slugger Rocky Colavito to Detroit for Harvey Kuenn, who had won the American League batting title the previous year. Colavito had shared the AL home run crown, and Cleveland fans loved him; with his good looks, powerful bat, and rifle arm, he was the city's heart throb. From a purely baseball standpoint, there were not many people in the game who thought the swap was a good one for the Indians. That mattered little to Lane, who made the phrase "Let's make a deal" popular long before the television show of that name.

In August 1960, he traded his manager, sending Joe Gordon from Cleveland in return for Detroit Tigers skipper Jimmy Dykes. At different times, he got rid of future Hall of Fame second baseman Red Schoendienst and Roger Maris, who would break Babe Ruth's single-season home run record. Lane even tried to swap the beloved Stan Musial, but was blocked by Cardinals owner Gussie Busch.

Joe L. Brown did not swing nearly as many trades as Lane, but he pulled off some very shrewd deals and seldom came out on the short end. Brown was the Pirates' general manager for 22 years, all but one in a stretch that saw Pittsburgh play in and win two World Series.

Piecing together the 1960 Pittsburgh Pirates was a masterful construction job, one shared by two different general managers in two dif-

THREE. *Building the Roster*

ferent ways. Branch Rickey, who had built a St. Louis Cardinals powerhouse with a farm system overflowing with prospects, joined the Pirates prior to the 1951 season at the age of 69.

His philosophy with the Cardinals was to sign every youngster he could, with the idea that there would be enough very good players to put together a roster capable of winning championships. It worked, and St. Louis did win World Series titles. In Rickey's short tenure as the Pittsburgh GM, he signed the double-play combination of Dick Groat and Bill Mazeroski, left fielder Bob Skinner, and first baseman Dick Stuart. All four would play significant roles in the Pirates' 1960 pennant drive. Both Groat and Mazeroski were signed as shortstops, with Mazeroski moving to second base.

Rickey's legacy with Pittsburgh, however, was his crafty acquisition of Roberto Clemente from the Brooklyn Dodgers. The date was November 22, 1954, and it was the most important transaction in Pirates history. No one would ever forget that Rickey broke baseball's color barrier with the signing and eventual call-up of Jackie Robinson, who played for the Dodgers and became the first African American in the major leagues. Pirates fans would likewise remember that the man called the Mahatma took advantage of a special

Roberto Clemente was the most talented of the 1960 Pirates. "The Great One" was on the brink of superstardom. His rifle arm was legendary, and he could do it all. He had speed, a potent bat, tremendous defensive ability, and reliability in the clutch. He led the 1960 Bucs in RBI and was second in batting, home runs, and runs scored. He had a hit in all seven games of the World Series. Clemente was to right field what Willie Mays was to center.

draft to pluck Clemente from the Dodgers. Playing for the Pirates, Clemente became the major leagues' first Hispanic superstar.

It was not the first time the Bucs had raided the Dodgers, and it would not be the last. Eight days after the monumental pickup, Rickey grabbed 21-year-old pitcher George "Red" Witt from Brooklyn. He added future relief ace Elroy Face as well, both also through the draft.

Two vital cogs in the Pirates' machine were already aboard before Rickey took over. Pitchers Vernon Law and Bob Friend were the long-standing veterans of the team, Law having signed his contract with Pittsburgh in 1948 and Friend following suit a year later. Both were signed while the Bucs' general manager was Roy Hamey, who would later become better known as the GM of the New York Yankees. Running the Pittsburgh club from 1946 to 1950, Hamey's best move was probably the trade that brought Danny Murtaugh to the Pirates from the Boston Braves along with Johnny Hopp in exchange for Al Lyons, Jim Russell, and Bill Salkeld. Murtaugh, a second baseman, had his best major league season as a Pirate. When he retired, he remained in the Bucs' organization and became very instrumental in their eventual success.

Also signing with Pittsburgh in 1952 was Fred Green, who was from New Jersey. The left-handed pitcher signed at the age of 18 after a workout in Forbes Field. His first pro season was at Brunswick, Georgia, of the Georgia-Florida League, and he won 20 games.

Joe Christopher, a speedy 19-year-old outfielder from the Virgin Islands, was the last player Rickey signed for the Pirates. That transaction took place in 1955.

Eleven of the 25 Pirates who played in the 1960 World Series were brought to the team by Rickey. The other 14 were the result of Joe L. Brown's work, most of it done in the trade market. Ten were acquired in seven separate deals he pulled off, while two were picked up in the Rule V draft and one was signed as a free agent after being released by another club.

Joe Gibbon, a southpaw pitcher, was the exception to Brown's wheeling-and-dealing style of building a team. An All-American basketball player at the University of Mississippi, he was the nation's second-leading scorer for the 1956–57 collegiate season. Gibbon then signed with Pittsburgh and reported to Lincoln, where he led the league in strikeouts despite pitching only half of the season. He was called up by the Pirates in 1959.

Brown's first big trade was one Frank Lane later said embarrassed him. In 1955, Bill Virdon played an outstanding center field for the St. Louis Cardinals, batting .281 with career highs of 17 home runs and 68 runs batted in. Virdon was voted the National League "Rookie of the Year." The next year, when he got off to a slow start, Lane, the Cards' GM, became frustrated and impatient. His trigger finger grew itchy, and he was ready to swap his young outfielder.

Meanwhile, another center fielder, Bobby Del Greco, had hit two home runs in one game for the Pirates against the Cardinals. He was a right-handed hitter, while Virdon batted left-handed. The St. Louis lineup was lefty heavy. So on May 17, 1956, Lane sent Virdon to Pittsburgh. In return, Brown packaged left-handed pitcher Dick Littlefield with Del Greco. Del Greco, who was 23, batted .215 for the Cards and .214 overall for the season. The 25-year-old Virdon, who had been batting .211 for St. Louis, hit .334 with eight home runs in 133 games for Pittsburgh. He finished with a .319 average, second to Milwaukee's Hank Aaron, who led the National League at .328.

In his first trade as a big league general manager, Brown clearly came out on top, not only for the 1956 season but for the long haul, as Virdon enjoyed a far better career than Del Greco. In 1957, Brown made a four-player trade with the Cubs. He swapped first baseman Dale Long and outfielder Lee Walls to Chicago for Dee Fondy, another first sacker, and infielder Gene Baker.

A pair of 1958 transactions by Brown strengthened the Pirates' bench. Pittsburgh swapped infielders Gene Freese and Johnny O'Brien to St. Louis for shortstop Dick Schofield and cash. Schofield, 23, had been the Cardinals' first bonus baby, getting $40,000 five years earlier. A switch-hitting part-timer, he was batting .213 in 108 at-bats at the time of the trade, both career highs. Freese, 24, divided time between second and third base for the Pirates. He showed promise by hitting 14 home runs as a rookie in 1955 and batting .283 two years later, but his meager stats when traded included a .167 batting average and one round-tripper. O'Brien's main claim to fame was that he was one of a set of big league twins—the other was named Eddie—signed as bonus babies by Pittsburgh in 1958. Both played the infield and pitched, with neither achieving appreciable success.

Rocky Nelson was the other 1958 addition. Just 13 days short of his 34th birthday when Brown selected him in the Rule V draft, Nelson was joining his fifth major league team in what would be his second stop in Pittsburgh. There may have been a few snickers from opposing GMs when Brown claimed Nelson from Toronto for $25,000, but the Pirates got the last laugh.

Although there were no comparisons to the impulsive Frank Lane, the young Pittsburgh general manager made one move that rivaled Trader Lane's swap of Colavito.

Brown raised many an eyebrow when he traded Frank Thomas, a Pittsburgh native and a Forbes Field fan favorite, to the Cincinnati Redlegs. It would take more than a year before Pirate followers would see that the deal was a very good one for their team. In fact, it provided three cornerstones of the Bucs' club that would win the 1960 World Series.

Brown made three trades in 1959, one to start the year and two to end it, obtaining five players who would figure prominently in the Pirates' 1960 success. The first would now be called a blockbuster, a seven-player deal with the Cincinnati Reds. The "name" player in the deal was Thomas, who was coming off the most productive season of his career. It earned him a selection to his third All-Star team in five years and a fourth-place finish in National League Most Valuable Player balloting.

He belted 35 home runs and drove in 109 runs in 1958 and was voted by Pittsburgh fans their most popular player.[1] As a 24-year-old rookie, Thomas had hit 30 home runs and had 102 RBI. At 29 years of age, he seemed to be in the prime of his career after averaging 27 homers and 91 runs batted in over a six-year period.

So it was a shock when Bucs fans opened up the sports pages of the *Pittsburgh Press* and the *Pittsburgh Post-Gazette* on the next-to-last day of January in 1959 and read with disbelief that Thomas had been traded. Brown shipped Thomas, pitcher Whammy Douglas, and outfielders Jim Pendleton and John Powers to Cincinnati for third baseman Don Hoak, catcher Smoky Burgess, and southpaw pitcher Harvey Haddix. Pendleton

Three. Building the Roster

and Powers were part-time outfielders, batting a combined .245 with 12 home runs in total at-bats in their combined major league stats at the time of the trade. Douglas was a right-hander whose only season in the major leagues was 1957, when he pitched 47 innings for Pittsburgh, posting a 3–3 record.

In Hoak, the Pirates acquired a fine fielding third baseman, a clutch hitter, and just as important, a fiery player who could inspire teammates and spark a team. Haddix was 22 when the St. Louis Cardinals signed him in 1947. Six years later, he won 22 games for the Cards, and less than two years after that, they traded him to Philadelphia, who dealt him to the Redlegs. Burgess was a wonderful addition. He would form a potent catching platoon with Hal Smith and provide an excellent left-handed bat off the bench.

Brown made two trades five days apart in December of 1959. First, he got outfielder Hal Smith from Kansas City. Then, he acquired Gino Cimoli and right-handed pitcher Tom Cheney from St. Louis for pitcher Ron Kline.

In six years with the Pirates, Kline had never had a winning season, but he was a fan favorite. The right-hander pitched more than 200 innings three years in a row and averaged nearly 12 wins over a four-year span. Pittsburgh fans hated to see him go. Cimoli signed with Brooklyn in 1947 and was 26 years old when he finally played with the Dodgers nine years later. He batted .293 and scored 88 runs in 142 games with Brooklyn in 1957, dropped to .246 the next year, and was swapped to St. Louis in a deal that sent Wally Moon to Los Angeles. Cimoli played in 143 games for the Cardinals in 1959 and hit .279. Cheney signed with St. Louis in 1952, pitched in four games with the Cardinals and had an 0–1 record in 1957, and did not make it back to the big team until 1959, when he again went 0–1.

Brown swapped pitcher Dick Hall, infielder Ken Hamlin, and a player to be named later to Kansas City for Smith. Catcher Hank Foiles went to the Athletics the next week to complete the deal.

Bob Oldis was known as a very good defensive catcher, but he never hit enough to earn much playing time. He was 25 when he arrived in the major leagues in 1953 with the Washington Senators, and he only had 46 trips to the plate in three seasons. He spent the next four years in the minors, changing employers in 1956 when the Yankees bought his contract. Brown picked Oldis in the Rule V draft in November of 1959.

The Pirates' general manager added the final two pieces to the club's world championship puzzle during the 1960 season. In late May, Wilmer Mizell, a left-handed starting pitcher, was swapped from St. Louis to Pittsburgh with infielder Dick Gray for second baseman Julian Javier and pitcher Ed Bauta.

Signed by the Bucs in 1956, Javier was a terrific prospect. He was a smooth fielder who possessed some pop at the plate. He was only 23, four weeks older than Mazeroski. Javier would become an All-Star, but no one was going to move Mazeroski out of the second base position in Pittsburgh. Brown needed another starting pitcher to give the Pirates a shot at winning the National League pennant. Mizell was available after a slow start with the Cardinals, so the deal was made on May 28.

Clem Labine had been a mainstay of the Brooklyn Dodgers pitching staff for several years. Two months into the 1960 season, he was traded by Los Angeles to the Detroit Tigers, who released him exactly two months later. Labine, who was 34, had gone 0–3 with a 5.82 earned run average in the American League. When the Tigers let him go, the New York Yankees called and promised to give him a job when one came open. Brown, who was shopping for bullpen help, called an hour later and told Labine that the Pirates wanted him right away.

For all of the discussion generated by the trades Joe L. Brown made, there was as much, if not more, conversation about a huge deal he did *not* make.

Searching for some power during the winter months following the 1959 season, the Pittsburgh general manager explored the possibility of acquiring Harmon Killebrew from the Washington Senators. When that hit a dead end, Brown talked with Kansas City. A proposed trade would have had Groat, Virdon, starting pitcher Kline, and catcher Hank Foiles going to the A's in return for outfielder Roger Maris, shortstop Joe DeMaestri, and Hal Smith.

Maris, a left-handed hitter, had belted 16 home runs for Kansas City the previous season and had hit 28 in 1958 for the A's and Cleveland Indians. As it turned out, Maris was shipped to the New York Yankees

Three. Building the Roster

with DeMaestri in a seven-player December deal. Brown obtained Smith and sent Foiles to Kansas City in a separate transaction, and he traded Kline to St. Louis.

While Pirates fans may have dreamed of having Maris hitting homers for their team—he swatted 39 in 1960 for the Yanks—they might have had nightmares thinking of what the season would have been like without their shortstop and center fielder. Adding the 100 home runs Maris hit in a two-year span would have been nice for the Bucs' offense, but it is hard to imagine that they would have been as successful if the trade had been made.

It was actually a done deal, Groat said years later. Joe Brown and Danny Murtaugh met with the A's brass and agreed to make the trade. The Kansas City guys asked them to step outside for just a few minutes while they discussed something. Groat said Brown and Murtaugh went out in the hall and shut the door and that Murtaugh told his general manager not to make the trade. The Pittsburgh manager was emphatic in saying he did not want the trade to be made. When they went back into the room, Brown announced that the deal was off.

And that was that.[2]

Groat once said that the 1960 Pittsburgh Pirates were Branch Rickey's team, his feeling based on the fact that Rickey had signed several players who were keys to the club's 1960 success and that the team could never have won a pennant and World Series without them. Clemente, Face, Groat, Mazeroski, and Skinner comprised a strong nucleus.

Brown's trades were just as important, however, with the players he added in the deals being just as instrumental in the 1960 league and world championships. Virdon, Hoak, Burgess, Haddix, Smith, and Mizell were much more than peripheral parts.

Four
Making Spring Count

As the Pittsburgh Pirates arrived for spring training in Fort Myers, Florida, they went virtually unnoticed by the rest of the baseball world.

What the baseball writers saw on the Pirates roster and their Grapefruit League lineup cards led them to make the same old assumption: somebody other than Pittsburgh would win the 1960 National League flag. The Bucs were not even viewed as contenders by most observers. Of 266 writers, only three picked Pittsburgh to win the 1960 pennant. National League players, in a poll taken by *Sport Magazine*, picked the Pirates to finish fourth behind San Francisco, Milwaukee, and Los Angeles.[1]

Arthur Daley of the *New York Times* wrote that the Pirates, the Cincinnati Reds, and the St. Louis Cardinals would be in a scramble for the bottom rung—fourth place—of the National League's first-division ladder. Citing a "rejuvenated" Stan Musial and "one of the finest all-round players in the game" in Vada Pinson, the well-respected Daley picked the Reds for fourth place, the Cards for fifth, and the Pirates for sixth, followed by the Chicago Cubs, with the Philadelphia Phillies destined for the basement. Daley predicted the Milwaukee Braves would win their third pennant in four years, finishing ahead of the San Francisco Giants and third-place Los Angeles Dodgers, who had beaten the Chicago White Sox in the World Series five months earlier.[2]

Being picked for sixth place was a slap in the face for the Pirates, who had shocked everyone by leaping to second place in 1958. Their 84–70 record was the team's best in 14 years. There was a even a parade in downtown Pittsburgh to commemorate such a high finish in the standings, and fans could not wait for the following year. High hopes were rewarded with a 1959 flop, with the Pirates finishing barely above .500.

FOUR. *Making Spring Count*

The 1960 Pirates were a young, but veteran, outfit. The average age of their eight position starters, with Smoky Burgess catching, was 28. It rose to 29 when first baseman Rocky Nelson joined him in a left-handed hitting platoon and dropped a half-year when Hal Smith was behind the plate. Second baseman Bill Mazeroski, at 23, was the youngest everyday player, and he had been a starter for three and a half seasons. Burgess was the oldest at 33, a year older than third baseman Don Hoak. Shortstop Dick Groat was 29, center fielder Bill Virdon and left fielder Bob Skinner were both 28, and first baseman Dick Stuart was 27. Right fielder Roberto Clemente was 25. Smith was 29, Nelson 35, and fourth outfielder Gino Cimoli 30.

Burgess had been in the majors 10 years; Hoak and Groat six each; Clemente, Skinner, Virdon, and Smith five apiece. Nelson had been up and down, spending parts of seven seasons in the big leagues. Stuart had been up for a year and a half. Utility infielder Dick Schofield was only 25, but had been in the major leagues seven years, beginning as an 18-year-old with the Cardinals because he was a bonus baby.

The pitching staff was old in terms of big league experience, but not in age. Bob Friend, 29, had pitched nine years for the Pirates, one more than Vernon Law, who was 30 years old. Harvey Haddix, 34, had eight years of major league service. Elroy Face, 32, had six.

While training in the warm Florida sunshine, the Pirates were looking for answers to several questions. Foremost on manager Danny Murtaugh's list was finding a fourth starting pitcher. Candidates included right-handers Bennie Daniels, George "Red" Witt, Curt Raydon, and Jim Umbricht, and left-hander Joe Gibbon. Witt and Raydon both showed immense promise as rookies in 1958, putting up some nice numbers for a team on the rise. Sadly, neither would ever come close to matching those performances. Witt started 15 games, completed five, pitched three shutouts, had a 9–2 record, and posted a 1.61 earned run average in 1958. The same season, Raydon made 20 starts, pitched two complete games and one shutout, with an 8–4 record and a 3.62 ERA. Both figured to be members of the Pittsburgh rotation for years to come, but they both hurt their arms. In 1959, Witt appeared in 15 games with the Bucs, making 11 starts. He was winless in seven decisions, pitched only 50⅔ innings, and had a 6.93 ERA. Raydon toiled in the minors the entire 1959 season and never returned to the majors. Unable to throw again without pain, he quit baseball and became a policeman.

Daniels, 27, appeared in 34 games with the Pirates in 1959, starting a dozen and compiling a 7–9 record with a 5.45 earned run average. It was very early—March 5 to be precise—when Murtaugh announced that Daniels would be his fourth starter. The Bucs' skipper said that four would normally be enough, but a fifth starter was needed because Haddix could not go with three days rest.[3] Umbricht looked like the obvious choice as the number five man in the rotation. He had a 14–8 record the year before at Salt Lake City, and he was throwing well in the spring. In a late call-up the year before, Umbricht started once, lasted seven innings, and was roughed up by Cincinnati for seven hits and five earned runs. Pittsburgh had obtained him before the 1959 season in a minor league deal with the Milwaukee Braves.

Players and scouts from opposing teams who watched the Pirates during the spring agreed that the club seemed to have enough offense and a strong enough defense to be a formidable National League competitor. They also agreed that pitching would be the key to the Bucs' success and that there were questions surrounding the back side of the rotation. Law was coming off a season that saw him pitch 266 innings. Haddix had worked 224⅓, allowing 189 hits and 49 walks, with a fine 3.13 earned run average. Friend had thrown 234⅔ innings, surrendering 267 hits in losing 19 games. For the Pirates to have any shot at first place, the three workhorses would have to stay healthy and continue to shoulder a large load. And they would have to get some dependable help.

The Pirates also needed some bullpen help. They knew they could count on Elroy Face, but reliable arms would be required to get to the diminutive closer. Left-handers Don Gross and Fred Green had relieved with some success the previous season, but Gross was experiencing arm problems and Green had only 37 innings of big league experience. Other possibilities were little lefty Alvin Jackson and Diomedes Olivo, a 41-year-old rookie southpaw. On March 7, Pittsburgh purchased him from Poza Rico of the Mexican League on the recommendation of scout Howie Haak. Jackson had gotten into eight games with the Pirates and was hit hard.

Right-handed options were Paul Giel, Ron Blackburn, Tom Cheney,

Four. Making Spring Count

and rookie Earl Francis. Giel, a Giants bonus baby whose biggest athletic headlines had been made in college football, was taken by Pittsburgh on waivers at the start of the 1959 season. He pitched seven and two-thirds innings in a season wrecked by a sore arm and was sent down to Columbus, where he split 10 decisions. Cheney had been roughed up in two starts and nine relief appearances with the 1959 Cardinals. Blackburn had pitched in 64 games for Pittsburgh over the past two years, all but two in relief, with a 3.50 ERA, three wins, and four saves. The Pirates began camp with 34 pitchers, 19 on the major league roster and 15 from minor league rosters.

In order for the Bucs to contend for the National League pennant, their outfield would need to be more productive. Expected starters Clemente, Skinner, and Virdon had combined to hit just 25 home runs and drive in only 152 runs the previous season. Clemente had batted .296, but was on the disabled list for a full month. Virdon hit a disappointing .254 and Skinner batted a respectable .280, but that was 41 points below the left fielder's 1958 average. Part of the reason was a back injury sustained in April when Skinner ran into a fence chasing a drive by Hank Aaron. He had fallen into some bad habits at the plate as a result of back pain and never found his normally smooth stroke the remainder of the 1959 season.

During the 1960 spring training, the Bucs proved to themselves that they could win. After losing their first three games, they rallied from an 11–0 deficit to outslug Kansas City, 17–13. They won the next day as Daniels and Umbricht combined to no-hit Detroit. The Pirates reeled off 11 victories in a row and showed a knack for coming from behind to win. It was a knack that would continue throughout their 1960 season.

Pittsburgh then lost six straight before getting three-run homers from Skinner and Clemente to beat Philadelphia. The next day, Joe Gibbon pitched seven innings without allowing an earned run, showing that he might be an able starter. Virdon homered in the spring finale as the Pirates finished 15–10, with only St. Louis better in the NL at 18–8. Witt went seven innings and gave up five hits and two runs, further lifting Murtaugh's spirits.

Pitchers Raydon, Jackson, Cheney, and Ed Bauta were the first

"Had 'Em All the Way"

players cut loose by Pittsburgh in the spring as all four were given minor league assignments on April 4. A few days later, four more hurlers—Francis, Blackburn, Williams, and Bob Lee—were sent down, along with first baseman R.C. Stevens, infielders Julian Javier and Dick Barone, and outfielders Henry Mitchell and Tom Burgess.

Gene Baker, a veteran who played second and third base, signed a Pittsburgh contract after proving his injured left knee was sound. Spring surprises for the Bucs were outfielder Joe Christopher and catcher Danny Kravitz. Christopher tied Virdon for the highest Grapefruit League batting average (.420) among Pirates with at least 30 at-bats, while Kravitz hit .462 in 26 trips to the plate. Gino Cimoli was named by Murtaugh as his fourth outfielder, an indication that Christopher would see very little playing time. The picture was more bleak for Kravitz as he was the fourth catcher behind Burgess and Smith, who would platoon, and Bob Oldis, a fine receiver who was a light hitter.

Paul Giel was recalled from Salt Lake City and added to Pittsburgh's roster. He had looked sharp during the spring, allowing two runs and striking out seven in nine innings of work. After a demotion to the Columbus Jets the previous year, Giel spent the winner learning to throw a slider and a screwball, and having more pitches increased his confidence. The Pirates returned Olivo, the elder rookie lefty, to the Mexican League, and he was then sold to Columbus of the International League.

Joe L. Brown wrote a pre-season article for the *Pittsburgh Post-Gazette*, and in it the Pirates' general manager cited injuries to Baker, Clemente, Mazeroski, Skinner, Burgess, Face, Witt, and Raydon, and said, without making alibis, that they had obviously contributed to the Bucs' 1959 disappointment. "We have a well-balanced club with no definite weakness showing now," Brown wrote. "We have a fine defense, fine speed, and adequate power. If we can keep our starting lineup free from injuries, we're going to please a lot of fans at Forbes Field this summer."[4]

Post-Gazette sports editor Al Abrams, in a column that ran on Opening Day, picked the Bucs to finish second in the National League behind San Francisco.

Four. Making Spring Count

Next to the Giants, I like the Pirates despite a couple of glaring weaknesses. This would be lack of consistent power and fielding deficiency at first base. The majority of experts believe Pittsburgh pitching will be weak because of the trade which sent a starter, Ronnie Kline, to St. Louis. From what I have witnessed at Fort Myers this spring, I look for Bennie Daniels, Jim Umbricht, and Joe Gibbon to more than fill this void.

As to the lack of power, this will be more than made up for by some fine hitting from the top to the bottom of the lineup. I look for Bob Skinner, Dick Groat and Bill Mazeroski to return to their 1958 batting form—and that would keep them on the bases and scoring often.[5]

Mazeroski, after being overweight and hampered by pulled muscles in 1959, shed some pounds and reported in good shape for the 1960 season. Bob Friend also lost weight and appeared to regain the form that made him a 22-game winner in 1958. Virdon hit extremely well during the spring, and he attributed his success to a switch from eyeglasses to contact lenses. Witt pronounced his right arm healthy again and said he was ready to pitch like he had two years earlier. Groat and Skinner, whose back was pain-free, both figured to be .300 hitters again.

As Opening Day approached, Murtaugh announced that he would not go with a set lineup, but would platoon at a couple of positions and would also change the batting order, according to whether the Pirates were facing a right- or left-handed pitcher. The early plan was to use Skinner in the leadoff spot against righties, with Don Hoak batting first when lefties were on the mound. The rest of the batting order would also change accordingly. Burgess would catch and Virdon would play center field against a right-hander. Smith and Cimoli would get the call vs. southpaws.[6]

Murtaugh's approach to spring training was a bit different from most managers'. He was not concerned, or didn't admit publicly to being concerned, about winning exhibition games.[7]

> We won the pennant in spring training. What happened is everybody hit camp at Fort Myers so full of pep and ginger, you'd have thought it was opening day. I figured we ought to save a little of that spirit and base hits for the games that counted later on.
>
> I just cut the veterans' time in the batting cage in half. We had the world's greatest bunch of pouters; they didn't want to miss their swings. But they didn't leave everything in Florida, either. When the season started, it was like opening a cage and letting the lions out.[8]

"Had 'Em All the Way"

An interesting footnote to spring training occurred on April 2. The New York Yankees and Pittsburgh Pirates met for the first and only time that spring. The Yanks took the game, 5–0, at Miller Huggins Field behind the pitching of Bob Turley.[9]

Five

A Fast Start

Pittsburgh opened the 1960 season on April 12 in Milwaukee, with Bob Friend and Warren Spahn as mound opponents. A crowd of nearly 40,000 attended the game at County Stadium. Other National League pitching match-ups that day pitted the Dodgers' Don Drysdale against Bob Anderson of the Cubs, the Giants' Sam "Toothpick" Jones against the Cardinals' Larry Jackson, and Cal McLish of the Reds against the Phillies' Robin Roberts.

The Pirates' opening-day lineup looked like this:

Bob Skinner, left field
Dick Groat, shortstop
Roberto Clemente, right field
Dick Stuart, first base
Don Hoak, third base
Gino Cimoli, center field
Bill Mazeroski, second base
Hal Smith, catcher
Bob Friend, pitcher

The County Stadium faithful had every reason to believe they were helping kick off a championship season. After all, their Braves had neared dynasty status over the past four years, sandwiching two National League pennants between two near-misses. After finishing a game out of first place in 1956, Milwaukee won the National League title in 1957 and 1958, then tied Los Angeles for first place in the 1959 regular-season standings, with the Dodgers taking the playoff series and then the World Series.

The Braves had plenty of pop and pitching as well. They led the National League with 177 home runs in 1959 as Eddie Mathews smashed

"Had 'Em All the Way"

a league-leading 46 and Hank Aaron hammered 39. Warren Spahn and Lew Burdette shared the league lead in wins with 21 apiece. It was the fourth of what would be six straight 20-victory seasons for Spahn, who is the major leagues' all-time winningest left-hander.

The crafty southpaw was in complete control through seven innings. He had a four-hitter going and a 2–0 lead as the Braves scored in the first on an RBI double by Joe Adcock and added a solo home run from Spahn in the seventh. The Pirates drew even in the eighth on a run-scoring single by Skinner and an RBI single from Clemente. Adcock slammed a two-run homer off Elroy Face in the bottom of the eighth, with the Bucs getting a run back on Smith's run-scoring double in the ninth. But their rally fell a run short, and Face was tagged with the loss, equaling his loss total for all of 1959. Pittsburgh outhit Milwaukee, 11–9, but committed two errors and hit into two double plays.

Two days later, the Pirates played their home opener, with 34,064 showing up at Forbes Field. Murtaugh changed his lineup all around, batting Hoak in the leadoff spot, dropping Skinner to third, Clemente to fifth, Cimoli to seventh, and Mazeroski to eighth. The left-handed-hitting Burgess, with Cincinnati right-hander Cal McLish pitching, was behind the plate for Pittsburgh.

Vernon Law was superb. He pitched a seven-hit shutout, walking no one and getting help from three double plays. All three were started with ground balls to the shortstop, who flipped to second, who relayed to first. Groat to Mazeroski to Stuart would become a defensive battle cry.

Pittsburgh's second baseman drove in four runs with a double and a home run. Clemente had five runs batted in on a 3-for-3 day that included a pair of doubles. Groat had three hits and scored three times as the Pirates pounded the Reds, 13–0.

The four-game series continued, with Cincinnati turning the tables and winning, 11–3. Pittsburgh trailed, 2–1, before the Reds scored four runs in the sixth inning off losing pitcher Umbricht. Giving up eight hits, four walks, and six earned runs in 5⅓ innings did not solidify his hold on the number-four starter's job.

April 17 is much too early to be called a turning point in a baseball season, yet that is exactly the way the Pirates would look back on their

Five. A Fast Start

doubleheader sweep of the Cincinnati Reds on that date. They based their feelings not just on the fact that they won both games, but more on the way they won them. Especially the second game. Just over 16,000 were in the Forbes Field stands for the Easter Sunday doubleheader, and they sure got their money's worth. Friend shut out the Reds on four hits in the first game behind two RBI each from Stuart and Clemente, who tripled and homered.

In the nightcap, former Dodgers great Don Newcombe and Raul Sanchez teamed to blank the Pirates on five hits through eight innings. Bill Henry came in to pitch the ninth for Cincinnati, which held a 5–0 lead. Henry, a left-hander regarded as one of the better late-inning relievers in the National League, was able to record just one out. Burgess, Virdon, and Mazeroski all singled, Mazeroski's hit plating the Pirates' first run. Pinch-hitter Hal Smith ripped a three-run home run, cutting the Reds' lead to one. Ted Wieand replaced Henry on the mound and retired Hoak, putting the Reds within an out of victory, before Groat kept the Pirates' hopes alive with a base hit. Skinner followed with a two-run homer that polished off a six-run rally and gave the Bucs a sweep of the twin bill. The comeback evoked memories of the previous season, when 46 of Pittsburgh's 78 wins resulted from the team wiping out a deficit in the sixth inning or later.

Friend thought that day was the building block for the season. He pitched as well in the first game as he ever did in shutting out a Reds team with all of those big bats—Frank Robinson, Vada Pinson, Gus Bell, and Ed Bailey—and he had very good stuff. Despite that, it looked like all the Pirates would get for the day was a split. Then they made that great comeback, one that Friend felt set the stage for the whole season. They came to be known as a come-from-behind team, and he thought it started with that second-game win over Cincinnati.

Friend talked about how the Reds pitchers had Pittsburgh shut out for eight innings, and the Pirates jumped up and scored six runs in the ninth. Not only that, but after scoring four times, they still trailed by a run and were down to their last out. Groat got a hit, Skinner hit it out, and all of a sudden, the Buccos had won. They had swept the doubleheader.

That rally got the Pirates believing, Friend said, adding that it also got the rest of the National League believing that the Pirates were never beaten until the third out in the ninth inning. They fed off that and never gave up the rest of the season. The right-hander said his club came from behind like the old Brooklyn Dodgers teams.[1]

The Phillies arrived in Pittsburgh with a new manager. Eddie Sawyer had resigned after only one game and was replaced by 34-year-old Gene Mauch.

Philadelphia won the first of its three games at Forbes Field, 4–3, as Jim Owens pitched a complete-game three-hitter. Harvey Haddix was sent to the showers in the third inning when the Phils batted around and scored all of their runs. Skinner answered with a three-run blast in the bottom of the third, but the Bucs could not score again despite four errors by Phillies infielders. Paul Giel was outstanding out of the Pittsburgh bullpen, throwing four and a third innings and allowing one hit. The loss, which evened the Pirates' record at 3–3, would be the last by the club in April.

Bob Skinner was often overlooked, but not by opposing pitchers. The lanky left fielder led the 1960 Pirates in extra-base hits and stolen bases and was second in RBI. He hit some big home runs, including a shot that capped a huge Easter Sunday rally the Bucs cited as a turning point in their championship season.

In the middle game, Law pitched his second complete game in as many tries in a 4–2 victory. Hoak had two hits, including a two-run homer, and scored twice as the Bucs made the most of just six hits.

Pittsburgh took the rubber game, 11–5, knocking out Philadelphia starter Curt Simmons in the first inning. Skinner had an inside-the-park home run with a man on, giving him three homers in four games. Smith slugged a three-run home run, and winning pitcher Fred Green hit his

Five. A Fast Start

first major league homer. Clemente and Stuart contributed three singles apiece to a 15-hit attack.

The Braves closed out the 10-game Pittsburgh home stand, and the Pirates swept all three games. Clemente remained red-hot with a two-run homer in the series opener and three hits in the third game. Friend threw a complete game, Haddix pitched into the ninth inning, and Joe Gibbon hurled three innings of shutout relief to win the second game. In Game Three, Skinner and Burgess swatted home runs. Burgess had gone deep the previous night, golfing a Lew Burdette low-and-inside delivery into the right-field stands. The little round man had five hits in seven at-bats in the series.

Pittsburgh began a grueling 19-day road trip in Philadelphia. Being away that long can be disastrous. A team can lose a few, grow dejected, and find itself just looking forward to returning home. On the other hand, a successful road trip can pave the way to a fine season. Friend felt the team's approach to a long trip helped immensely. Most of the Pirates were pretty level-headed; they didn't get overly excited or dejected. That's the way they were all the time. That kind of attitude means a lot when you're playing day after day on the road.[2]

The first game in Philly was rained out, but the two clubs still got together off the field. At least, their general managers did. The Pirates' Brown, in search of a starting pitcher, talked with John Quinn of the Phillies about a possible trade. During the spring, Brown had offered fourth-string catcher Danny Kravitz and utility infielder Dick Schofield to the Phils for relief pitcher Dick "Turk" Farrell. Now, Quinn said, Pittsburgh was seeking a front-line hurler, meaning a starter. One name that popped up was Gene Conley, the former Milwaukee right-hander who had started and relieved. Others mentioned were right-handers Jim Owens and Don Cardwell.[3]

Law and Friend both pitched complete games and improved to 3–0 as the Pirates swept the abbreviated series from the Phillies. Law allowed seven hits in Pittsburgh's sixth consecutive victory, equaling the club's longest winning streak of 1959. Friend tossed a four-hit shutout and struck out 11 as the streak reached seven.

The first of a three-game series in Cincinnati was washed out, depriving Red Witt of his first start. The Pirates made it nine in a row by taking the remaining two games at Crosley Field. Clemente and Mazeroski belted home runs in each contest and drove in seven runs apiece, leading a Pittsburgh offensive barrage that totaled 25 runs and 26 hits in the two games. Mazeroski had six hits, while Clemente slugged a grand slam and a three-run shot. The Pirates right fielder also sparkled defensively in the second game. He gunned down Gus Bell at the plate when the Cincinnati outfielder tried to score from second base on an Ed Bailey single. Clemente also prevented an extra-base hit when he ran down a long drive to right-center off the bat of Eddie Kasko. Those gems helped Law notch his fourth win in as many decisions, all of them nine-inning jobs. A 10-run Pirates second inning in the first game paved the way for Bennie Daniels to earn what would be his only victory of the season.

At the end of April, 11–3 Pittsburgh led San Francisco by a game and a half, with Milwaukee three games back, and St. Louis and Los Angeles both three and a half games out of first place.

Hal Smith and Smoky Burgess, the catchers, led the team in batting with respective averages of .435 and .407, and each had two home runs. Clemente, who was hitting .386, led the club with 22 hits, two more than Groat. Skinner was tops in homers with four and in RBI with 16. Clemente had knocked in 14 runs and Mazeroski had driven in 13.

Murtaugh predicted that 88 wins would win the National League pennant and that the Bucs would remain in the thick of the race all season along with the Giants, Dodgers, and Braves.

Six

The Little Irishman

Casey Stengel was an entertainer, John McGraw was known as "Little Napoleon," and Connie Mack wore a necktie in the dugout. Leo Durocher was always talking, while Walter Alston had very little to say.

All of those managers were successful, proving there is no formula for how to run a ball club. Baseball managers' personalities dictate their individual styles, with flamboyance working for some and a low-key approach for others. The key is to have the players' respect. Being a genius—coming up with innovative strategy—is overrated, with only a handful of games over the course of a season decided by shrewd moves. Charlie Dressen, when he was managing the Brooklyn Dodgers, was quoted as saying that if his players kept the game close, he would figure out a way to win it. Danny Murtaugh, on the other hand, said, "Don't expect me to out-manage anybody. If you keep me close in the eighth inning, I'll blow it every time."[1]

Instead of putting pressure on himself as Dressen did with his statement, Murtaugh took himself off of the hot seat and eased into his job as the skipper of the Pittsburgh Pirates. The old "dumb like a fox" description fit him like a glove, and his constant hound-dog facial expression masked what was a wily countenance that was perfect for dugout leadership.

The ultimate compliment for a manager is to be called "a player's manager." Players love to play for him, knowing he will never criticize them in public or embarrass them in any way. That is not to say such a skipper never gets upset with his players. But he does it behind closed doors, man-to-man. He treats players with respect and always goes to bat for them.

Murtaugh was that way. The Pirates appreciated the way he treated

"Had 'Em All the Way"

them, and they reached down for something extra on the playing field as a result. The little Irishman knew his players and how to get the most from them. "I know what it's like to be cussed in front of the team," Murtaugh said. "It hurts more than it helps. If we do any cussing, it'll be in my little office and private."[2]

"If you did your job," Elroy Face said of Murtaugh, "he just left you alone. If you didn't, he let you know. He knew his players, the ones he had to pat on the back and the ones he had to kick in the butt. He knew everything about them, on and off the field."[3]

The Pittsburgh Pirates Encyclopedia places Murtaugh second behind Fred Clarke in its ranking of the Bucs' all-time managers. In four separate stints as the Pirates skipper, Murtaugh compiled a record of 1,115–950 and a .540 winning percentage, with National League pennants and World Series championships in 1960 and 1971. He led Pittsburgh to division titles in 1970, 1971, 1974, and 1975.

After spending five years of his playing career with Philadelphia, Murtaugh was traded to Pittsburgh. In 1948, his first season with the Pirates, he established career highs with 146 games played, 514 at-bats, 149 hits, 71 RBI, and a .290 batting average. He led National League second basemen in putouts, assists, and double plays, and his fielding percentage was just one point behind league leader Jackie Robinson.

In 1948, injuries limited

Danny Murtaugh was the perfect manager for the 1960 Pirates. His low-key approach, dry sense of humor, and patience reflected his roster. They were ingredients for a locker room filled with friendship and respect, both of which helped mold the "team" personality that underlined late-game comebacks. Murtaugh pretty much let his players play. He was slow to criticize them and never did it to the press.

Six. The Little Irishman

Murtaugh to 74 games, and his batting average fell to .203. Following the 1951 season, he became the player-manager of the Pirates' New Orleans farm team, and it was there that he met Joe L. Brown, the Pelicans' general manager. The two would work together again down the road.

Murtaugh later managed at Charleston, where he was fired in 1955. The next year, he was coaching on Bobby Bragan's staff in Pittsburgh. In 1957, the Pirates dumped Bragan and wanted to name Clyde Sukeforth their new manager, but he said no thank you. Murtaugh was hired for the final two months of the season, and when the Bucs played above .500 in that span, he was invited back.

Possessed with an uncommon modesty and an Irish wit, Murtaugh was known as much for his hangdog looks and his ability to spray tobacco juice on an unsuspecting reporter's shoes as he was for his handling of the pitching staff.[4] Elroy Face, who had been a mediocre starting pitcher, worked exclusively out of the bullpen once Murtaugh took over as the Pittsburgh manager in 1957. Face never started another game in a big league career that lasted 11 more years. "One year," Face recalled, "Stan Musial beat me with a homer in the 10th inning in St. Louis to end my 21-inning scoreless streak. After the game, Danny Murtaugh came by my locker, looked me in the eye and said, 'Relief pitcher, my ass.' I couldn't get mad at Murtaugh because that was his way of making me feel better."[5]

Dick Groat had endured a frustrating relationship with Bragan when he was the Pittsburgh manager. Bragan, who had a habit of blaming players for losses, told writers that the Pirates had a Triple-A infield and, citing Groat's lack of speed, said he was more suited to play third base than shortstop. He stayed on Groat, who found it difficult to relax and just play his game. He felt whatever he did was never enough for Bragan. So it was with great relief that the Bucs shortstop learned Murtaugh had been named manager in August of 1957.

> Danny didn't waste any time. The next day [after he became manager], I read in the papers where Dick Groat and Billy Mazeroski were going to be the Pirate shortstop and second baseman for a long time. Danny told the writers how pleased he was with this combination. All these things were things that hadn't been said over the years by Bragan. It gave me a

phenomenal lift, a whole different mental turnaround. There's no way I can't say I didn't enjoy my five years with the Pirates under Danny. He meant so much to me, particularly in the field of confidence.[6]

Danny Murtaugh was a great leader our title year. He got the best out of 25 players, which is the key to good managing. He handled people exceptionally well and played the game, right down the line. Whether I played in or deep was his decision, but otherwise Danny left me alone. For instance, in all the years he managed me, he never knew my hit-and-run sign or when I was going to put it on. He never asked. No one knew my sign except for the base runner, usually Billy Virdon.[7]

New York Times columnist Arthur Daley personified Murtaugh as a guy who had clawed his way to the top.

The going was rough all the way. As a soldier, he was ambushed by German snipers. As a shipyard worker, he was pinned against a bulkhead by a falling metal plate and had hot rivets dropped inside his shirt. As a volunteer fireman, he barely escaped entrapment inside burning buildings. As a ballplayer, he had to scramble for even bare survival. So when admirers tossed a testimonial dinner for him one winter, they staged a skit: "This Is Your Miserable Life, Danny Murtaugh."[8]

Daley wrote that the Pirates manager was anything but the prototypical tough guy, or, for that matter, the prototypical baseball manager. After all, he drank milk and not beer.

Desperate Danny hardly fits the popular conception of the Captain Kidd type of pirate chief—swaggering, ruthless, domineering, rollicking, and calling for a yo, ho, ho, and a bottle of rum. Instead, he's a mild-mannered man with a placid disposition, a sly sense of humor, a tendency toward self-effacement, an ability to inspire fierce loyalties, a total lack of color, and an ingrained distaste for any drink stronger than ginger ale.[9]

Daley stressed that Murtaugh was the settling influence the young Pirates needed.

When Murtaugh succeeded the brilliant and imaginatively restless Bragan as manager in 1957, it was a stopgap appointment. The Bucs of that season were still young, still in their formative years. They were unsettled by Bobby's daring and impetuous strategic moves. He over-managed them. The easy-going Murtaugh, comfortable as an old shoe, gave them the relaxed feeling they never had under Bragan. He restored confidence and brought out the best in his athletes.[10]

There had been hints in 1958 and 1959 that the Pirates were putting it all together, that young players with promise were realizing their

Six. The Little Irishman

potential. The main reasons for the optimism were maturity and experience, and some of that was due to a manager who believed patience paid off in the long run. "Danny has the patience," Pittsburgh general manager Brown said, "to go along with a player not until he fails, but until he succeeds."[11]

Bob Friend credited his manager with knowing his players well, saying his best asset was his ability to read personalities. Murtaugh handled every player differently, and he gave them all a lot of confidence. The Pirates were a pretty close-knit ball club, and much of that had to do with their manager. There were never closed-door meetings to air things out. There was no need for that because the skipper kept everything relaxed and running smoothly.[12]

Danny Murtaugh was very much a fundamentalist, Groat said. He preached doing the little things and making the routine plays. He also handled people extremely well. People talk about strategy, but the most important things a manager can do are to know his players and handle each one the right way. Murtaugh did that.

Groat credited him with keeping his career alive, recalling that before Murtaugh became the Pirates manager, he was doubting himself, wondering if he belonged in the big leagues. Groat was even wondering if he had chosen the right sport. He always loved basketball and remembered walking the streets in Cincinnati and St. Louis, thinking maybe he should go back to the NBA. He said Murtaugh changed everything, especially the way he felt about himself.[13]

Murtaugh remained even-tempered, and that helped the Pirates to be the same way. They never got too high or too low, whether riding a winning streak or mired in a losing streak.

The Bucs' nine-game win streak ended at St. Louis on the second day of May, a rare one-game visit that saw Elroy Face force in the deciding run by issuing a bases-loaded walk in the ninth inning. Face's record dropped to 0–2, while former Pirate Ron Kline pitched a complete game for his first victory as a Cardinal.

With Pittsburgh holding a one-game edge over the Giants atop the National League standings, Arthur Daley wrote a column in the *New York Times* in which he proclaimed the Bucs' fast jump out of the gate as nothing short of miraculous. He also belittled them. "The extraordi-

"Had 'Em All the Way"

nary start of the Pirates has the experts rubbing their eyes in disbelief," Daley wrote. "They obviously are not that good, but it will take considerable doing to chop them down to size. The class teams are humming along in tight pursuit, meaning the Giants, Braves, and Dodgers."[14]

The *Times* columnist must have felt like a prophet when Pittsburgh dropped one of two games in Chicago and all three in San Francisco, relinquishing the league lead to the Giants on May 8. First, San Francisco's three Willies—Mays, McCovey, and Kirkland—all hit home runs in handing Law his first loss of the season. The next day, Haddix could not hold a five-run lead as San Francisco scored six times in the seventh inning to win. In the finale, the Pirates committed seven errors, three by Groat, in getting stomped, 13–1, as the Giants grabbed a one-game lead in the National League.

Among the headlines in San Francisco newspapers the day after the sweep was this one: "Pirates Leave Stadium in Need of Fumigation." The Bucs' frustrations were further escalated by what they felt was questionable work by the umpiring crew as four Pittsburgh players were given the heave-ho in the three-game series.

When the Pirates made four more miscues and lost their first game in Los Angeles, they had dropped six of seven. The lone win during the slide was a 9–7 slugfest in Wrigley Field, decided by pinch-hitter Bill Virdon's two-run triple in the ninth inning after Clemente had singled, tripled, homered, and driven in three runs. George Witt started for Pittsburgh, but lasted only two innings after giving up six hits, two bases on balls, and six runs, only two of them earned. Murtaugh got excellent work from his bullpen as Umbricht allowed a run in four innings, Green pitched two shutout frames, and Face tossed a scoreless ninth.

The Pirates' win spoiled the Cubs managerial debut of Lou Boudreau, who replaced Charlie Grimm. The pair had switched places, with Boudreau moving from the broadcast booth to the dugout and Grimm trading his uniform for a microphone.

Pittsburgh stopped a four-game slide on May 10 by nipping the Dodgers, 3–2. Law pitched his fifth complete-game victory in improving to 5–1, with Groat playing superb defense as he handled a dozen chances flawlessly. Hal Smith smacked a solo home run and Mazeroski won it with a two-run shot. The win put the Bucs back in gear as they beat L.A.

Six. The Little Irishman

again the next day, then took three out of four from the Braves to finish the road trip with a 10-7 record. In winning the rubber game in Los Angeles, Pittsburgh rallied for five runs in the last two innings to win, 6-3. Trailing by two, the Bucs scored three runs in the eighth after two were out, ex-Dodger Cimoli singling in what proved to be the winning run to beat his old team. Face gained his first victory by throwing three one-hit innings.

May 12 was a Thursday, and Pittsburgh was idle prior to a four-game weekend series in Milwaukee. The club got down to the roster limit by sending two outfielders to the minors, as Joe Christopher went to Salt Lake City and Roman Mejias to Columbus. The moves left the Pirates with four outfielders and four catchers. Kravitz appeared to be the odd man out behind the plate as it was only a matter of whether he would be traded or sent down.

That same day, the Braves nipped the Cardinals, who had lost all 10 of their road games since the season began. St. Louis manager Solly Hemus ripped two phones off the wall in the dugout before steaming into the dressing room. The Cards would fall to 0-12 on the road, dropping their first two games in Chicago, before beating the Cubs in Wrigley Field. That win came in the first game of a doubleheader, but Hemus had more to kick about in the second game as Don Cardwell pitched a no-hitter in Chicago's 4-0 shutout.

Groat went six-for-six, and the Pirates erupted for eight runs in the seventh inning to beat the Braves, 8-2. Groat collected three singles and three doubles in raising his batting average from .277 to .318. Dick Stuart clouted a two-run homer and Mazeroski launched a three-run blast. Friend was the beneficiary of a 17-hit attack, going the distance and allowing five hits for his fourth victory.

However, Bill Mazeroski was carried off the field in the ninth when he injured his right leg sliding into second base. Despite the win, Pittsburgh was two games behind the Giants, who blanked L.A. for their seventh straight triumph. Mazeroski was out of the lineup the following night with a pulled ligament when the Bucs won on a two-run triple by Clemente in the 11th inning. All of Milwaukee's scoring resulted from four solo home runs. The Pirates concluded their road trip of nearly three weeks by splitting a doubleheader with the Braves. Bob Skinner,

Don Hoak, and Stuart homered as the Bucs extended their winning streak to five games before losing the nightcap.

The Pirates were glad to get a day off and to return home for two weeks. A number of Pittsburgh players were hot, none hotter than Clemente, who was riding a 12-game hitting streak that had boosted his batting average to .374. Clemente went hitless in the first game of the home stand, but he still found ways to help the Pirates defeat the Cubs, 11–6. He stole two bases, scored two runs, and made an outstanding running catch.

Friend won for the fifth time, although he was hit harder than he had been all season. Mazeroski returned to the lineup after missing three games to contribute a hit, two runs scored, and an RBI. The win was the first of four straight for Pittsburgh. Law outpitched his old teammate, Kline, and went nine innings for the seventh time in eight starts. The Deacon's record was 6–1 after he beat the Cardinals, 4–2, the sixth outing in which he had allowed two runs or less. Law was helped by a couple of sparkling defensive plays. One by Mazeroski saw the second baseman dive to his right to stab a shot off the bat of Joe Cunningham, and while on his stomach, flip the ball to Groat for a force-out. The other was pulled off—quite surprisingly—by first baseman Stuart, who extended his 6-foot-4 frame to come up with a bullet smacked inside the foul line by Carl Sawatski and then toss to Law covering first.

The victory, which came on May 18, pulled Pittsburgh even with San Francisco. The next night, the Pirates edged ahead of the Giants, taking a half-game lead in the National League standings. Pittsburgh again topped St. Louis, 8–3, while San Francisco did not play. The Bucs returned to sole possession of first place after an 11-game absence. The Roberto Clemente Showcase was on display in the win, featuring his bat and his arm. Clemente had four of the Pirates' 13 hits, with two singles and two doubles, scoring twice and knocking in a run. In the second inning, Cardinals third baseman Ken Boyer ripped a drive off the right-field wall for what looked like a sure double. Clemente, who knew every crevice and cranny on the Forbes Field right-field fence, played the carom perfectly and fired a bullet to Groat at second base. Groat was waiting with the ball and the tag, and Boyer was out.

Al Abrams wrote in his *Pittsburgh Post-Gazette* column that he

Six. The Little Irishman

thought the Pirates had what it took to capture the National League flag, but with one exception.

> As the club is set up presently, it can't go all the way. It's not deep enough in pitching strength to win the pennant. It can win, I add, if a deal is made for a starting pitcher to take his place alongside Bob Friend and Vernon Law. Even then, it will be tough going. Frankly, I'm not as high now on the Pirates as I was this spring at Fort Myers. At the time, I thought either Jim Umbricht or Bennie Daniels (or both) were ready to take over starting roles in the mound rotation. So far the two youngsters haven't come up to expectations.[15]

Seven
Invasion of the Giants

It was only May 20, too soon to place too much importance on one series, but there was no telling that to the fans in Pittsburgh. San Francisco was paying a weekend visit to Forbes Field, and the place was quivering with excitement. The Pirates held a half-game lead over the Giants in the National League standings, so there was that. And there was the matter of revenge. The Giants had swept Pittsburgh out on the coast earlier in the month, and followers of the Buccos wanted payback.

A paid crowd of 39,439—the second-largest for a night game in Forbes Field history—was on hand for the Friday night opener. They sure got their money's worth and more. Three free innings and a victory. Lefty Harvey Haddix was masterful as he allowed just four hits over seven and two-thirds innings. He left with a 3–2 lead, turning the game over to Elroy Face in the eighth.

The Baron of the Bullpen got Willie Mays to open the ninth on a foul out to Bob Oldis, who had replaced Smoky Burgess behind the plate. But Willie McCovey quieted the Forbes faithful with a blast to right field, his ninth home run of the season, tying things, 3–3.

It stayed that way until the top of the 12th. Fred Green, the tall southpaw in his third inning of work, gave up a two-out, run-scoring single to light-hitting Hobie Landrith, and the Giants had the lead. With Billy O'Dell on the mound for San Francisco, Gino Cimoli pinch hit for Green and grounded out to short. Don Hoak singled to right and came all the way around on Dick Groat's opposite-field double. Score tied. After four nearly flawless innings of relief, O'Dell was done. Three hitters later, so were the Giants. Right-hander Billy Loes intentionally walked Bob Skinner and breathed a sigh of relief when Dick Stuart's fly ball was gathered in by left fielder Orlando Cepeda at the base of the scoreboard.

Seven. *Invasion of the Giants*

Roberto Clemente then laced a hard two-out single to right field that plated Groat with the game-winner. It was Clemente's third hit of the game and his second run batted in, raising his batting average to .378 and the Pirates' league lead to a game and a half. In 32 games, the Bucs right fielder had 31 RBI. There was such euphoria over the victory that, as the crowd trooped out of Forbes Field, one would have thought the Pirates had won the pennant.

Game Two of the series was a pitchers' duel won by Giants southpaw Johnny Antonelli. Cepeda provided him with all the runs he needed, hitting a homer off Bob Friend with McCovey aboard in the second inning. The 3–1 win gave Antonelli a lifetime record of 23–10 against Pittsburgh. Clemente knocked in the Pirates' only run in the loss and drove in two more in the rubber game as the Bucs nipped San Francisco, 8–7. In a game held up more than an hour by two rain delays, Pittsburgh trailed, 4–0 and 7–5, before Bob Skinner belted a two-run home run to tie the score in the ninth. Hal Smith won it with a pinch-hit, two-out RBI single in the 11th. Face pitched three scoreless innings for the win. Clemente's three hits gave him seven for the series, along with five runs driven in. The Pirates' lead was one and a half games.

After the game, Danny Murtaugh sat in his clubhouse office with his shoes off and his feet propped on his desk. Shaking his head, he said, "Never walk out on us in the late innings. That's when we get real tough."[1] The three-day series with the Giants drew almost 100,000 fans to Forbes Field.

As Clemente's star reputation grew, so did his aches and pains. Over the course of his career, there was a long list of injuries which sometimes kept the right fielder out of the lineup. Even when he played, Clemente was bothered by nagging injuries. Unfortunately, because he continued to perform at such a high level, there were people—particularly sportswriters—who did not believe Clemente was hurt. Some even wrote that he was a hypochondriac, that his health problems were mostly in his mind. Those charges hurt him deeply.

During his rookie season in 1955, Clemente began to experience back trouble, and it continued throughout his career. He explained that he had a disc out of place, causing him pain. In 1959, he missed nearly two months with a sore elbow on his throwing arm. Because of the problem, he learned to be economical with his throws. If he had to make many of them in a game, the pain would return. So he would frequently use an underhand motion in returning the ball to the infield after catching a fly ball with no one on base.

One of baseball's storied franchises, the Dodgers were a very different ball club from when they were Brooklyn's beloved Bums. As different as the West is from the East, literally, but the transformation was more than geographical. When the team moved from Brooklyn to Los Angeles for the 1958 season, it was already getting old. The "Boys of Summer" were sliding into autumn, and as they did, speed replaced power as the main offensive ingredient. Jackie Robinson was long gone, retiring after the 1956 season rather than report to the hated Giants, to whom he had been traded. In January of 1958, catcher Roy Campanella was in an automobile accident and would be in a wheelchair for the rest of his life. The three-time MVP was the Dodgers' anchor. Their heart was Pee Wee Reese, the captain. For the team's first season in Los Angeles, he was listed as "an infielder," not "the shortstop." It was Reese's final season.

By 1960, the Dodgers' regular lineup did not include Gil Hodges at first base, Duke Snider in center field, or Carl Furillo in right. All three were on the roster when the season began, but Furillo played his last game on May 7. Hodges backed up singles-hitting Norm Larker at first. Snider, moved from center to right the previous season, was now the club's fourth outfielder, though he finished second on the team in home runs that year with 14. The Dodgers, no longer known as sluggers, turned to pitching as their bulwark. It served them well, never better than in that series with Pittsburgh.

But that had not been the case heading into the series. The defending World Series champs were five games under .500 and trailed the first-place Pirates by eight and a half games. Los Angeles had not won back-to-back games in almost a month. Knowing that pitching could change a club's fortunes in a hurry, and that the Dodgers had the arms to do just that, Danny Murtaugh did not want to discuss the Dodgers' troubles. The Pirates' skipper didn't think they would last, and he didn't want to jinx his team by stirring the pot. He knew the Los Angeles pitching staff could roust the Dodgers right out of hibernation.

SEVEN. *Invasion of the Giants*

Sure enough, that is what the L.A. hurlers did. Sandy Koufax, Johnny Podres, and Don Drysdale all threw complete games in a three-game Dodgers sweep, combining to hold the Pirates to three runs and 14 hits.

Koufax, winless in four decisions to that point, pitched a one-hitter and struck out 10. Losing pitcher Bennie Daniels had the only Pittsburgh hit, a second-inning single. Koufax, who was wild early, provided a glimpse of the dominating pitcher he would become. After walking five in the first three innings, he permitted just one base runner over the final six. Daniels gave up four hits in seven innings in what was by far his best outing of the season.

Podres was not as sharp as Koufax, but he made big pitches when he needed them. Thirteen Pirates reached base, but just two scored, one driven in by Clemente. Drysdale scattered five hits in the series finale and got home run support from Don Demeter, John Roseboro, and Frank Howard. Howard, who played the outfield, and first base later in his career, could hit a baseball a long way. Doing so eventually molded him into baseball's Paul Bunyan. One of his tape-measure blasts came in that series-sweeping win over the Pirates. Bob Friend had been scheduled to be Drysdale's mound opponent, but he was sidelined with a throat infection. Jim Umbricht took Friend's place and threw a fastball that Howard deposited into Schenley Park behind the left-field fence at Forbes Field. Travel distance was estimated at 550 feet. A mammoth blast. Howard was a giant of a man. Gentle, humble and well liked by everyone, he would blush as quickly over mention of how far he hit a ball as he would from talk of his swinging and missing a pitch out of the strike zone, which he did a lot. He struck out more than 100 times (with a high of 155)—at a time when that was not so easily accepted—and he sent a large number of baseballs into orbit, one an estimated 560 feet.

Howard, at six-foot-seven and 255 pounds, had been an All-American in basketball and baseball at Ohio State University. He still holds the school record for rebounds in a game with 32. The Philadelphia Warriors picked him in the NBA draft. He had three great nicknames, Hondo, in tribute to a John Wayne movie character, and "The Washington Monument" and "The Capital Punisher" during his stay in D.C.

"Had 'Em All the Way"

The 1960 National League "Rookie of the Year," Howard averaged 24 home runs over five seasons for the Los Angeles Dodgers. Traded to Washington, he hit 237 homers in seven years with the Senators, including 136 from 1968 to 1970—44, 48, and 44. Howard once homered in six straight games and in one stretch, hit 10 home runs in 20 at-bats. He finished with 382 home runs and 1,460 strikeouts, with a career .273 batting average, in 16 years in the majors.

Pittsburgh had a day off after the Dodgers left town, while the Giants were winning their third straight over the Phillies. San Francisco and Pittsburgh had again switched places in the standings, with the Giants on top of the National League and the Bucs a game and a half behind.

Almost from the beginning of the season, there were constant murmurings about the Pirates' shortage in the starting pitching department. Back on April 26, Al Abrams wrote in his column,

> The club needs more pitching.
> There's no getting away from this until the time Bennie Daniels and Jim Umbricht prove they can take regular starting turns on the mound without getting bumped off the majority of the time. Murtaugh can't keep going with Law and Friend alone plus an occasional winning trick from Haddix. Hitting, the type no one thought the Pirates possessed, has carried the team this far. But will it continue?
> Unless negotiations fall through at the last minute, the Pirates will come up with a pitcher through a trade in the near future. Brown has been talking to the Phillies for some time in an effort to pry a pitcher out of them. The chances are good that he will. That is, the chances are good, if the Phils don't change their minds because of their recent victory surge.[2]

Four days later, Pirates beat writer Jack Hernon of the *Post-Gazette* had written more about a rumored Pittsburgh-Philadelphia deal:

> Trade conversation which started during spring training resumed last night as the teams were idled by a heavy rain. Joe Brown still is trying to pry loose a starting pitcher from the Phils and had a talk with local boss John Quinn yesterday.
> Quinn said Brown was interested in a front-line pitcher, "not a sixth or seventh man on the staff." Which would eliminate any interest in a relief hurler, as that's what a "sixth or seventh man" does on a ball club. Don Cardwell and Jim Owens might be tough cookies to get out of this town to set up residence in Pittsburgh. So maybe the guy Quinn is willing to part with would be Gene Conley.[3]

Seven. *Invasion of the Giants*

Conley, a 6-foot-8 right-hander, had pitched for the Milwaukee Braves, helping them win the National League pennant in 1957, before being swapped to Philadelphia.

May 27 was a gray day in Pittsburgh, but it was a bright day for the Pirates. Heavy rains drenched Forbes Field, postponing the game with Philadelphia. The Pirates were idle, but their general manager was not. "The Trade" finally happened, but it wasn't the one the Pittsburgh writers were expecting. Brown finally acquired a much-needed starting pitcher, sending heralded prospect Julian Javier to St. Louis for left-handed hurler Wilmer "Vinegar Bend" Mizell and utility infielder Dick Gray. In announcing the deal, Brown said he was "shooting everything for this year" in trading Javier, a talented second baseman who was playing with Pittsburgh's farm team in Columbus. He would go on to become a two-time All-Star with the Cardinals and help win three pennants.

At the time of the deal, the 29-year-old Mizell had a 1–3 record and a 4.55 earned run average in 55 innings spread over nine starts for St. Louis. Skeptics said it was a terrible move by Brown since Vinegar Bend had apparently soured, with his best days behind him. The day before he was traded to Pittsburgh, however, Mizell pitched seven innings for St. Louis against Milwaukee and struck out 10 Braves. It was the best he had felt on the mound since July of the previous season, when he was selected to the National League All-Star team.

"I was 10–2," he recalled, "and I was pitching when we had a sudden downpour. They didn't get the pitcher's mound covered. When I went back out, on the first pitch I made, my foot slipped out from under me. Man, I felt things pull from my hips to my shoulders. I went on to pitch about seven innings. The next day I got muscle spasms, the kind that squeeze the breath out of you. I struggled through the next spring training."[4]

In reality, the Pirates were getting the old and rejuvenated Vinegar Bend, the one who had averaged more than 11 wins and nearly 194 innings per season in six years with the Cardinals. The 6-foot-3 southpaw won 10 games as a rookie in 1952. He pitched a career-high 224⅓ innings and was a 13-game winner the next season, and went 14–14 in 1954.

"We are shooting for 1960," Joe L. Brown said. "We are giving up one of the finest young prospects in the minor leagues in Javier, but we are trying to do this job in 1960 and let the future take care of itself. In Mizell, we are getting an established major league pitcher with good equipment."[5] Talking about the trade, Murtaugh said, "We gave up a good prospect in Javier, but we're looking at the present in acquiring Mizell. He's got to be of help to us." Harvey Haddix agreed, saying, "It has to be a good trade for the Pirates. When you get an established pitcher and don't give anyone off your own [big league] club, it's a good trade. I understand he had some back trouble last year. If he is sound, we've got ourselves a pretty good pitcher. Especially in this ball park."[6]

A couple days off and the departure of the Dodgers combined to awaken the Bucs' bats a bit. After being virtually silenced by Los Angeles pitching, Pittsburgh resumed a long home stand against the Philadelphia Phillies. The Pirates bounced back to hit the ball hard, erupting for 60 hits in their next five games to close out the month on a winning streak.

Igniting the hot streak was an extra-inning victory over the Phillies. Bob Friend and Philadelphia's Jim Owens matched zeroes for seven innings before the Pirates scored two unearned runs in the eighth. Friend couldn't get anybody out in the ninth, surrendering four straight singles that tied the score. Elroy Face prevented further damage, thanks to Bob Skinner's arm. Face relieved Friend with none out, Jim Coker on first base and Bobby Del Greco on second. Joe Koppe flied out to center, Del Greco moving to third. Pinch-hitter

Wilmer "Vinegar Bend" Mizell was the much-needed fourth piece of the 1960 Pirates' starting rotation. After joining the club in a late–May trade, the left-hander went 13–5 with a 3.12 earned run average, eight complete games, and three shutouts.

Seven. *Invasion of the Giants*

Wally Post lifted a fly ball to left, and Del Greco tagged up and headed home. He didn't make it. Skinner's throw to catcher Hal Smith cut down the potential go-ahead run.

Face pitched three shutout innings and Jim Umbricht two. In the bottom of the 13th, with Phils relief ace Turk Farrell working his fifth inning, Bill Mazeroski lined a one-out single to center field. Pinch-hitter Smoky Burgess, batting for Umbricht, flied to left. That brought leadoff batter Don Hoak to the plate. Mazeroski stole second base, getting himself into scoring position. Hoak, who was 0-for-5, ripped a two-run homer to right. His third home run was the game-winner.

The Sunday afternoon game was far less dramatic. Vernon Law survived three Philadelphia home runs, while the Pirates scored six runs in the first two innings. Robin Roberts was knocked out of the box in the second. Law won for the seventh time in eight decisions. Clemente made a sparkling catch of a sinking line drive that saved two runs. Fred Green came out of the bullpen to pitch two-hit ball over two and two-thirds innings and provided some breathing room by smacking a home run. The win, combined with San Francisco's loss at St. Louis, left the Bucs and Giants dead even atop the National League standings.

The Braves made a one-day stop at Forbes for a Memorial Day doubleheader, but the second game was rained out. They watched their number-one starting pitcher receive almost the identical rough treatment from the Pirates as Robin Roberts got, as Warren Spahn lasted two innings, giving up five runs. Haddix was the beneficiary of a 14-hit attack in an 8–3 Pittsburgh win. Dick Groat had four of the hits, Burgess and Gino Cimoli adding three apiece, with Cimoli getting four RBI. Face came on with one out in the ninth to put down an uprising by Milwaukee, which scored three runs after being shut out for eight innings.

The Pirates capped off a 16–11 May by nipping Cincinnati in 11 innings. It was Pittsburgh's fifth extra-inning win in five tries for the season. The Reds used 23 players, their roster stretched by the extra innings and by the thumb of home plate umpire Frank Secory. Groat had five more hits, giving him nine in two games, and Clemente singled in the winning run. Face won his fourth straight decision, pitching two innings and extending his scoreless-inning streak to $11\frac{2}{3}$ over six appearances.

"Had 'Em All the Way"

Vinegar Bend Mizell made his Pittsburgh debut and was staked to an early lead when the Bucs scored three runs in the first two innings. He pitched into the ninth inning, leaving up by a run with men on first and third and nobody out. Lefty Fred Green retired the side, but not before Cincinnati tied the score. It stayed that way until the bottom of the 11th as Face threw two shutout innings.

Pinch-hitter Burgess opened the inning for the Pirates by drawing a walk from Cal McLish. Bill Virdon ran for Burgess. Left-hander Claude Osteen was brought in to pitch to Bob Skinner, and he walked him. Reds catcher Dutch Dotterer argued the ball-four call by home plate umpire Secory and got tossed out of the game for his trouble.

Following a long delay that saw Reds manager Fred Hutchinson storm onto the field, Groat beat out a bunt to load the bases with no outs. Righty Jay Hook became the eighth Cincinnati pitcher, and Clemente lined a single to center field to plate the game-deciding run. The final was 4–3.

Although he let a win slip away, Mizell's performance against the Reds was the start of one of the most impressive stretches of pitching in the left-hander's career. In winning eight of his next 10 decisions, he beat the Cubs four times and the Giants three. He allowed two or fewer earned runs in the last six of those victories.

After a sour start to the season with St. Louis, Vinegar Bend was making the old change-of-scenery trading theory look mighty good.

The next day, it was announced that Pittsburgh had sent catcher Danny Kravitz to the Kansas City A's for former Bucs catcher Hank Foiles and cash. The Pirates filled the roster spot by recalling outfielder Joe Christopher from Salt Lake City, where he was hitting over .400. The following day, Pittsburgh traded Foiles to Cleveland for outfielder John Powers.

The Pirates' 27–14 record had them in first place, one and a half games ahead of the Giants, who had dropped three of their last four. The only dark spot for Pittsburgh during the month of May was its defense. The Bucs committed 29 errors and only had 11 errorless games. They went through a horrid stretch in which they made 18 errors in seven games. That week was particularly disastrous for Groat, who had five errors in two days and seven in seven games. He then played flaw-

Seven. Invasion of the Giants

lessly for the next 28 games. Dick Stuart lived up to his reputation with an error in three straight games, giving him seven in his last 22 games.

Clemente, whom *Pittsburgh Post-Gazette* sportswriters started referring to as Mr. Clutch late in the month, hit safely in all but three of Pittsburgh's 27 games in May. He was named National League "Player of the Month" after batting .336 and leading the club with 25 RBI. Among Clemente's 39 hits were eight doubles, three triples, and three home runs. Skinner hit safely in 23 games, also batting .336, with six doubles, four triples, and three homers. Groat had 39 hits and batted .315. Mazeroski hit just .230, but belted six home runs and drove in 16 runs.

Murtaugh received a pleasant surprise from Cimoli, who led the team with a .355 batting average. After beginning the season in a platoon with Virdon, Cimoli became the everyday center fielder in May. Virdon struggled with four hits in 26 at-bats in May. Trade rumors started brewing, but Murtaugh would say only that he felt confident Virdon's hitting would come around and that he would make a big contribution.

Pittsburgh's starting pitchers pitched into the seventh inning in 20 out of 27 games, and had 10 in which they lasted at least eight innings. Friend pitched seven or more innings in all six of his starts for the month, while Haddix went six and a third or longer in each of his five starts.

In addition to their perfect record in extra-inning games, the Pirates had already come from behind to win six times after trailing in the seventh inning or later.

> It was a miraculous club. We just wouldn't concede to defeat. It was a case of 25 professionals. Maybe not super spectacular, but they did the ABC things Danny talked about. Sure, we had Clemente, Mazeroski, the best in their field, but there were a lot of us, the Skinners, Hoaks, Burgesses, Virdons, Hal Smiths, all who did a lot of things well, but not the super-great talent. We did the ABC things. We took the extra base, threw the ball to the right base. I can't ever recall Virdon throwing to the wrong base at the wrong time. This club played the way Murtaugh wanted it to. I feel the 1960 Pittsburgh Pirates were as close to the beliefs and philosophies of Danny Murtaugh as any team could be.[8]

"Give me a club that makes those ABC plays every day," Groat quoted Murtaugh, "and I'll show you a club that's going to be a contender." Danny would preach that. Oh, sure, he loved the Mazeroskis who could make the outstanding plays, the Bill Virdons to run down the fly balls, the Bobby

Clementes—but more important, in his eyes, was the team that made the double play when it should, a team that would throw to the right base when it should. Put the ball in the relay man's hands, not giving up the extra base. Danny never fussed about physical errors. Mental errors upset him greatly, which is the right way I feel you should look at baseball.[9]

Friend called the Pirates a team of execution, saying they didn't beat themselves. They usually got runners in from third base with less than two out and got bunts down, and their fielders made the routine plays. Making the routine plays routinely is what a club must do to be strong defensively, Friend said, stressing that it was not the sensational play which characterized a defense because every club gets some of those now and then. It's catching and throwing the baseball, and the Pirates did that. The intangible things win you a lot of ball games, the pitcher noted, saying the Bucs did so many things that never showed up in the box score. That's the way they won.

When a team plays that kind of baseball, Friend said, you can look at its manager. That's where it all starts.[10]

Eight
Heart of the Pirates

Dick Groat and Bill Mazeroski were born 50 miles and nearly four years apart. Joined together in the middle of the baseball diamond on a Pittsburgh Pirates team that was the doormat of the National League, they would become the heartbeat of the 1960 World Champions of baseball.

As the 1960 season slipped into summer and the pennant race began to take shape, National League managers, general managers, and players knew something many fans might not have realized. They knew the Pittsburgh Pirates had a couple of trump cards. Second baseman Mazeroski and shortstop Groat were like granite; they were solid in the field and at bat. Analyses of baseball teams always rate pitching and hitting, with defense often overlooked. Those close to the game have never overlooked it, and the Bucs' double-play combination figured to be a key factor in the chase for the NL championship flag.

Bill Mazeroski was born in Wheeling, West Virginia, the son of a coal miner. His dad, Lew, had a reputation in the Ohio Valley as an outstanding shortstop. When he was 17, Lew Mazeroski was invited to the Cleveland Indians' spring training camp, but he never made it. He lost part of a foot after a quarter-ton rock fell on him. "But there's going to be a Mazeroski in the big leagues yet," Lew declared.[1]

He proved quite a prophet and an equally fine teacher, showing Bill how to field ground balls and how to avoid base runners sliding into second base. Young Bill learned how to turn a double play at a very young age. He also learned how to get rid of the baseball quickly and throw accurately from any position and any arm angle. The Indians, White Sox, Red Sox, and Phillies were the teams showing interest in Mazeroski. He was also offered basketball scholarships to Ohio State,

"Had 'Em All the Way"

West Virginia, and Duquesne. When his dad read about Branch Rickey's reconstruction program in Pittsburgh, he asked Al Burazio, "What about the Pirates?"[2] So Burazio, Mazeroski's high school coach in Tiltonsville, Ohio, drove his star shortstop to a Pirates tryout camp where he was seen by Rickey. The Mahatma loved the way the 17-year-old fielded. He was impressed by his strong arm and his body control.

After Mazeroski graduated from high school in 1954, he signed with Pittsburgh for a $4,000 bonus and was sent to Williamsport, Pennsylvania, in the Class A Eastern League. Although he batted just .235, he was promoted to Hollywood of the Triple-A Pacific Coast League in 1955. But after hitting .170 in 21 games, he was sent back to Williamsport, where he batted .293. He then played winter baseball in the Dominican Republic. Back in Hollywood the next summer, Mazeroski was hitting .306 when he was called up by the Pirates in July of 1956.

He was one of a half-dozen shortstops at the Pirates' 1955 spring training camp. One day, for an intrasquad game, he was moved to second base. "Some left-handed pull hitter hit a ball to the shortstop," Mazeroski recalled. "I was playing way over. I ran to second base, caught the ball and threw it to first, all in one motion. Branch Rickey saw that and said, 'Leave that kid at second. He is now a second baseman.' That's how I became a second baseman in professional ball."[3]

Bill Mazeroski will forever be remembered for hitting THE home run in the 1960 World Series and for his quick release when turning a double play. "The Prince of the Pivot" was an outstanding all-around second baseman and a fine hitter out of the No. 8 hole in the lineup—keeping innings alive and driving in runs, even when he couldn't always afford to be very selective.

Eight. Heart of the Pirates

Dick Groat was an All-America basketball player at Duke University. In those days, freshmen could not play Division I varsity football or basketball. So all of his college hoops totals are for three years. He ranks 18th on the all-time scoring list for one of the elite basketball programs in the country, with 1,886 points and a career average of 23 points per game. He averaged 26 points his senior season (1951–1952), when he was named the National College Player of the Year. Groat was an All-America selection as a junior and senior. His jersey No. 10 was the first in Duke athletic history to be retired. He was also a two-time All-America in baseball, playing shortstop and batting .386 his junior season at Duke, .370 as a senior.

Through the years, Groat has emphasized that his first love was basketball, but that his father always wanted him to play baseball and always hoped he could play for the Pittsburgh Pirates. He was a hometown boy, having grown up in Wilkinsburg, Pennsylvania, just a few miles from Pittsburgh. Following his senior baseball season at Duke, Groat signed with the Pirates for a $25,000 bonus and a salary of $5,000 a year for five years. "I remember the negotiations in Mr. Rickey's office," he said. "I had asked him for more than the minimum wage. He smiled, but he wasn't laughing. 'It's unheard of, Dick,' Mr. Rickey said, 'that a rookie would play for more than the minimum!' The fact that my father had wanted terribly to see me play in the major leagues, the fact this was my hometown and I wanted badly to play for the Pirates, meant a great deal to me. The money wasn't nearly as important to me at that time. Just getting to the big leagues was."[4]

Three days after signing, Groat was in the Bucs' starting lineup at shortstop.

He was taken with the third pick of the first round of the NBA draft and played for the Fort Wayne Pistons in 1953, averaging 11.9 points in 23 games. Following his rookie season with the Pirates, Groat missed two years of baseball while serving in the military. When he got out, he planned to continue his NBA career while also returning to the Pirates.

> I promised [Pistons coach Charlie Eckman] I would sign, but only after speaking with Mr. Rickey. Next to my father, no one influenced my life more than Mr. Branch Rickey. I felt in my heart that he would give me his blessing to play both sports, but he had no sense of humor about it. I used

"Had 'Em All the Way"

Gene Conley [who pitched for the Milwaukee Braves and played forward and center for the Boston Celtics] as an example, but Mr. Rickey said, "Conley pitches every fourth day and is just a backup basketball player. You'll play 150 games for us and you would be a starting guard for the Pistons. It's too much."

He couldn't force me to quit, but I wasn't going to fight him. So I gave up basketball. I confess that one reason I chose baseball was that my father didn't like basketball. He loved baseball. He threw out his arm pitching when I was just a boy, and he dreamed of having a son be a major league baseball player. He never missed a game when I was with the Pirates.[5]

Any synopsis of the Pittsburgh Pirates' 1960 season would obviously include Mazeroski's World Series-deciding home run and Groat's Most Valuable Player award. Perhaps more significant, however, were the day-to-day contributions of those two men over the course of 155 games. They formed the nucleus of the team's defense, while stabilizing the top and bottom of the Bucs' batting order with big hits and runs driven in. Maz and Groat. Groat and Maz. They made the Pirates go. Groat frequently ignited the offense by executing the hit-and-run, shooting a single to right field that sent Bill Virdon scampering around to third base. Mazeroski, hitting in possibly the most difficult spot in the lineup, sacrificed batting average points to knock in some awfully big runs from the eighth position.

Neither man was flashy. Both were solid defensively. And, oh boy, could they turn a double play. Mazeroski, of course, was the master, the Prince of the Pivot. He did it so smoothly and so quickly. Someone seeing him make the turn for the first time might blink twice, wondering if maybe he was seeing things, or if he missed seeing something. The Pirates grew accustomed to watching Maz Magic. It was never that his teammates did not appreciate Mazeroski or that they did not marvel at the amazing way he played second base.

When they took the time to think about it, the rest of the Pittsburgh Pirates knew they were watching something special. But because they watched it day in and day out, every day over the course of one long season after another, perhaps they took his excellence for granted. Yet, to a man, each could give a testimonial for the second baseman extraordinaire.

Mazeroski played second base like an extremely talented musician

EIGHT. *Heart of the Pirates*

plays an instrument. That comparison may come the closest to describing the day-in, day-out performances by the Hall of Fame second sacker. He was truly gifted, a virtuoso. The way he operated on the right side of the Bucs infield was a unique combination of grace and ability. His game was polished to a brilliant shine—God-given skill honed by hard work and dedication. He used a small glove (easier to get the ball out) that was so worn that it looked like an old rag. Teammates laughed at it. They wondered why Mazeroski did not use a newer one since he had other gloves broken in. Big leaguers do that during batting practice and infield, saving their "gamers" for actual games.

"I lost my gamer," Mazeroski said, "after the 1960 World Series. Next spring training, I'm using my second glove, and Clemente shows up with my gamer. It had been put in his bag after the Series by mistake. Roberto told me he'd tried to give that old glove away in Puerto Rico. None of the kids would take it."[6]

A seven-time All-Star, Mazeroski had a .983 lifetime fielding percentage. He led the National League in assists nine times and in double plays eight times. He won eight Gold Glove Awards and participated in 1,706 double plays in his 17-year career, all with Pittsburgh. He helped make 161 double plays in 1966 when the Pirates set an NL record with 215.

He had a high fielding percentage, but that does not tell the whole story of Mazeroski and his defense. There have been players whose lofty fielding percentages were misleading because they did not try for a lot of balls, either playing it safe or simply lacking range. Mazeroski had outstanding range, and he tried for everything. As a result, he led the National League in chances eight times and had more than 900 chances five times, with a high of 957 in 1966.

Groat called Mazeroski

> the perfect second baseman for any shortstop that ever lived. I remember Maz as the greatest second baseman that ever played the game. Not just that he turned the double play better than anybody else ever turned it, but he had marvelous range; he had great instincts; he never threw to the wrong base; even his rookie year, his mistakes were so few and far between that it was unreal. He's the greatest defensive second baseman in the history of the game of baseball.

"Had 'Em All the Way"

Groat talked about his double-play partner's extremely strong legs and the way he stayed at the bag despite knowing he was going to get hit. The shortstop said when a ground ball was hit, he would just catch it, get rid of it, and Mazeroski would do whatever had to be done. He had even seen Maz take the throw off the short hop and turn it into a double play. There was no way, in Groat's mind, that anybody could compare with Mazeroski turning the double play. The Bucs captain said his second-base buddy always gave him the ball where he could handle it and never made him a sitting duck on a play at the bag. He said Maz did so many little things better than any second baseman that ever played the game.[7]

Gene Alley was the Pirates shortstop after Groat was traded, and he explained why Mazeroski was called No Touch. "Maz never really caught the ball, never really closed his glove over it, turning the double play. He could tilt his glove at an angle and hold his hand just so. It was a wonder the ball stayed in there—then it would slide out into his hand just like that. He was the only one I saw do it like that. I tell you, he could field a ground ball."

Alley remembered the first time he saw Mazeroski. He was 20 years old, and it was the first time he went to spring training with the Pirates. He watched Maz taking ground balls and thought, "Man, if you have to be this good to be in the major leagues, I'll never make it." Alley said he never saw Maz make a play that looked hard, that Maz could do it and make it look like it was nothing.

Known for his hands, Mazeroski also had quick feet, Alley said, adding that you can't throw the ball unless your feet are planted. That's what made him so quick. He was quick with his hands, but he was quicker on his feet—that's what made him stand out. Mazeroski was not flashy, Alley said, but just went out and played. Guys would slide into him, try to take him out of a double play. He always had cuts and bruises on his legs and shins. He probably didn't play a game when he didn't have something wrong with his legs. Those legs were big and strong, and his first step to the bag was quick.

Alley recalled one day when Pete Rose came down, trying to break up a double play. Maz had caught the ball and stepped to throw. Rose did a block slide and just slid down him, like somebody trying to do a

EIGHT. *Heart of the Pirates*

body block against a tree. "I don't think I ever saw anybody take him out who hurt him," Alley said. "Once Maz had thrown the ball, he would do a little hop. They didn't catch him with his feet planted, which is when runners will hurt you."[8]

Dick Schofield recalled getting to know Mazeroski after being traded from St. Louis to Pittsburgh in 1958.

> I knew who he was. Everybody would talk about how he could make the pivot on the double play better than anybody who had ever played second base. Maz had fantastic hands. He made every play look very easy. You can't teach what he had: his reactions, the unique way he did things. The good Lord gave him these abilities. Maz making the double play was text book. He'd take some throws that would be terrible and still turn the double play. Spectacular was the norm for him. He was unassuming and reliable. You knew he would be there to play, even if he was hurt. Maybe Bill didn't hit as much as most guys in the Hall of Fame. But they didn't play second base like Bill did.[9]

When Mazeroski was selected to his first All-Star team in 1958, American League players stopped what they were doing to watch him during infield practice. National Leaguers already had witnessed his lightning release as he turned double plays. The American League players had heard about it, but they stood awestruck as they saw with their own eyes that No Touch caught the ball and got rid of it like no one else.

Total Baseball includes a statistic called fielding runs that takes into account all major fielding statistics for a player and compares them to the league average. Its purpose is to determine the best fielders. Mazeroski's career total of 362 fielding runs is second only to Napoleon Lajoie, regardless of position. His total player rating (another stat in *Total Baseball* that takes a player's major statistics and puts them into a single calculation in an attempt to rate the best overall players) is 36.3, which ranks him 62nd all time in the major leagues.[10]

Mazeroski was durable. He played in at least 152 games seven times, including 159 in 1962, 162 in both 1964 and 1966, and 163 in 1967. While batting eighth most of his career, he drove in 64 or more runs six times, with a high of 81 in 1962. He hit at least 10 home runs six times, belting 19 in 1958. His lifetime batting average of .260 was achieved with 2,016 hits.

"Had 'Em All the Way"

There were many times that he was less than selective at the plate because of where he hit in the batting order. He swung at bad pitches in an attempt to knock in teammates rather than take a walk and have the pitcher come up next. It was one more example of the kind of team player Mazeroski was. His sub-par 1959 season was caused, in large part, from being overweight. Thinking additional weight would help his batting, and hampered somewhat by a charley horse, Mazeroski fell to a .241 batting average. Two weeks before the 1959 season ended, Pittsburgh general manager Joe L. Brown patted the second baseman on the stomach and said, "You're too fat. Trim down." Mazeroski dropped 10 pounds to his norm of 183 for the 1960 season.[11]

Mazeroski was inducted into the Hall of Fame in 2001, an honor that many baseball people felt was long overdue. During his induction speech at Cooperstown, he thanked the Veterans Committee for voting him into the Hall mainly because of his defensive prowess. Mazeroski did not get much farther into his speech. Overcome with emotion, he broke down crying and left the podium, evoking heart-felt sobs and a tremendous ovation from other Hall of Fame members and fans on hand. His uniform number "9" has been retired by the Pirates.

Like his double-play partner, Groat experienced a bad season in 1959. After he batted .315 and .300 the previous two years, his average plummeted to .275. He rebounded to raise that average 50 points, but more importantly, he was one of the best clutch hitters on a 1960 club that produced big hits in bunches.

Groat was never considered a five-tool player. He wasn't that fast, he didn't have a powerful arm, so on and so forth. What the observers of Groat always did say in his defense was that he had a great desire and phenomenal natural instincts. Always known as a smart ballplayer, he knew hitters and their tendencies. That allowed him to position himself in a way that made up for being a step slower than some shortstops. As a result, he made all the plays, many of them considered routine because of his being in the right place instead of having to range far to field a ground ball.

Groat proved that it's not always the A-plus talents who make great professional athletes. Whatever it was—instinct, desire, intelligence, or natural athletic prowess—Richard Morrow Groat ended his athletic

Eight. Heart of the Pirates

career not only as one of the great shortstops of his era, but as one of the finest college basketball players ever to grace the landscape.[12]

Anybody with even a remote interest in college basketball knows that a guy does not become a star hoops player at Duke University unless he is tremendously talented. Too often, however, people equate the words "talented" and "athletic" to a thoroughbred racehorse. Groat seldom outran anybody. He did outsmart and outmaneuver a lot of folks, on the hardwood and on the baseball diamond. He might not have been fast, but he was quick. He also knew where he was supposed to be before he had to be there.

"Groat didn't have a lot of range," Elroy Face said, "but he was very smart. He played the [shortstop] position really well so the ball was always hit to him. He knew the hitters and how to play them."[13]

"Dick Groat was a student of the game," Mazeroski said. "He played the hitters well, had good hands and an accurate arm. He was great at feeding me for the double play. He also hit .300 most of the time. Dick was a great hit-and-run man who hit to the opposite field with the best of them. A real team player and a winner."[14]

The reason Groat isn't highly regarded by many as a fielder is, in large part, due to his own shrewdness. He knew the hitters and where they usually hit the ball.

"There are two kinds of shortstops," said Alvin Dark, a standout shortstop himself before becoming a major league manager, "the flashy ones and the smart ones. Groat is smart. All I want from my shortstop is to stop the ball and get it away as fast as possible. Groat's fielding doesn't have the fans screaming. But he makes easy plays out of hard ones. I have to say he plays the position as well as anyone I ever saw."[15]

Dark has often been cited by Groat as a huge influence on him and his career. "Alvin and I became close personal friends," Groat said. "He taught me a lot about the hit-and-run and how to play the game. I will never forget it."[16]

Groat was getting spiked frequently by runners going into second base, usually in double-play situations. "I was getting torn to ribbons around second base on double plays," Groat said. "My right leg was all scarred up. I was getting it from everybody—coming in hard at the Pittsburgh rookie."[17]

"Had 'Em All the Way"

Dark was playing for the Giants, and one night after he reached second base, he said to Groat, "I'll see you in the runway after the game."

"After the game," Groat said, "Alvin spent about a half-hour with me. He had gotten a base bag, put it down, and explained to me what I should be doing, how I should be getting away from the spikes. I wasn't making the pivot properly, and Alvin saw this. To take his time like he did was something special for me. Alvin Dark was that kind of player, a class man."[18]

Pittsburgh center fielder Bill Virdon, who roomed with Groat and teamed with him on so many hit-and-run plays, said, "Dick is the player who catches a right fielder too far back and drops a single. The next hitter bounces into what looks like a double play. Dick busts up the double play, keeping a rally alive. You don't read about that in the box scores. But it can mean more than a home run."[19]

"There was never anybody better at handling the bat than Dick Groat," Virdon added. "I didn't get thrown out at second, because if Groat swung and didn't get a hit he'd foul it somehow. Didn't always get me to second base, but he did most of the time."[20]

Groat never played a day in the minor leagues. Branch Rickey had promised him that if he signed with Pittsburgh after he completed his basketball and baseball eligibility at Duke, he would be the Pirates' starting shortstop right away. When Groat signed on June 16, 1952, the Pirates were playing the New York Giants at the Polo Grounds. He pinch-hit on June 19, and the next night he was in the starting lineup. He played in 94 games at shortstop and batted .284 that first season, while making 25 errors. Following two years in the Army, he played almost every day, and he committed 32 miscues in 1955 and 34 in 1956. He hit .315 with a career-high seven home runs in 1957 and batted .300 with 66 RBI the next year.

"Dick knew how to play baseball," Bob Friend said. "When a man was on second base with nobody or one out, he always advanced him to third. It was easy to see from the time he came up that he was going to be a leader. Dick held things together."

When Murtaugh was promoted from coach to manager of the Pirates in 1957, one of the first things he did was to name Groat as the team's captain. "Any time you want to move an outfielder, or do anything

EIGHT. *Heart of the Pirates*

during a game, you can," the new skipper told his 26-year-old shortstop. "Just have a reason for doing it. And if it isn't a good idea, we'll talk it over after the game and decide whether or not to do it again."[21]

Having such responsibility and confidence bestowed upon him was a far cry from the treatment Groat had received from his previous manager, Bobby Bragan. Murtaugh expected his captain to be an example, which meant sometimes being criticized in front of the rest of the team.

> In St. Louis, Danny called me into his suite. "Dick," he said, "you're playing well, doing a super job, but I'm warning you at tonight's clubhouse meeting, you're the one I'm going to make an example of. So, don't be upset. Forget everything I'll say. It's for the benefit of the rest of the team. I'm telling you now I'm going to be on your back." Danny had an awareness that he could do this to me and instead of feeling hurt, I'd accept it as a tremendous compliment.[22]

When Groat was chosen captain, he tried to lead by example. He advanced runners and took strikes to protect runners. He showed that a batter could do all the right things for the team and still hit .300. Something like that becomes contagious.[23]

Talking about his own special gift, his ability to hit behind the runner, to execute the hit-and-run as well as perhaps anyone in major league history, Groat set the record straight on one presumption. He said the idea of him, or anyone else, being able to see who is covering second base—the shortstop or the second baseman—and then hitting into the open area was vastly overrated. Groat said that if a hard thrower was pitching, he would just try to get the bat on the ball, to stay on top of the ball and hit it on the ground. He said it was different with a soft thrower. Then he could kind of pick his hole. He said he was an inside-out hitter, always an opposite-field hitter, even when he played in college. That was natural for him.[24]

A baseball proverb preaches that the double play is a pitcher's best friend. In that sense, the 1960 Pittsburgh staff had 163 "best friends," with Mazeroski involved in 127 of them and Groat 92. The shortstop and second baseman combined to handle 1,576 fielding chances, while committing 34 errors. That is a .978 fielding percentage for the so-called keystone combo, two of the key defensive players on the field.

"Had 'Em All the Way"

They helped win a whole lot of ball games with their defense and did their share on offense as well. Both were clutch hitters who were tough outs with men on base, especially in the late innings of close games.

Groat and Mazeroski were the heart of the Pirates.

NINE

Staying in Front

Any baseball manager will tell you that his ongoing goal is to win the next series. Consistently taking two out of three and three out of four will always mean pennant contention and often will win a pennant.

In the first two months of the 1960 season, the Pirates won 10 of 14 series, lost three, and split one. Two long winning streaks fueled that success. The Bucs won nine straight in April and concluded May with a four-game win string that reached six early in June.

On the first day of June, the Bucs were wrapping up a 14-game home stand and were facing former Pirate Bob Purkey. Cincinnati sent the knuckleballer to the mound in an attempt to split a two-game set. Bob Friend was the starting pitcher for Pittsburgh, which owned a one and a half game lead in the National League. The Bucs scored two runs in the first inning and two more in the third, when they kayoed Purkey. Roberto Clemente doubled in a pair of runs as Pittsburgh rapped out 11 hits. Friend was brilliant. He allowed three hits, all singles, in a 5–0 victory, his sixth of the season. The Pirates concluded the home stand with a 10–4 record, and it was time to go on the road for more than two weeks.

Road trips worried Pittsburgh fans. The previous season, the club was a disaster away from home—15 games under .500, a .403 win percentage. It was no secret that if the Pirates were going to remain in contention for the 1960 National League title, they would have to play better away from Forbes Field.

Pittsburgh had a 10–8 road record in 1959 when it began a 16-game trip June 3 in Philadelphia. It started well. Vernon Law pitched an eight-hitter in winning for the eighth time as the Pirates shut out the Phillies.

"Had 'Em All the Way"

Following a rainout, the teams played a Sunday doubleheader, and the Phils won both games. Dick Stuart's home run was the only Pittsburgh scoring in 18 innings.

After a day off, Law was back on the mound, and the big leagues' top winner didn't have a thing. Neither did his defense. The Bucs committed four errors that helped send Law showers in the second inning, and the Cubs cruised, 13–2.

The long ball and a short reliever got the Pirates back on track.

Elroy Face stood five-feet-eight inches tall, and some Pirates executives had their doubts about that height. There were no doubts about his stature as a relief pitcher. He inherited a full-blown jam in the second game of the series after Bucs starter Vinegar Bend Mizell had pitched six shutout innings. Staked to a 5–0 lead on the strength of a Bob Skinner home run and a Dick Stuart two-run shot, the left-hander began the seventh by walking Walt Moryn. As is the case so often, a free pass to the leadoff man opened the gates for big trouble. Three hits later, the score was 5–2, and Danny Murtaugh was bringing Fred Green in from the bullpen. Green gave up a run-scoring hit and got an out before issuing a walk that loaded the bases.

Exit Green. Enter Face.

The first batter he saw was Ernie Banks, the National League RBI leader at the time. There was only one out, the bases were filled, and the potential tying run was in scoring position. Face got Banks on a pop fly to Bill Mazeroski at second, then completed his escape act as Ed Bouchee bounced back to the mound. To notch his seventh save and help Pittsburgh even the series, Face pitched two and two-thirds scoreless innings. The two-thirds, of course, were the toughest as he had to retire the Cubs' three-four hitters with the bases loaded.

The next day, June 9, Friend earned his seventh victory in the Wrigley Field rubber game, but threw a scare into the Pirates when he departed after seven innings. He felt something in his right groin while pushing off of the pitching rubber. The diagnosis was a slightly pulled muscle, and his condition was listed as day-to-day.

The Bucs lost three of four games in St. Louis, leaving them clinging to a half-game edge over San Francisco. In the losses, Pittsburgh pitchers were pounded. Harvey Haddix and Bennie Daniels were manhandled

NINE. Staying in Front

for seven runs in two innings; the bullpen blew a two-run lead in the ninth; and Mizell gave up three runs in four innings.

The Pirates' lone victory in the series was recorded by Law in the first game of a Sunday doubleheader at Busch Stadium. He became the majors' first nine-game winner and went the distance despite being raked for 13 hits. Stuart belted two home runs and added three singles to drive in five runs. Dick Groat and Smoky Burgess had four hits apiece as Pittsburgh rapped out 23 hits and won, 15–3. Perhaps the most remarkable statistic of the game—in light of the plodding pace which turns most of today's baseball games into marathon-like ordeals—was that it took only two hours and 33 minutes. And that was with the teams combining for 36 hits.

The Pirates arrived in San Francisco with a one-game lead over the Giants and had to win two out of three games to leave the City by the Bay in sole possession of first place. The offense was healthy enough, boasting four of the league's top 10 hitters: Burgess at .367, Clemente at .346 and second in the league with 44 RBI, Bob Skinner at .330, and Groat at .325.

Friend put the Bucs at ease by making his scheduled start, opposing Sad Sam Jones in the first game at Candlestick Park. Jones, a right-hander who possessed a wicked curveball, lasted only five innings. Errors by second baseman Don Blasingame and shortstop Ed Bressoud led to four unearned Pittsburgh runs in the first two innings. Friend threw a complete-game seven-hitter to lift his record to 8–3 as Pittsburgh prevailed, 6–3.

There are not many times a pitcher allows a dozen hits and is still around for the 27th out. But Harvey Haddix did. His nifty 12-hitter earned him the win because the Pirates battered six San Francisco pitchers for 19 hits of their own. The result was a 14–6 rout. Haddix contributed mightily at the plate by getting four hits and knocking in a pair of runs. Groat also had four hits, with Hoak driving in four runs. The down side was the defense. Pittsburgh made four errors, all in the infield.

The following afternoon, Pittsburgh cruised into the ninth inning with an eight-run lead, then had to hold on as the Giants scored five times. Bill Virdon singled in two runs, and Skinner blasted a grand slam. "Doggie" had three hits and five RBI on the day. Fifteen more hits gave

"Had 'Em All the Way"

the Pirates 34 in two games and 42 for the series. Two more errors gave them eight for the series, all by infielders. The sweep in San Francisco increased Pittsburgh's lead over the Giants to four games.

The Bucs traveled almost 400 miles down the coast of California to Los Angeles for a weekend series with the Dodgers. Vernon Law improved to 10–2 in the opener with a six-hitter as he outdueled Stan Williams in what was a historic and comedic day in baseball. On June 17, in the third inning at Cleveland Stadium, with Willie Tasby on first base, Boston's Ted Williams slugged a pitch from Indians right-hander Wynn Hawkins over the wall in left-center field for his eighth home run of the season. More importantly, it was the 500th homer of the "The Kid's" illustrious career.[1]

The comedy was staged at Chicago's Comiskey Park. Earlier in the season, White Sox owner Bill Veeck had unveiled a $300,000 scoreboard that exploded with fireworks when a Sox batter hit a home run. So when Clete Boyer homered for visiting New York, Yankees manager Casey Stengel led the Yankees as they marched around the field carrying lighted sparklers.[2]

A Saturday night Memorial Coliseum crowd of over 50,000 watched Danny McDevitt shut out the Pirates for eight innings. Holding a 3–0 lead, the Dodgers lefty retired the first two batters in the ninth, Roberto Clemente and Dick Stuart, on ground balls. Gino Cimoli kept the Pirates alive with an infield single, and catcher Hal Smith drew them within a run by hitting a two-run homer to left-center. Don Hoak lined a single to left field, and Bill Mazeroski walked. Danny Murtaugh called on Gene Baker to bat for Jim Umbricht, who had relieved Bob Friend after seven innings. Los Angeles manager Walter Alston had seen enough, and he summoned closer Larry Sherry to get the final out. He didn't get it. Not right away, at any rate. Sherry, who threw right-handed, didn't face the right-handed hitting Baker. Instead, it was the left-handed batting Smoky Burgess, one of baseball's all-time best pinch-hitters. Burgess ripped an opposite-field base hit, bringing home Hoak with the tying run. Sherry finally retired the side, and Elroy Face did likewise for Pittsburgh, sending the game into extra innings.

Clemente led off the 10th with a single, moved to second on a one-out walk to Cimoli, and scored on a single by Smith, who grounded the

NINE. Staying in Front

ball sharply between short and third. The part-time catcher had kept the Pirates alive with a two-out, two-run homer in the ninth, then won it the next inning with an RBI single. Face set the Dodgers down in order, and Pittsburgh had its fifth road win in a row.

Bennie Daniels got the start for the Pirates in the L.A. finale. He entered the game with an earned run average of 7.32 and pitched like it. The Dodgers racked him for five earned runs in two and two-thirds innings. They sent 10 men to the plate in a six-run third and had a five-run lead with Sandy Koufax on the mound. Stuart erased all but one run of that lead with a grand slam in the fifth. When Koufax walked the next batter, his day was finished, two outs short of the five innings required of a starter to be credited with the win. The Dodgers picked up a couple more runs and won, 8–6, ending Pittsburgh's five-game winning streak. The Pirates' 9–7 trip left them four games over .500 on the road for the season. They were four games ahead of San Francisco and four and a half in front of the Milwaukee Braves.

There was big major league news away from the stadiums as Bill Rigney was fired on June 18 as the Giants' manager. Tom Sheehan, the 66-year-old director of San Francisco's scouting system, was named as Rigney's replacement. Sheehan had never managed in the big leagues. Rigney, who was in his fifth season in San Francisco, had been rumored on the way out. Leo Durocher, who had managed the Giants

Dick Stuart led the 1960 Pirates in home runs and was third in RBI. Some of his blasts were tape-measure jobs that gave Forbes Field fans a lot to talk about. Unfortunately, so did his poor defense. The first baseman had a few hot streaks at the plate that proved crucial in the Bucs' drive to the National League pennant.

and the Dodgers, was one of those reportedly being considered as his successor.

In announcing the change, Giants president Horace Stoneham said, "It wasn't necessarily that Rigney wasn't managing well, but something had to be done." Rigney had come under fire when San Francisco was swept in a three-game series at home by league-leading Pittsburgh. The Giants had lost eight of 12 games before the move. The 41-year-old Rigney said he was surprised at the firing, but added, "We played bad for several days and then worse for several more."[3]

The Giants won their first game under Sheehan, then dropped five in a row to fall six and a half behind the Pirates and into third place in the National League standings. San Francisco was four back of the Braves, who leapfrogged into second place by winning nine out of 10.

Pittsburgh began a 13-game home stand with exceptional performances by their starting pitchers. Vernon Law matched up with future Hall of Famer Bob Gibson, a hard-throwing right-hander making his first start since being recalled from Rochester. Law was in control through eight innings before giving up three successive St. Louis singles in the ninth. Elroy Face saved Law's 11th victory in a 3–2 win after inheriting a mess in the ninth. The Cardinals had a run in, two runners on base, and no outs. Face picked off Curt Simmons, who was pinch running for Carl Sawatski at second base, and struck out Daryl Spencer and Stan Musial to end the game.

"I hate to think of where our team might have been in 1960 without Elroy Face," said Groat, adding that the little reliever was terribly overlooked and underrated. The Bucs captain said he even thought Face should be in the Hall of Fame. The statistics for saves were different back then. Getting them was not so easy.

There were many times Elroy would come into the game in the eighth, or even the seventh, inning with men on base. Maybe the tying run would be on third and the go-ahead run would be on second. He would get out of that jam and then finish the game, pitching two or two and two-thirds innings. He might be back out there the next night, Groat recalled. "He didn't just come in to start the ninth with nobody on base. He inherited a lot of base runners, a lot of jams, and he was amazing the way he got out of most of them."[4]

NINE. Staying in Front

Friend also lauded the Pirates' relief ace, saying they had Face, and he got Pittsburgh out of many, many jams. And he didn't just pitch the ninth inning. He had long saves. He was the best.[5]

In 1960, Face appeared in 68 regular-season games, all in relief. He worked 114⅔ innings, allowing 93 hits and walking only 29, with a 2.90 earned run average. His record was 10–8 with 24 saves. His average appearance was one and two-thirds innings, roughly the same as it was in his astonishing 1959 season. In his five busiest relief-only years (1958–1962), Face pitched in 307 games and worked 475 innings.

Face was indirectly responsible for the save becoming an official major league statistic. Jerome Holtzman, a long-time sportswriter, invented the save in 1960, when he was covering the Cubs. Chicago had a very good bullpen duo in right-hander Jim Brosnan and lefty Bill Henry, neither of whom received much attention for the job they did in protecting leads.

In looking back at the 1959 season, Holtzman noted that, of Face's 18 wins, 10 came after he had allowed the opponent to score, only to pick up victories when Pittsburgh scored in the late innings. As a result of his glossy record, Face was lauded by many writers as the best relief pitcher in baseball, praise that was not deserved based solely on the won-lost record, in Holtzman's opinion. Holtzman pointed out, however, that Face had been better in 1958, when his record was 5–2. The only criterion, other than the wins and losses, for judging relievers was earned run average, and that was also not an accurate barometer since what happened to inherited runners was not reflected in a pitcher's ERA. Holtzman came up with the idea of awarding a save to a relief pitcher who entered a game with the potential tying or winning run on base or at bat and who then finished the game without relinquishing the lead.

Holtzman presented his idea to Lou Boudreau, a future Hall of Fame shortstop who was a Cubs broadcaster at the time. Boudreau liked it, and Holtzman passed along his save proposal to J.G. Taylor Spink, the publisher of *The Sporting News*, the magazine that was known for so long as the "Baseball Bible." Spink also liked the idea of saves, and he began giving a trophy to the top reliever in both the American and National League. The first "Fireman of the Year" winners, chosen by

The Sporting News in 1960, were the Cardinals' Lindy McDaniel and Mike Fornieles of the Red Sox.

The Baseball Association of America appointed Holtzman chairman of a group to propose to the committee for official scoring rules that the save be included in box scores and be made an official statistic. That did not happen until 1969. For the nine intervening years, Holtzman wrote a weekly *Sporting News* story in which he listed leaders in the race for the "Fireman of the Year," including the save as an unofficial stat. When it was adopted, the save became the first new major statistic since the RBI was added in 1920.[6]

It should be noted, for the purpose of accuracy, that saves, in regard to the 1960 season and Pittsburgh pitchers' career statistics, were retroactively assigned. Researchers dug into old box scores and awarded saves using extremely lenient criteria. So, a save did not appear in a box score appearing in the newspaper the day after a game.

So, when it is written that Elroy Face or Clem Labine notched a save for the Pirates in 1960, that actually happened after the fact. Long after. Use of terms like "posted a certain number of saves" or "was credited with a save" are not accurate in the sense that said saves had not been born at the time being referenced but are accurate after researchers went back and awarded saves.

In the case of Face, the save did not even become an official statistic until the final year of his major league career. Yet, his stats over 16 years in the majors show him with 193 saves.

On June 22, Bob Friend pitched his fourth shutout of the season for his ninth win. He allowed St. Louis eight hits and did not walk a batter, while Dick Groat rapped out four hits and Roberto Clemente lined a two-run double. The Cardinals snapped the Pirates' seven-game home win streak, cashing in on Groat's bobble for two unearned runs. Those runs were the margin of defeat, making a tough-luck loser of Harvey Haddix, who singled in the Pirates' only run.

Vinegar Bend Mizell pitched a seven-hitter, Pittsburgh downing the Cubs, 4-1, to open a four-game series. The complete game was Mizell's first of the season, and he helped his own cause with a pair of RBI singles. The Pirates nipped Chicago the next day, then were swept by the Cubs in a Sunday doubleheader as they beat both Friend and

NINE. Staying in Front

Law. A four-run ninth-inning rally fell a run short in the first game. Smoky Burgess came off the bench to slam a two-run homer in that rally. It was his 11th career pinch home run, equaling George Crowe's major league record.

Monday, June 27, was an off-day for both the Pirates and Giants before starting a three-game series at Forbes Field on Tuesday. Monday night, Tom Sheehan held court in his suite at the Carlton House in downtown Pittsburgh. Sheehan's record as the San Francisco manager was 3–6, but that did not dampen his spirits. He was talking to Al Abrams, a sportswriter for the *Pittsburgh Post Gazette & Sun Telegram*. "I thought this team [San Francisco] was the best in the National League before I ever dreamed I would take it over," Sheehan said. "I still think it's the best. We'll just have to prove it. All a team's gotta do is win a few games and you're back in the race just like that. Naw, we're not discouraged. We got a long way to go. We're gonna make it."[7]

Jumping out of his chair and waving his arms to make a point, Sheehan said, "Those blankety-blank errors. I've never seen so darn many errors in my life. Poor Rig [Bill Rigney] would still be around but for those errors. He left, but I'm still plagued with 'em. But this is too good a club to stay down. Let us get over that error binge, and we'll be okay, I'll tell you."[8]

The Giants trotted out of their dugout at Forbes Field bent on cutting into their six-game deficit in the standings, but managed no more than a split in the three-game series. Split a three-game series? Sounds impossible, but that is exactly what happened.

That's because the opening game was stopped by a curfew with the score 7–7. It went into the record book as a tie, with the game to be replayed in its entirety. The next night's game was rained out, forcing a Thursday twin bill. The Giants jumped all over Friend, who gave up six earned runs for the second straight start, neither of which lasted five innings. Jack Sanford tossed a three-hitter in an 11–0 cakewalk. The nightcap belonged to Dick Stuart. The first baseman enjoyed a career performance by clouting home runs in each of his first three at-bats and adding a two run single to drive in seven runs.

The brassy Stuart had started the season slowly, to say the least. He did not hit a home run until his 26th game, and that brought out the

Forbes Field boo birds. They were very vocal when Stuart struck out as a pinch-hitter in the first game of the doubleheader against the Giants, mired in a 2-for-34 slump. He turned the jeers to cheers with his three shots over the left-field fence, highlighting a 4-for-5 day that raised his batting average to .244, his home run total to a team-high 11, and his RBI count to 43.

At the end of June, Dick Groat led the Bucs in hitting with a .334 average, one point better than Roberto Clemente, who was tops on the club in RBI with 51. The right-fielder was back on track after struggling through an 8-for-38 stretch in the middle of the month, the heat and fatigue causing him to lose 12 pounds in a span of two weeks. Still, he continued to hit, consistently driving in clutch runs, and to make phenomenal plays in right field.

Pittsburgh made some changes in its pitching staff, involving four right-handers. The Pirates optioned Jim Umbricht and Bennie Daniels to Columbus of the International League, while promoting Tom Cheney and Earl Francis from the same team. Danny Murtaugh said he planned to give Cheney a chance to start and use Francis out of the bullpen. Francis, who had been impressive in the spring, made his debut against the Giants and allowed seven hits and three runs in five innings.

Sport Magazine conducted a poll of National League managers who rated the league's players at each position, and not a single Pirate ranked number one. Stuart placed sixth at first base; the Dodgers' Charlie Neal was ahead of Bill Mazeroski at second; Hoak was behind Eddie Mathews of Milwaukee and St. Louis's Ken Boyer at third; and Chicago's Ernie Banks, the Redlegs' Roy McMillan, and the Braves' Johnny Logan made Dick Groat number four at shortstop.

In the outfield, Clemente was second to Milwaukee's Hank Aaron in right; Willie Mays of the Giants and Cincinnati's Vada Pinson ranked ahead of Bill Virdon in center; and Bob Skinner was third behind San Francisco's Orlando Cepeda and Gus Bell of Cincinnati in left. Hal Smith was fourth and Smoky Burgess fifth at the catcher position, with the Braves' Del Crandall, the Redlegs' Ed Bailey, and the Dodgers' John Roseboro one-two-three in the voting. Pittsburgh's pitching ranked fifth in the National League behind Los Angeles, Milwaukee, San Francisco, and St. Louis.

Ten
A Friend, a Face and the Law

If there had been a poster boy for the Pittsburgh Pirates of the 1950s, it would have been Bob Friend. The handsome right-hander grew up with the Bucs, maturing as a pitcher and gradually improving and gaining prominence along with his ball club.

Maturity and improvement were watchwords for the Pirates' pitching staff as a whole in 1960. They allowed the fewest runs—and fewest earned runs—in the National League. One of the main reasons was that they also issued the fewest bases on balls. Two 1960 Pirates pitched more than 270 innings, with two others throwing more than 150. All four starters in the regular rotation won at least 11 games. The staff pitched 47 complete games and had an earned run average of 3.90, both numbers third-best in the league.

Friend could certainly appreciate such collective accomplishments. He had pitched for the Pirates when they were terrible, when they were arguably the worst team in the major leagues. He made 109 starts before he turned 25 years of age for teams that finished seventh once and eighth, or last, four times. In the three following seasons, Friend started 118 games, averaging 36.8 starts over a 10-year period. He was durable and reliable. He always took his turn.

"I didn't miss starts," Friend said. "I always took the ball, and I'm proud of that. It's true I did not have any serious arm problems, but it's also true that I did not beg out of a start just because I felt a little twinge. I burned up the innings."[1]

The great thing when he was just starting out with the club, he said, was that he got the chance to start. And he got the chance to get better in the major leagues instead of in the minors. As Friend got better, so did his supporting cast, with his victory total increasing in direct proportion to the additional offensive and defensive support he received.

Friend could see the team was making progress, and so was he. As young and inexperienced as he was, to go to the mound as many times as he did, he knew he had to learn something. He learned how to throw strikes more consistently and not to make those strikes too fat. He also learned there were times when a hitter would help because he was so eager. Times like that, he didn't have to throw strikes; the hitters would swing at balls off the plate. Always a competitor, he said he learned how to compete—how to pitch out of trouble and how to minimize damage.

At the same time, Pittsburgh's other players were learning how to win. They had a strong nucleus—Groat, Maz, Clemente, Skinner, Virdon—guys who knew how to play baseball and who could play it pretty well. It was just a matter of getting the experience.[2]

Friend's teammates and his statistics will tell you that he was as fine a pitcher when he was a 19-game loser as when he was a 22-game winner. And he was always a workhorse. "I like to think I was dependable," Friend said. His manager and teammates always knew they could count on him to give them innings, to pitch pretty far into the game most of the time, and he did that. After all, he said, that's what pitchers were supposed to do, what they were getting paid to do.[3]

A native of Lafayette, Indiana, Friend was reportedly close to signing with Brooklyn. Stan Feezle, a Dodgers scout, had already signed Carl Erskine and Gil Hodges out of

Bob Friend was a poster boy for the Pirates, literally growing up with the team. He gave the 1960 club a strong one-two pitching punch, winning 18 games on the way to being named the National League "Comeback Player of the Year." The right-hander never missed a start, routinely pitched deep into games, and could be counted on for 200-plus innings every season.

Ten. A Friend, a Face and the Law

the state of Indiana, and he figured to have an inside track on Friend. Feezle, a great salesman and scout, landed the right-hander all right, but for the Pittsburgh Pirates in 1949. Branch Rickey had left the Dodgers and gone to Pittsburgh, taking Feezle with him. Friend thought it was a great opportunity to sign with the Pirates for an $18,000 bonus, pretty good money then.[4]

A talented all-around athlete, Friend was an all-state halfback and pitcher, and he also played basketball and golf in high school. He was offered a football scholarship by Purdue University, which his father had attended. Friend had every intention of accepting the offer and playing for the Boilermakers. Instead, he signed with the Pirates out of high school in 1949. He later returned to Purdue and earned his degree, attending classes during the off-season for eight years. His bachelor's degree, received in 1957, is in economics.

After signing with Pittsburgh, he was assigned to the Pirates' Class B team in Waco, Texas, in the Big State League. Sporting an 11–9 record, Friend was told that he was being promoted to Indianapolis. That same day, he went out and pitched a no-hitter against Wichita Falls. He finished the year with the Indianapolis Indians of the Triple-A American Association, going 2–4.

In 1951, he had a good spring with the Bucs and was kept with the big team, becoming one of their starting pitchers at the age of 20. Pittsburgh was at or near the bottom of the National League standings every year back then, but the good thing from Friend's perspective was that he had the opportunity to pitch regularly early in his career rather than having to wait in line, or in the minors. He started 22 games and won six as a rookie, added a victory to his total each of the next two years, and had the meager total of 28 wins after four big league seasons.

Friend enjoyed a breakthrough campaign in 1955, posting a 14–9 record and a sparkling 2.83 earned run average while pitching 200⅓ innings. The ERA was the lowest in the National League, making him the first pitcher ever to lead his league in earned run average while pitching for a last-place team.

He threw at least 222 innings each of the next 10 seasons, averaging 256. Friend worked a Herculean 314⅓ innings in 1956 when he started 42 games and finished 19 of them, putting together a 17–17 record that included four shutouts. He even relieved seven times that year and saved two games.

Nicknamed "Nervous" by his Pirates teammates during his rookie season, Friend could not sit still on days of his scheduled starts. He would pace the clubhouse while bending his right arm and massaging it with his left. Many years later, he was asked about getting tensed up when he was going to pitch. "Sure, I'm a little keyed up when I pitch," Friend replied. "When I'm not, I don't pitch very well."[5]

Also known for his determination, he was once tested for confidence by Branch Rickey. Following a 7–12 season in 1954, Friend was called into the office of the Pittsburgh general manager. Rickey suggested that maybe it would be a good idea to send the pitcher back to the minors. "I wanted to see his response," Rickey said. "If he had been doubtful, I probably would have sent him down. But he had a definite, firm feeling that he should not go back."[6] The next year, Friend had that breakthrough season, leading the National League in earned run average for another last-place team. "Nineteen fifty-five was the turning point," Friend said years later. "That is when I arrived as a pitcher. Experience had taught me a lot, and I had learned how to pitch."[7]

Friend pitched in an era when starting pitchers were expected to finish games. They threw a lot of pitches and usually pitched deep into games. Pitchers back then didn't know how many pitches they had thrown. There was no "quality start" stat. For him, a quality start was when he pitched a complete game and the Pirates won.[8]

Vernon Law and his brother, Evan, who was a catcher, led Meridian High School to the Idaho state baseball and football championships. Vernon once struck out 25 batters in an American Legion game, and no less than nine major league teams sent scouts to visit the Law home.[9] Herman Welker recommended Law to the Pirates in 1948. Welker, an attorney and future Idaho senator, telephoned singer/actor Bing Crosby, a part-owner and vice president of the Pittsburgh team. Crosby, a college classmate of Welker, phoned the Bucs' front office, and scout Babe Herman was dispatched to take a look at Law. Law recalled:

> The reason I signed with the Pirates was that all the other scouts that came in didn't leave too good of an impression with my parents. They would come in smoking cigars. My dad allowed no smoking in the house; he'd

Ten. A Friend, a Face and the Law

say, "You can come in, but that cigar's got to stay outside." Babe Herman and Herman Welker were the last ones to come in. They brought a box of chocolates and a bouquet of flowers for my mother. Halfway through the conversation, the phone rings. On the other end of the line is Bing Crosby! My mother just about fainted on the spot. It wasn't until I'd been in the big leagues a while and the Dodgers had moved to L.A. that Bing Crosby happened to be in the clubhouse when I was pitching and said, "I want to tell you something about your signing that you probably don't know. Babe Herman and Herman Welker bought a big box of cigars and passed them out to all the other scouts who didn't know about the Mormons, that they didn't smoke or drink!"[10]

Law, who is an elder in the Mormon church, signed in 1948 and began his pro career that year with Class D Santa Rosa, California. When the Pirates signed the pitcher, they had an agreement with him that he would not have to pitch on Sundays. During that first season at Santa Rosa, Law did not go to the ball park on any Sunday. "I thought it was a permanent agreement," he said, "but the next year, my manager at Davenport scheduled me to pitch on a Sunday, so I pitched. I realized it couldn't be any other way. I can't take Sunday off—there are twenty-four other guys on the club who would like to have the day off too."[11] Law spent a year at Davenport, a Class B team in Iowa. Bill Burwell, a former major league pitcher who managed the Pirates for one game in 1947, helped Law develop. Burwell taught the 18-year-old right-hander to change speeds and showed him how to throw a changeup. The pair would work together again in 1960, when Burwell was the Pirates' pitching coach.[12]

Law was called up by Pittsburgh in June of 1950 and remained in the big leagues. He started and relieved during the early years of his career, which was interrupted by military service in 1952–1953. In 1955, he started 24 games and relieved in 19, pitching 200 innings and going 10–10. After that, he was a regular member of the starting rotation. Beginning in 1957, he enjoyed winning records for four straight seasons. Law pitched a career-high 20 complete games in 1959, when he went 18–9 over 266 innings. "My dad was quite an amateur ballplayer," he said. "One day he pitched a doubleheader and won both games. I'm sure I got some of those genes."[13]

Apparently. On July 19, 1955, against the Milwaukee Braves, Law pitched 18 innings and didn't get a decision. He gave up nine hits and one earned run, walking two and striking out 12. Bob Friend, who pitched the 19th, was the winning pitcher when the Pirates scored twice in the bottom of the inning as Pittsburgh won, 4–3. Five days later, Law pitched a 10-inning four-hitter in beating the Cubs, 3–2. So he pitched 28 innings in six days.

Law did not throw at hitters and only brushed one back occasionally. He had a theory about that. "I don't think a duster does one bit of good. Maybe there's one or two or three or four batters in the league you can shake up with a duster, but not many. When you throw at a guy, you're liable to wake him up and he'll wallop your next pitch."[14]

Danny Murtaugh smiled wryly when he heard stories about Law not knocking a batter down. Speaking at a Bucs Fan Club luncheon, the Pittsburgh manager said,

> So, I'm talking to one of my pitchers and I says, "Look, when the other pitcher comes up there, I want you to knock him down." And my pitcher [Law] was one of those fellows who is well versed in the Bible, and he tells me, "Skip, turn the other cheek." So I looked at him and said, "All right with me. I'll turn the other cheek. But if this guy don't go down, it's gonna cost you a hundred bucks." So my pitcher looked at me and said, "They that live by the sword die by the sword."[15]

A good-hitting pitcher who was used a dozen times as a pinch-hitter, he hit 11 home runs and batted .216, with 191 hits, for his 16-year career.

Another pitcher who knew what to do with the bat was Harvey Haddix, who batted .212 over 14 big league seasons. He, too, was occasionally called upon to pinch-hit.

Explaining how he became a pitcher, Haddix told this story:

> I went to a Cardinal tryout camp in Columbus, Ohio. They handed us forms to fill out—name, age, address, home town, position, and so forth. Where it had position, I put down "Pitcher, First Baseman, Outfielder."
>
> Well, this scout looks at my card and he says, "Boy, you can't be all three." I had pitcher down first, so he just took his pencil and scratched out the other two positions. So I pitched and they signed me and I've been a pitcher ever since.[16]

Haddix had to wait a while before reaching the big leagues. Signed by the St. Louis Cardinals in 1947, the left-hander did not pitch in a

TEN. A Friend, a Face and the Law

major league game until five years later. In his first year of pro baseball, Haddix was named the Most Valuable Player of the Carolina League. He was honored for a season in which he went 19–5 with a 1.90 ERA, struck out 268 batters in 204 innings and pitched a no-hitter for Winston-Salem.

After two years in the minor leagues and two years of military service, he got out in late 1952 and pitched 42 innings for the Cards. One of his teammates that season was Harry Brecheen, a 37-year-old pitcher who was near the end of an outstanding career. Also a southpaw, the five-foot-ten, 160-pound Brecheen was similar in stature to Haddix, who was five-nine and 170. Brecheen was called "Cat" because of his quickness and agility. So Haddix, who was also quick and agile, was nicknamed "Kitten."

A fine fielder and good base runner, Haddix helped himself in a lot of ways, especially at the plate. He had 169 career hits, including 21 or more three times. In 1953, he rapped out 28 hits, scored 21 runs, and batted .289. That same season, he was a 20-game winner and had a 3.06 earned run average, while pitching 253 innings. He was selected to his first of three straight All-Star teams and finished second in "Rookie of the Year" voting behind Brooklyn infielder Junior Gilliam.

Haddix won 18 games in 1954 and fell to 12–16 in 1955. Less than a month into the 1956 season, St. Louis sent him to Philadelphia as part of a five-pitcher deal. He won a dozen games for the Phillies, while pitching over 200 innings for the fourth straight year. After he went 10–13 in 1957, the Phils traded him to Cincinnati for slugger Wally Post. Haddix went 8–7 in 1958, his only season with the Reds.

It was May 26, 1959, during his first season with Pittsburgh, that Haddix tangled with the Braves' Lew Burdette in a monumental pitching duel at Milwaukee's County Stadium. They matched zeroes for 12 innings, but the shocker was that Haddix did not allow a base runner, not even a walk. Pittsburgh didn't make an error. The Kitten had pitched a 12-inning perfect game. Burdette was giving up hits, but escaping one jam after another.

A Pirates error ended the perfect game in the 13th, when the Braves scored to take a 1–0 win. Haddix pitched a one-hitter, with that lone hit leaving the park on a blast by Joe Adcock. A mix-up on the base paths resulted in Adcock passing Hank Aaron and being credited with an RBI double instead of a three-run homer.

Many have called Haddix's performance the greatest game ever pitched.

As Dizzy Dean would have said, Wilmer "Vinegar Bend" Mizell was "a right fair country pitcher." Put plenty of accent on the word "country." The tall left-hander was born in Leakesville, Mississippi, but gained notoriety and fame growing up and playing baseball in nearby Vinegar Bend, Alabama (population, 50). Hence the nickname. After playing two years with a team comprised of family members, he attended a Cardinals tryout camp. Mizell recalled:

> It was in Biloxi, Mississippi. Six of us loaded up in a little automobile and went down. Must have been 1,000 boys in that camp, from all over the South. I was the last pitcher of the day. They brought my brother in to catch. I threw nine pitches and struck out three men. That's all the scouts saw me pitch. They called the camp off for the day; that night there was a hurricane bouncing around in the Gulf. Rained so hard the next morning they had to call the camp off. Buddy Lewis was the scout in charge.
>
> Next spring, the day I graduated from high school, Buddy Lewis showed up in Vinegar Bend and got someone to bring him out to the country, where we lived. My first cousin and I were getting our baths down in the swim hole, to go to graduation exercises. We got out and by the time we got back to the house, Buddy said, "I'd just like to see you warm up." My brother caught for me, about five or ten minutes or so, then Buddy said, "I would like you to go to Albany, Georgia, and pitch Class D baseball this summer—if you will, I've got a contract for you, $175 dollars per month."
>
> I didn't know what to say to Buddy. This was a surprise. In those days scouts didn't talk to high school boys, so I hadn't heard anything from Buddy over the winter other than a Christmas card. Buddy must have thought I was holding out on him—he said, "Well, when you get to Albany, I'll see that they give you $500." I almost broke his arm getting the pen to sign that contract. Uncle Irvan had to sign for me. I was still underage. He put me on a train that night to Albany, Georgia. I didn't even go home after graduation exercises.[17]

That was in 1949. Mizell was pitching for the Cardinals three years later. He pitched 190 innings his rookie year and won 10 games, but he was a bit on the wild side, issuing 103 walks to lead the league. The next season, he won 13 games and had a 3.49 earned run average. He struck out 173 in 224⅓ innings, but walked 114.

TEN. A Friend, a Face and the Law

Mizell was in the Army in 1954 and 1955, and he pitched in the Cuban Winter League in the 1955–1956 season, setting a league record for strikeouts with 206 in 179 innings. "Shucks, those guys [in the Cuban Winter League] couldn't understand the language I was pitching to them in," he explained. "That's why I struck out so many."[18]

He was the Cardinals' Opening Day pitcher in 1956, becoming the first to do that after not having played the previous two seasons. An All-Star in 1959, Mizell was 1–3 with a 4.55 ERA for the Cardinals in 1960 when they traded him to Pittsburgh. He had been a double-figure winner in five of his six full seasons with St. Louis, but his career record at the time of the trade was 69–70.

There were numerous stories about the man called Vinegar Bend and his country connections. When he pitched for the Winston-Salem (N.C.) minor league team, Mizell rode around the baseball field one night on a mule and sang country music over the public address system. "I walked behind more mules than I walked batters, and that's saying a lot," he said.[19]

Playing for Houston of the Texas League in 1951, Mizell struck out 18 in one game. His team's management held a Vinegar Bend Night, flying in 32 people, reportedly "the town's total adult population."

Frank Lane, the wheeler-dealer general manager, talked once about calling Mizell to his office to discuss a contract. "I was looking for a typical Ozark Ike type," Lane recalled. "Vinegar told me how he had turned most of his earnings over to his family to put them on their feet, how he had bought his brother a truck, and now that he was married and expecting his first child, he thought it was time to get something for himself.

"I never had a chance to open my mouth for the next half-hour. He signed for more than I had intended to give."[20]

Elroy Face was ahead of his time. There was no "save" or "closer" designation when he pitched in the major leagues, no thunderous sound effects, flashing lights, and rock music when he entered a game, and no stardom associated with what he did. What he did was save the necks—and wins—of Pittsburgh pitchers. There was little, if any, fanfare. He did not have saves handed to him on a silver platter; there was none of that three outs to protect a three-run lead stuff.

"Had 'Em All the Way"

Many times, Face walked into full-blown jams—tying and/or winning runs on base and one out or nobody out. He frequently inherited such messes in the seventh or eighth inning and pitched the rest of the way. He had no set-up man. The little right-hander with the ruthless forkball was his own set-up man, often pitching the last two or more innings.

Face wasn't always a relief specialist, however. Like most pitchers, he began as a starter. For a long time, relievers were looked upon as second-class citizens. (Hoyt Wilhelm was an exception on both counts as he started out as a relief pitcher and brought respect to the job.)

It was 1948 when the Pirates picked up the man considered to be their all-time best relief pitcher. Branch Rickey actually drafted Face twice, first getting him for Brooklyn from Philadelphia in 1950, then taking him for Pittsburgh from the Dodgers on December 1, 1952, for a $7,500 price tag. Face was 20 years old when the Phillies signed him. Face said,

> I quit school when I was eighteen and joined the Army. I was on a team and we would call another town and if they weren't playing that Sunday, we would either go to their field or they would come over to our field and play. I had consecutive games when I struck out seventeen and eighteen batters. A scout on vacation for the Phillies read about it in the paper, came over and watched me pitch a ball game on Labor Day, 1948. In the seventh inning, he signed me up to a contract.[21]

That scout, Fred Mathews, saw Face pitch in a sandlot game in Massachusetts. Mathews liked what he saw, but had some reservations because of Face's size (five-foot-eight and about 150 pounds). The Phils' scout liked the up side, however, having read in a newspaper that the pitcher was 17 years old. When Mathews offered Face a contract, he mentioned that his parents would have to sign off on their approval. Face's father, a garage mechanic who was out of work at the time, asked why. Then he told the scout that he was 20 years of age, not 17. Mathews decided to sign him anyway.

Face spent two years at the Class D level, pitching in Bradford, Pennsylvania. He played in Pueblo, Colorado, which was a Class A team, and for Class AA Fort Worth, Texas. After being chosen by the Pirates in the draft, he pitched for them in 1953. He went back to the minors the next season, then returned to the majors for good in 1955.

Ten. A Friend, a Face and the Law

Face learned how to throw the forkball from Joe Page. The premier relief pitcher for the New York Yankees from 1944 to 1949 was attempting a comeback with the Pirates in 1954 following a three-year absence from the majors. At that time, Face, who had started 13 games and relieved in 23 more for Pittsburgh in 1953, was a fastball-curveball pitcher, who needed an off-speed pitch. He would spend the entire 1954 season in the minor leagues trying to perfect such a pitch. Rickey had sent him to New Orleans to work on finding a third pitch.

Face had already found it before he left the Pirates in the spring. He learned the forkball (now known as the split-fingered fastball) from Page. Face developed the forkball in the minors and returned to the big leagues a better pitcher in 1955. Forty years after he retired from baseball, Face was asked the difference between his forkball and Bruce Sutter's split-fingered fastball. "About four million dollars," he said.[22]

Face lowered his earned run average a full three runs in 1955 and earned the first two saves of his career, while continuing to divide time between starting games and finishing them. His ERA dropped every season for the next four years as he was used exclusively as a reliever after 1957. He was credited with 20 or more saves three times, with a high of 28 in 1962, but the season for which he is most remembered is 1959. That year, Face had an 18–1 record, his .957 winning percentage the all-time best for a single season in the major leagues. He added nine saves that season and finished 47 of the 57 games in which he pitched, all out of the bullpen.

> They used to accuse me of throwing a spitball because it would sink. If it was working, I might use it sixty or seventy percent of the time. If it wasn't, I may have used it twenty percent. But I would throw it on any count—three and two, three and one—it wouldn't make any difference. If I got them looking for that, then I could throw the fastball by them and if they were looking for the fastball, they'd be out in front of the forkball.[23]

Face had a few weapons in addition to his sinking pitch that induced ground balls. He was a very good fielder, was hard to bunt on, and possessed an excellent pickoff move. That helped him hold runners close and also bailed him out of trouble at times. Once, he went into a game with two runners on and no outs. He picked the man off second, the other runner off first, and retired the hitter on the first pitch. One pitch and three outs.

Elroy Face could find a lot of ways to get the job done.

Clem Labine was a terrific pickup for the 1960 Pirates. He not only had a great deal of experience, he also had biggest-game experience. The right-hander had pitched in four World Series with the Dodgers and had performed suberbly. Just the year before, he had helped Los Angeles defeat the Chicago White Sox. His other three Series were with Brooklyn.

Pittsburgh added Labine on August 16, which meant he would be eligible for the World Series. It was a spotlight in which he had thrived. In 10 previous Fall Classic games, nine in relief, he had a 1.67 earned run average. Labine's one World Series start came in 1956 with the Yankees leading the Dodgers, three games to two. With the pressure of Brooklyn's possible elimination on his shoulders, he pitched a seven-hit shutout in Game Six.

Relief was Labine's main job in nine years with the Dodgers, and he did it well. He posted 83 saves for them, with a high of 19 in 1956. He pitched more than 900 innings and had a 70–52 record. He knew how to pitch, and he could do it under pressure, making him a big help to the Pirates and taking some of the load off Face.

Fred Green's best season in the majors was 1960. The left-hander pitched seven years in the minor leagues after signing with Pittsburgh when he was 18 years old. He threw more than 200 innings in both of his first two years of professional baseball. He won 20 games in 1952 for Class D Brunswick as an 18-year-old and 13 the next season at Class B Waco. Green also made stops at Williamsport, New Orleans, Hollywood and two Triple-A farm clubs, Salt Lake City and Columbus. He started and relieved along the way before finding a place in the Pittsburgh bullpen late in 1959 at the age of 25.

Joe Gibbon could have played pro basketball. He was drafted by the Boston Celtics after being the second-leading NCAA scorer. The six-foot-four Gibbon averaged 30 points and 14 rebounds per game for Mississippi in 1957 and earned first-team All-America honors. He was voted the Most Valuable Player in the Southeastern Conference in a poll of the players. He was All-SEC in basketball and baseball. He is in the

Ten. A Friend, a Face and the Law

state of Mississippi Sports Hall of Fame as well as the Ole Miss Hall of Fame.

Gibbon, a lefty, signed with Pittsburgh in 1957 after his senior year of college. He went 9–4 with a 1.83 ERA at Class A Lincoln, then pitched at Columbus the next two years, winning 16 games in 201 innings in 1959. He was a rookie with the Pirates in 1960.

Eleven

The Great One, Billy and Bob

As daylight brought a new year on January 1, 1973, I awoke from what I thought was a terrible dream. It was of Roberto Clemente dying in a plane crash. I was single in those days and always kept the radio on all night. That way, I would go to sleep listening to music and hear it when I woke up. I was half asleep when the newscaster announced that Clemente had been killed when an airplane went down in the Atlantic Ocean. It had been carrying supplies to earthquake-stricken Nicaragua, and Clemente was on board to make sure the food and other materials reached deserving victims.

When I shook off the cobwebs of sleep and realized my nightmare was reality, hearing the report of the tragedy once again, I was stunned. I recalled Clemente's many exciting feats on a baseball field and his many humanitarian efforts off it. I also recalled my treasured conversation with him, and I treasured it even more.

It was with great joy that I read in August of 1973 that the Baseball Writers' Association of America had held a special election and waived the mandatory five-year waiting period for Clemente, voting him into the Hall of Fame. He compiled a .317 lifetime batting average with 240 home runs, 1,305 RBI, and four batting titles. Clemente became the first Hispanic player inducted at Cooperstown.[1]

In a eulogy for Clemente, Baseball Commissioner Bowie Kuhn said, "He gave the term 'complete' a new meaning. He made the word superstar seem inadequate. He had about him a touch of royalty."[2]

Mention the New York Yankees, and Babe Ruth comes to mind. With the Braves, it's Hank Aaron; Ted Williams with the Boston Red Sox; Willie Mays with the Giants; and Stan Musial with the St. Louis Cardinals. The names are synonymous with the franchises.

ELEVEN. *The Great One, Billy and Bob*

So it is with Roberto Clemente and the Pittsburgh Pirates. He is an unquestioned legend, one whose character and stature as a person match his athletic stardom. Famed Pirates broadcaster Bob Prince anointed Clemente "The Great One," and it stuck. It was the perfect *title*, because a nickname seemed beneath such a regal man.

On Saturday, November 6, 1952, the Dodgers held a tryout camp at Sixto Escobar, a stadium in Santurce, Puerto Rico, located just off the ocean on Puerta de Tierra, the long finger of land leading to Old San Juan. Seventeen-year-old Roberto Clemente, who came from Carolina, Puerto Rico, attended the tryout along with 71 others.

Al Campanis, the Dodgers' chief scout in the Caribbean, ran the tryout. "This one kid throws a bullet from center on the fly," Campanis said. "I couldn't believe my eyes." He asked the youngster to make another throw, estimated at nearly 400 feet. "And he does it again."[3] It was Clemente who made the throw. Campanis had recognized what many scouts would rate the greatest throwing arm they ever saw exhibited by a baseball player. Clemente then ran the 60-yard dash in 6.4 seconds. Campanis sent the other 71 players home. Thoroughly convinced of Clemente's speed and throwing ability, Campanis wanted to know if he could swing the bat. In batting practice against an accomplished minor league pitcher named Jose Santiago, Clemente ripped several line drives.

Noticing that he liked to stand far away from home plate, Campanis doubted that the youngster could reach pitches on the outer half of the strike zone. So he instructed Santiago to throw the next series of pitches, preferably curveballs, toward the outside corner. Clemente responded by ringing another set of line drives. "The kid swings with both feet off the ground and hits line drives to right and sharp ground balls up the middle," marveled Campanis. "He was the greatest natural athlete I have ever seen at a tryout camp."[4]

Five major league teams eventually showed interest in Clemente, including the Boston Red Sox, New York Giants, St. Louis Cardinals, and Boston Braves, as well as Brooklyn. It came down to the Braves, who offered the largest bonus, the Giants, and the Dodgers. Clemente wanted to play in New York, where he had relatives and friends. Any signing over $6,000 would make him a "bonus player" and would mean

"Had 'Em All the Way"

the team signing him would be required to keep him on its major league roster or risk losing him in a supplemental draft after his first year in the minor leagues. The Giants kept their offer under the bonus line. The Dodgers offered a $10,000 bonus and a first-year salary of $5,000. Brooklyn planned to send Clemente to its top farm club in Montreal. As talented as the Dodgers' scouts and executives felt he was, part of their mission was to keep him from playing for the Giants in the same outfield with Willie Mays.

On February 19, 1954, Roberto's father, Melchor Clemente, sent a telegram to the Brooklyn Baseball Club, saying he would sign a contract with Montreal of the International League on behalf of his son. At the bottom of the telegram were the words "signed, Melchor Clemente, father, Roberto Clemente, son."

Clemente was in the Montreal starting lineup for its home opener against Syracuse. Playing center field and batting fifth for the Royals, he got three hits in four trips to the plate and knocked in a run. He blasted a 400-foot home run in Montreal, becoming the first player in Royals history to clear the left field wall at Delorimier Downs. The next day, he was on the bench. A week later, he was back in the lineup, only to be removed in the first inning for a pinch-hitter when Montreal loaded the bases. Clemente had three triples in another game and was back on the bench the following day.

Clemente's playing time had nothing to do with his performance. It was hard for him to understand why he was sitting so much when he was playing so well. The Dodgers were seemingly hiding him from other teams' scouts. At the same time, the Brooklyn hierarchy appeared bent on not helping to develop the future star outfielder when a rival club might reap the benefits.

Max Macon, the Montreal manager, denied that he was being told (by the Dodgers) whom to play, but few took that claim at face value. Glenn Cox, a pitcher on the team, said players always knew about other players, and it was obvious to all of them that Clemente was something special and deserved more playing time. "Macon had orders, and that was that," said Bob Watt, who served as road secretary for the Royals. "Whenever we'd spot a scout in the stands, that would be the end of Clemente for that day. He never had the chance to show what he could do."[5]

ELEVEN. *The Great One, Billy and Bob*

The thinking in Brooklyn, Buzzie Bavasi (the Dodgers' general manager) acknowledged later, went like this: "Since we were going to lose him anyhow in the draft, why should we spend so much time developing him for somebody else? We used other players and Clemente went in only on defense in the late innings or played sparingly."[6]

In one six-game series in Havana, Clemente never got off the bench. During batting practice, he hit with the Royals' pitchers. At one point, he grew so disenchanted that he wanted to go home. Campanis, who was responsible for Brooklyn signing Clemente, was in Montreal with Bavasi for a few games, and he urged Clemente to stick it out, that his chance would come. Campanis must have known that chance would not come with the Dodgers.

The Dodgers' attempt to hide Clemente did not work. Branch Rickey was the major roadblock. He had worked with Brooklyn from 1942 until joining Pittsburgh after the 1950 season. He obviously knew the goings-on of the Dodgers and their personnel. When Rickey took the Pirates' GM job, he brought Clyde Sukeforth and Howie Haak with him from Brooklyn. Both men were considered excellent scouts and talent evaluators. With Rickey's intimate knowledge of the Dodgers and their system, and with his scouts on standby to go wherever he needed them, there was no way a prospect like Roberto Clemente, dangling out there, ready to be drafted at the end of the year, was going to escape their notice.

During the summer, Rickey dispatched Sukeforth and then Haak to report on Montreal's bonus baby. As Sukeforth later told the story, he checked on the Royals during a series against Richmond. Just observing Clemente in outfield practice, when he unloosed one stunning throw after another, and at the plate during batting practice, when he kept drilling shots back through the box, was enough. It hardly mattered that Macon kept Clemente on the bench.

Having finished last in the National League standings in 1954, the Pirates would get the first selection in the draft of minor league players. "We had the draft meeting at Mr. Rickey's farm outside of Pittsburgh," Sukeforth recalled. "He called the meeting to order. 'We have the first draft choice, as you know. Who are we going to draft?' Two or three guys spoke up. One guy wanted a fellow in the Southern League. Another

"Had 'Em All the Way"

wanted a fellow on the coast. Mr. Rickey said to me, 'Clyde, what would your choice be?' I said, 'Clemente is definitely our man.'"[7]

Rickey traveled to Puerto Rico to watch Clemente play winter baseball. He was playing in the same Santurce outfield with Willie Mays, and the two were battling for the league batting title. On November 22, 1954, Rickey followed the advice of Sukeforth and Haak and drafted Clemente from the Brooklyn Dodgers for $4,000. The Rule V draft stipulated that players selected must remain on their new teams' major league rosters for the entirety of the following season. So Clemente was to be a Pirate in 1955.

In addition to being a superb hitter, extraordinary outfielder with an arm rated by many as the best ever among outfielders, and a tremendous base runner who was both speedy and smart, Roberto Clemente was a very proud and a very sensitive man. He was passionate about being one of the best baseball players of all time and about representing his country, Puerto Rico. He wanted to show the world what a fine person and athlete his home country had produced.

Much has been written and said about athletes—especially professional athletes—"playing hurt," performing in spite of injuries because that is what they are paid to do. Athletes who sit out with ailments perceived by the press and public to be minor have often been maligned. Clemente was one such athlete. He was called many things, among them a hypochondriac and complainer, in sports columns. Some writers even made fun of the way he spoke by writing words exactly as Clemente pronounced them, making him look foolish in the process. His first few years in the major leagues were also his first few years in the United States, and he was having to learn to speak English while being interviewed by people who wrote his words down for the public's digestion and inspection.

He felt he had been terribly misunderstood and thought many Latin ballplayers were misunderstood. They were thought to be moody, very temperamental. Every time they voiced an opinion or a feeling that did not go along with everybody else, Clemente said that label of moody was thrown at them. That was not fair.

Clemente said, however, that for him, it was more than that. He said sportswriters write it and then other people say that he whined

Eleven. The Great One, Billy and Bob

and complained about every little thing that bothered him, every little ache and pain. He emphatically said that he played baseball very hard … as hard as anyone, harder than most. "I give everything I've got," Clemente said, "running after fly balls, making throws, hitting the baseball, and running the bases. Sometimes I crash into walls catching balls or trying to catch them. I have even had stitches as a result. To me, it is the only way to play; it is the only way to do anything."[8]

One of the greatest Pirates of all time said he did everything to the best of his ability, never loafing or taking it easy, no matter the score or his team's place in the standings. Often, when Clemente missed a few games, writers would suggest that he must be in a bad mood because he had not been hitting or because he was not receiving enough attention. Some columns went farther, saying if he was in a certain frame of mind, he did not try his hardest. He responded that giving everything was a matter of pride, the only way he knew, and that he didn't want anyone to say that Roberto Clemente gave less than his best. But he felt that was exactly what detractors were saying when they talked about his being a hypochondriac and accused him of making excuses for not playing.

Clemente explained that when he missed a game, it was because he was not physically able to give his best. He said if he tried to play and could not get to a fly ball, could not run fast enough to a base, could not swing the bat to hit the ball hard because something hurts, then that would not be the true Roberto Clemente.[9] The Pirates' right fielder said staying in the lineup and going through the motions would be a sham, just a show to prove he could play when not feeling 100 percent physically. To him, that would be hurting the team. He could have also gotten himself hurt worse and ended up missing many more games. He thought it was the smart thing to miss a game or a few and get healthy. Then the Pittsburgh Pirates would have the real Roberto Clemente back in the lineup. He thought that was what the Pittsburgh Pirates and their fans would want.

He said he did not like to miss baseball games, that he loved baseball and loved to play it. Clemente also loved showing that men from Puerto Rico could play baseball very, very well, rhetorically asking why would he want to miss a chance to do that. Playing halfway because his shoulder or back hurt would mean less than a whole Roberto Clemente. It would

"Had 'Em All the Way"

have bothered him if he played poorly—not getting to a ball or hitting one—because he was hurt.[10]

Clemente said he had tried many times to explain himself to sportswriters, who would seem to be understanding while at his locker, then attack him in print for being soft and selfish. The writers would nod their heads, like they agreed, in his presence. Then they wrote in their newspapers that Roberto Clemente was a hypochondriac, that he looked for reasons to stay out of games. That made him sad and it made him angry. But what could he do?[11]

Bill Virdon personified the 1960 Pittsburgh Pirates. He was very quiet and very underrated. One of the finest defensive outfielders in the major leagues, "The Quail" turned potentially spectacular catches into routine ones as he made chasing down and grabbing fly balls look easy. At the plate, his modest stats defied a knack for coming up with big hits in big situations.

Bill Virdon, a Michigan native, played in a summer league in Kansas and was seen by legendary New York Yankees scout Tom Greenwade. The Yankees signed Virdon in 1950 and sent the 18-year-old outfielder to Class D Independence, Kansas, moving him up to Class B Norfolk, Virginia, the next year. He played with Class A Binghamton, New York, in 1952 and split the 1953 season between Kansas City, Missouri, and Double-A Birmingham, Alabama. In 1954, the Yankees traded Virdon and two other players to St. Louis for Enos Slaughter. Virdon batted .333, smacked 22 home runs, and had 98 RBI for Rochester, New York, of the Triple-A International League. After five years in the minors, he was kept by the Cardinals in 1955.

Bob Prince dubbed him

ELEVEN. *The Great One, Billy and Bob*

"The Quail" because of his lanky appearance and his graceful movements in the outfield. Highly regarded for his defensive prowess, Virdon could run down drives into the gaps as well as anyone. He always got a tremendous jump on the ball, a valuable asset and one which allowed him to turn would-be eye-popping catches into routine plays.

There were those, among major league players, managers and coaches, who believed his defense was on a par with that of Willie Mays. Of course, Mays had a stronger arm and a much bigger bat, and he was certainly the better all-around player. Bob Friend said Bill Virdon was every bit the center fielder as the three everybody talked and wrote about (Mays, Mickey Mantle, and Duke Snider), but that he did not play in New York where everything was noticed. But he could go and get the ball, prevent hits, and cut off singles to keep them from being doubles. He could do those things as well as anyone, better than most.[12]

Bob Skinner was signed by the Pirates in 1951 at the age of 19. Playing first base for Mayfield, Kentucky, of the Class D Kitty League that summer, he batted a sizzling .472 in 106 at-bats and earned a promotion after 29 games. At Mayfield, he was paid $250 a month and was lucky to get it. "They'd have 300 people in the stands every night," Skinner said. "The same 300. On payday once, they told us to come around the next day. They had to hold a town council meeting to get up the payroll money."[13] He hit .283 for Waco, a Class B team, and then served two years of military duty with the Marine Corps.

When he got out, Skinner made the Pirates team in 1954 as a first baseman, but was back in the minor leagues for the 1955 season. He was leading the Southern Association that year with an average of .346, but broke his left hand and missed the rest of the season.

In 1956, he returned to the majors to stay. In 1958, his .321 batting average was fifth in the National League. Skinner was a talented player whose skills surprised folks at times. Not considered a power hitter, in 1958 he became the fourth player to hit a ball over the right-field stands at Forbes Field during regular season. He was much faster than his gangly stature would have suggested, and his throwing arm was one of the best among big league left fielders.

Prince called him "Dogie," although writers and announcers sometimes referred to him as "Dog" and "Hound."

Twelve

The Road Through Milwaukee

It could be said that the road to the National League pennant from 1956 through 1960 had to go through Milwaukee.

The Braves won 453 games during that five-year period, most in the league. That was 35 more than the next winningest team, the Dodgers of Brooklyn and Los Angeles. The St. Louis Cardinals were third with 392 wins. Milwaukee was on the verge of forming a dynasty over that stretch, with two National League flags and three runner-up finishes. One of the seconds was really a first as the Braves tied the Dodgers for the top spot in 1959.

With the Braves featuring the same cast of stars, there was every reason to think they could win their third pennant in four years, though San Francisco was the pre-season favorite of the majority of baseball writers. Fence busters like Aaron, Mathews, and Adcock, and a pitching big three of Spahn, Burdette, and Buhl provided solid arguments for leaning toward Milwaukee. Before the month of July ended, the Braves had a lot of baseball folks looking over their shoulders. Including the Pittsburgh Pirates.

The Pirates had their own troubles, but no one on the club was sounding off. That was typical of their manager. Danny Murtaugh didn't say a whole lot. He usually didn't have to. His Pirates were a veteran team with good leadership. Dick Groat and Don Hoak would talk to teammates if there was a need. They knew how and when to do it, and they had the respect of the rest of the guys in the clubhouse. But there wasn't much said by the Bucs regarding their most glaring deficiency. Everyone knew the problem.

Defense. It was erratic, leaky, downright shoddy at times. In June, it was horrendous. Pittsburgh committed 30 errors in 27 games, with

Twelve. The Road Through Milwaukee

only 10 errorless outings. Twice they made four miscues in one game. Pirates infielders made 19 of the June errors, eight by third baseman Don Hoak. Outfielders had eight misplays, the catchers two. The good thing was that Pittsburgh remained in first place and that timely hitting and consistently good pitching were staples of the club.

When asked about the defense, Murtaugh simply said that he expected it to improve, that his guys were just going through a bit of a bad time. And the Pirates did improve, making only two errors in the first 10 games of July. Meanwhile, they continued two very pleasing habits, coming from behind to win and mowing down opponents in extra-inning games. Vernon Law and Johnny Podres both pitched into the 10th inning on July 1. Law got the first two outs before Charlie Neal gave the Dodgers a 3–2 lead with a solo home run. In the bottom of the inning, Joe Christopher's one-out double ended Podres' day, bringing on Larry Sherry. He got Dick Groat on a fly to left. Roberto Clemente singled up the middle, plating Christopher with the tying run. Then, with two outs, Dick Stuart singled to right field. Clemente was running on the pitch, and he came all the way around to score when Frank Howard's throw was wide of the plate. The win made Pittsburgh 7–0 in extra-inning games.

The Dodgers won the next two games to take the series. Once again, they got masterful pitching, with Stan Williams and Don Drysdale throwing complete games and allowing one earned run apiece.

The All-Star teams were announced, and left-fielder Bob Skinner and second baseman Bill Mazeroski were elected as starters for the National League. The voting was done by players, managers, and coaches, and they could not vote for members of their own team. The eight position starters for each league were decided by the ballots. The managers—the Dodgers' Walter Alston in the National League and Al Lopez of the White Sox in the American League—named 22 additional players, including pitchers, for both teams.

There was some controversy—that is usually the case with any kind of all-star selections—as Alston did not pick either Warren Spahn or Lew Burdette, the Braves' outstanding pitchers. It was suggested that their omission was a slap in the face of Milwaukee manager Charlie Dressen, who was a former Dodgers coach under Alston. Spahn's record at the time was 8–4. Burdette was 7–6.[1] Rounding out the National League starters were catcher Del Crandall, first baseman Joe Adcock, third baseman Eddie Mathews, and right fielder Hank Aaron, all of Milwaukee; Cubs shortstop Ernie Banks; and Giants center fielder Willie Mays.

American League starters included catcher Yogi Berra, first baseman Moose Skowron, center fielder Mickey Mantle, and right fielder Roger Maris, all of the Yankees; second baseman Pete Runnels and third baseman Frank Malzone, both of the Red Sox; White Sox left fielder Minnie Minoso; and rookie shortstop Ron Hansen of Baltimore.

Alston picked three Pittsburgh players as reserves, including shortstop Dick Groat, right fielder Roberto Clemente, and catcher Smoky Burgess. He also selected three Pirates pitchers, starters Vernon Law and Bob Friend and reliever Elroy Face. Pittsburgh, with eight, had the most players on the National League All-Star team.

On July 4 the Pirates finally lost an extra-inning game. They let a five-run lead get away, with Elroy Face losing the game. The Braves got a game-tying home run from Del Crandall in the bottom of the ninth and also scored the game-winner off Face in the 10th.

Harvey Haddix ended a three-game Pittsburgh skid with a complete-game win in the nightcap of the doubleheader. The split left the Pirates three and a half games in front of Milwaukee and five ahead of San Francisco on Independence Day, the date traditionally viewed by the baseball world as the halfway point. In reality, that was still nearly a week away. Rocky Nelson's second home run of the game came in the 10th inning and proved the difference as Pittsburgh nipped the Braves on July 5. The game would have ended in the bottom of the ninth if not for a perfect throw to the plate by Bucs left fielder Bob Skinner. The Braves, trailing by a run, had the bases loaded with two outs with Face on the mound. Crandall lined a single to left, driving in the tying run, but pinch-runner Eddie Haas was cut down as Pittsburgh reserve catcher Bob Oldis applied the tag.

Shut out for eight innings by Carlton Willey, the Pirates rallied for three runs in the ninth to take the lead. Nelson led off the inning with a home run, and one out later, Don Hoak hit a two-run shot. Nelson's second homer of the game followed a two-out single by Skinner. Paul

TWELVE. The Road Through Milwaukee

Giel surrendered a run in the 10th before Bob Friend recorded the last two outs to wrap up the victory.

On July 6, Bob Purkey was sailing along with a two-hitter before running into what had floored opposing teams all season: Pittsburgh's proclivity for late-inning miracles. The Reds led, 1–0, when Don Hoak led off the eighth with a walk. Bill Mazeroski singled, and after striking out pinch-hitter Dick Schofield, Purkey issued a bases on balls to Bill Virdon to fill the bases. When he also walked Dick Groat to force in the tying run, Fred Hutchinson had seen enough. The Cincinnati manager called on his left-handed relief specialist, Bill Henry, to pitch to Bob Skinner, who had struck out twice.

Near the end of a career punctuated by short stays with several major league clubs and monumental success in the minors, Rocky Nelson enjoyed his best big league season with the 1960 Pirates. His home run early in the seventh game of the World Series helped write the story of one of the greatest Fall Classic games ever.

Many of the old ball parks had their own personality traits, nooks and crannies that resulted from squeezing a baseball field between already existing city buildings and onto a piece of property that was asymmetrical because it was the land that was left. Those quirks added spice to the old ball yards and to games played in them, sometimes causing unusual things to happen.

Cincinnati's Crosley Field was such a stadium. It was what was commonly referred to as a "band box" because of its small size and short distances to the fences. Crosley's measurements were a mere 328 feet down the left field line, 366 to right, and 380 to center. Its main personality trait was an incline in left field, a gradual rise up to the wall. More than one outfielder had fallen down out there. One of them was Wally Post.

"Had 'Em All the Way"

Skinner got an outside pitch from Henry and lined it toward the left-field line. Post, the Reds' left fielder that day, ran in and attempted to make a shoestring catch, but missed. His flailing try left him skidding to the turf while the ball rattled around the base of the fence. Mazeroski scored easily. So did Virdon. Then came Groat. Skinner, whose stature belied deceiving speed, rounded second base and charged into third, arms and legs going every which way. That's where he saw third-base coach Frank Oceak excitedly windmilling him to the plate. Skinner made it, his inside-the-park grand slam giving the Pirates a 5–1 lead.

Reds catcher Ed Bailey homered off Paul Giel in the ninth. Billy Martin singled and pinch-hitter Jerry Lynch walked. Murtaugh waved in Face to get the final out, and he did as Frank Robinson grounded out to Hoak at third. Tom Cheney got his first major league win after pitching a strong seven innings.

Skinner was the man the next night, too, smacking a two-run double in the ninth inning to turn defeat into victory and giving Pittsburgh a sweep of the two-game series at Crosley.

The Pirates next split a doubleheader in Philadelphia, with Bill Virdon banging out five hits that included two doubles, a triple, and a home run. After dropping below .200 in early June, the center fielder had raised his batting average to .261.

Gene Conley was the answer to a trivia question: Which major league pitcher played on three straight world championship teams in another sport? The six-foot-eight right-hander, an All-American basketball player at Washington State University, was a backup big man for the Boston Celtics when they won NBA titles in 1959, 1960, and 1961. The man he primarily backed up was center Bill Russell, perhaps the all-time NBA MVP.

Conley averaged 8.3 rebounds and 6.7 points per game while playing about 19 minutes a contest in 1959–1960, his best season in the NBA. He also won 14 games for the 1954 Milwaukee Braves and helped them win pennants in 1957 and 1958. He was the winning pitcher for the National League in the 1955 All-Star Game after striking out the side in the 12th inning. Traded to Philadelphia in 1959, Conley hooked up in a pitching duel with Vernon Law on July 9. Conley four-hit Pittsburgh, winning, 2–1, when the Phillies scored a run in the bottom of the ninth

Twelve. The Road Through Milwaukee

inning. One night later, the Bucs gained a split in the four-game series by scoring four times in the ninth to beat Robin Roberts.

The Pirates carried a five-game lead over Milwaukee into the All-Star break. St. Louis and San Francisco were both eight games out. The break is baseball's traditional halfway point, when writers and fans talk about the team that is in front being the one to beat for the pennant. Never mind that more than 70 games are left on the schedule, which is exactly the reminder always tossed out by the first-place managers. "I'm sure not talking pennant at this point," Murtaugh said. "During spring training, I did not dream we would be in first place now. It is too early to be thinking about the pennant."[2]

There were two All-Star Games, played on July 11 and 13. The National League won both, 5–3 in Kansas City and 6–0 in New York. Pirates pitchers were the starters and winners in each game. Friend pitched three one-hit shutout innings in the first contest, with Law getting the last two outs. Like his teammate, Law also gave up just one hit as he pitched two shutout innings in Yankee Stadium.

Other Pirates fared well, too. Face pitched one and two-thirds perfect innings in Kansas City. Skinner had one hit in each game. Mazeroski had an RBI single. Clemente walked and was robbed of an extra-base hit on an outstanding catch by Jim Lemon of the Washington Senators. Not so well for Burgess, 0-for-3, and Groat, 0-for-1. Mays went 3-for-4 in each game, hitting a home run in New York. Stan Musial, playing in his 17th All-Star Game, belted a solo home run as a pinch-hitter in Yankee Stadium and, afterward said he felt the homer coming. Stan the Man had a pinch single in the Kansas City game. Ted Williams had a single while batting once in each game.

Following a three-day break to play the two games, major league teams resumed the regular season on July 14. In what was supposed to be a day off, the Braves made a one-day stop in Pittsburgh to make up a Memorial Day rainout. Their manager, Charlie Dressen, tried to pull a fast one. He announced Warren Spahn as his starting pitcher, then warmed up both Spahn, the left-hander, and right-hander Bob Buhl. Dressen sent Buhl to the mound, and he blanked the Bucs for eight innings, with Lew Burdette completing the five-hit shutout in one-two-three fashion. Pittsburgh lost again the next night, falling to the Reds at

"Had 'Em All the Way"

Forbes Field, while Milwaukee was winning in Philadelphia. That reduced the Pirates' lead over the Braves to three games.

Sparking the Reds' win over the Bucs was speedy center fielder Vada Pinson, who had three hits, an RBI, and a stolen base. He also made a brilliant catch that robbed Bob Skinner of an extra-base hit. Pinson had been an instant sensation, but his star status slipped away at the age of 27, when it seemed he would be reaching his prime. He broke in with Cincinnati at the age of 19, and his career got off to a blistering start a year later. Playing in all of the Reds' games, his 205 hits, 131 runs scored, and .316 batting average were strong National League "Rookie of the Year" credentials. But the 1959 award went instead to Willie McCovey, a unanimous selection despite playing in just 52 games.

Two years later, Pinson batted .343, finishing second in the National League batting race and third in the MVP voting (behind teammate Frank Robinson and runner-up Orlando Cepeda) as Cincinnati won the 1961 National League pennant. Compared to Mickey Mantle because of his sprinter's speed—3.3 seconds from home plate to first base—and home run power, the left-handed Pinson was beautiful to watch. He glided into the gaps to chase down fly balls and was a graceful blur racing from first to third. He compiled a stat sheet from 1959 to 1965 that was better than Mantle's and every other big league center fielder, with the exception of Willie Mays.

The three-game margin in the standings stayed that way as the Braves and Pirates both won on Saturday, with the Bucs staging more of their late-inning magic. They wiped out a three-run deficit by scoring four runs in the final three innings. Cincinnati's Jay Hook had been sailing along, throwing five shutout innings after Pittsburgh scored twice in the first. Trailing, 5–2, the Pirates got a home run by Bill Mazeroski in the seventh inning and a two-run single by Don Hoak in the eighth to tie the score. Dick Stuart won it with a pinch-hit home run off Jim Brosnan with one out in the ninth. The game story in the *Pittsburgh Post-Gazette* said, "Dick Stuart doesn't get many cheers, but when he gets them, they're BIG ones. 'It was all or nothing,' he said in the clubhouse. 'Brosnan was throwing hard, and I was swinging hard.'"[3]

Stuart's 13th homer made Earl Francis a first-time winner and a loser of Brosnan. It was only the second blown lead of the season for

Twelve. The Road Through Milwaukee

the Reds' right-hander, who was considered an eccentric because he spoke openly of the virtues of reading and thinking. Brosnan also had the audacity—at least, that was the word best describing the way "baseball people" viewed the author and his work—to write an inside-the-game book. It was a diary he kept during the 1959 season. Brosnan wrote about things players and managers discussed and did in the locker room, the dugout, and the bullpen. Stuff that had always been sacred among the big league fraternity. It was a *Ball Four* piece of literature a decade before Jim Bouton.

Brosnan's book, *The Long Season*, was well written and informative, a very good read. A review that appeared in the *New York Times* was kind but not applauding. The review took on the defensive stance and tones of a former ballplayer, including lines such as "Had Jim Brosnan done less thinking, he might have been a more effective pitcher."[4] Brosnan would finish with numbers proving he was quite effective in 1960: 57 games, 99 innings, a 7–2 record, 12 saves, and a 2.36 earned run average. In 1961, the basis for a second book titled *The Pennant Race*, he was 10–4 and "saved" 16 games for a Reds team that won the National League title. The only trouble with Brosnan was that he dared to be different.

In the opening game of the Sunday doubleheader, Pittsburgh once again staged a late rally. They scored four runs in the eighth inning, but came up one run short. The Pirates' consistent come-from-behind feistiness had folks talking, and one of them was Reds manager Fred Hutchinson. "They give you hell," he said of the Bucs. "They force the issue at all times, and if you give them any kind of break, they climb all over you and before one knows it, you're licked." Hutch was speaking from experience as he had seen Pittsburgh wipe out large Cincinnati leads to beat the Reds four times already during the season. "The Pirates don't only have a good club," he said. "They have a fighting club."[5]

The second game of the Sunday doubleheader had a strange beginning. Pre-beginning, to be specific. Don Newcombe was warming up as Cincinnati's starting pitcher. Big Newk was the Brooklyn Dodgers ace during his heyday, winning 47 games in a two-year span after notching 39 victories in his second and third seasons in the majors. A National

League "Rookie of the Year," he was the league's Cy Young Award winner and the Most Valuable Player in 1956 when he won 27 games.

Newcombe, 34 and well past his prime, was now struggling to get batters out. He had been traded to Cincinnati by the Dodgers two years earlier, and had recalled good memories in 1959. He went 13–8 with a 3.16, but would never come close to double figures in wins again.

As the big right-hander took his tosses from the mound minutes before the game was to begin, Danny Murtaugh approached the umpires. He pointed out that the pitcher's shirt sleeves were two different lengths. Citing a rule that required sleeves to be approximately the same length (in order not to pose a distraction) for the batter, the Pittsburgh skipper demanded that Newcombe change shirts. The umpires agreed and instructed the pitcher to do so. Newk went bananas and was ejected from the game without throwing one pitch. Reds manager Fred Hutchinson made Cal McLish his emergency starter.[6]

Back in April, the Pirates had knocked McLish out of the box in the third inning on the way to a rout. This time, he lasted seven innings, but was again the losing pitcher. Bill Virdon slammed McLish's first pitch over the fence, and Dick Groat had three hits to give him seven for the twin bill. Tom Cheney, a right-hander who began the season in the minors, threw a four-hit shutout. The Braves, behind Burdette's 10th victory, won in Philadelphia as they crept within two and a half games of Pittsburgh.

Monday was an off day, but there was baseball business in Chicago, where the National League voted unanimously to expand to 10 teams. That was contingent upon the proposed founding of a new major league called the Continental League. "We feel that, if there isn't anything in the offing for the Continental League to go ahead, we're prepared to go ahead," said National League President Warren Giles. Ford Frick, the Commissioner of Major League Baseball, said that any expansion plan would include New York. National League representatives agreed that New York City was virtually assured of getting one of the new teams when the time came.[7]

During the All-Star break, American League representatives had announced that there was absolutely no thought of adding teams. "It never came up," was the official word following a league meeting.[8]

Twelve. The Road Through Milwaukee

Strangely enough, the American League expanded first, adding the Los Angeles Angels and the Washington Senators for the 1961 season. The National League's expansion took effect in 1962, with the addition of the New York Mets and Houston Colt .45s.

The Pirates' margin was whittled to one and a half games when they lost in Los Angeles while Milwaukee downed the Cardinals at home. The Bucs had a four-run lead after five innings, but Friend couldn't hold it. Fred Green gave up a game-winning home run to Norm Larker. It was just the second homer for the Dodgers' first baseman, who had three hits and raised his league-leading batting average to .359. The Dodgers inched past St. Louis into third place in the National League. Pre-season favorite San Francisco was in fifth place, just two games over .500. The Braves extended their winning streak to seven games and moved within a half game of the league lead on July 20 as the Dodgers again downed Pittsburgh. Warren Spahn shut out the Cardinals on seven hits, while Hank Aaron and Joe Adcock hit home runs.

The Pirates' loss dropped them to 9–10 for the month, and their bullpen was letting them down. During that 19-game stretch, their starting pitchers were solid, but their relievers were awful. Starters pitched seven or more innings 11 times in the 19 games, with Harvey Haddix going eight or more in all three of his starts. He, Bob Friend, and Vernon Law each pitched a complete game. The starters had pitched 129⅓ innings, with a collective 3.40 earned run average.

There were 29 appearances by relief pitchers during the 29 games. They were scored upon more than half of those appearances—16—and allowed 22 earned runs. Bullpen ace Elroy Face pitched in nine games and had at least one earned run charged to him in five. He gave up two earned runs twice and three on another occasion. The Pittsburgh bullpen's earned run average for 45 innings over the 19-game span was 4.40, exactly a full run higher than the starters' ERA.

Law took care of any bullpen worries by five-hitting the Dodgers on July 21, and batterymate Hal Smith slammed two home runs for the second straight night. The three-game series drew nearly 154,000 fans, boosting Los Angeles home attendance to 1.4 million. The Braves lost to St. Louis, then lost to the Cubs while the Pirates won in San Francisco as Wilmer Mizell threw a complete game, the second in a row for Pitts-

"Had 'Em All the Way"

burgh. That stretched the Bucs' National League lead to two and a half games.

Two days later, Pittsburgh was out of first place.

The Pirates were introduced to a 23-year-old pitcher named Juan Marichal, and they were dazzled by the right-hander with the high leg kick. The Giants' future Hall of Famer had made a spectacular major league debut earlier in the week when he pitched a one-hitter against Philadelphia. Pittsburgh managed four hits and four walks, but were done in by four San Francisco double plays. Willie Mays' two-run homer and a solo shot by catcher Bob Schmidt gave the Giants a 3–1 win. Milwaukee moved within a game by shutting out the Cubs at Wrigley behind another 23-year-old pitcher, left-hander Juan Pizzaro.

On July 24, the Giants again downed the Pirates, while the Braves took two from the Cubs. Mays and Schmidt hit home runs for the second straight game, backing Billy O'Dell's two-hit performance over eight innings. The Bucs rallied for three runs in the ninth, but came up short. Warren Spahn and Bob Buhl pitched complete games in Milwaukee's doubleheader sweep.

Those results left Pittsburgh and Milwaukee dead even in the games-behind column, but the Braves were on top of the National League standings by .001 of a percentage point (.590 to .589). It was the first time in 56 days that Pittsburgh had not been in first place.

The Pirates were back on top the very next day. Bob Friend beat the Cardinals for his 11th win. Roberto Clemente, Bill Virdon, and Bob Skinner all homered. Elroy Face came in to get the final out with the tying runs on base. Milwaukee, which was idle, slipped a half-game back and into second place.

Face saved another game the next night, but had to pitch one and two-thirds innings. He retired all four batters he faced, using a double play to preserve the 13th victory for Vernon Law, who beat St. Louis for the 10th time in a row. Virdon clouted a pinch-hit two-run home run off reliever Bob Gibson that proved the difference in a 5–4 triumph. The Braves kept pace with a win at San Francisco, their fourth straight, but then lost three straight games and seven out of eight.

The Pirates cooled off the Cardinals, who had been red-hot with 11 wins in their last 14 games. The Bucs concluded a sweep in St. Louis

Twelve. *The Road Through Milwaukee*

and won the opener of a three-game set at Wrigley Field for a four-game win streak that built their lead back to three games. In the final win over St. Louis, the Bucs lost a couple of right-handed pitchers. Starter George Witt left the game after one inning with pain in his right elbow. Earl Francis came on and pitched well, allowing an unearned run in three innings. But he, too, was forced from the game with discomfort in his right shoulder. Lefty Fred Green pitched four shutout innings for his fifth victory.

At Chicago, Vinegar Bend Mizell pitched his second straight complete game, a two-hit shutout, while Don Hoak took care of the offense. The third baseman homered and drove in three runs. Mizell, who had experienced control problems at times during his career, was almost flawless. He retired the first 17 batters he faced before a single by Cubs pitcher Jim Brewer. The left-hander walked one and faced 29 batters, just two over the minimum.

The Cubs won the next two games, leaving Pittsburgh with a July record of 15–14 and a two-game lead over Milwaukee. The worst part of the losses was a bad outing by Elroy Face. It followed a solid week by Pirate relievers in which they allowed two earned runs in 14⅔ innings. Face, entering in the seventh with his team down, 2–1, was hammered for four hits and four earned runs in an inning. His earned run average ballooned to 3.52.

Danny Murtaugh must have been wondering about Face. He knew the Baron had to be tired from pitching in 45 of the Pirates' 96 games. Murtaugh also knew there wasn't anyone better for tough late-game situations and that he would rather hand the ball to a tired Elroy Face than a rested anyone else in the Pittsburgh bullpen. So, the Bucs' manager did a mental head-shake and just hoped the little guy with the big heart would be able to revive his ability to get clutch outs as the club headed for the stretch drive.

Milwaukee manager Fred Haney was doing some head-shaking of his own. Having Warren Spahn, Lew Burdette, and Bob Buhl in his rotation was like an insurance policy against long losing streaks. One of the three would usually salvage a win every turn through the rotation, preventing the losses from piling up. But all three lost from July 27 to July 29, just when the Braves were breathing down the necks of the Pittsburgh

"Had 'Em All the Way"

Pirates. Milwaukee had won four in a row and, after slipping a percentage point ahead of the Bucs in the National League standings, was just a half-game back. The successive setbacks by the Braves' big three dropped them three games behind the Pirates and started a week-long slide that came at the worst time.

Thirteen
Dog Days and Doubleheaders

"Dog days" are a part of baseball folklore, representing that grueling period during the final third of a long season when players are exhausted, when the end is not really close, and when what fans think of as "just a game" can become a grind. Although there is no definite period with such a designation on the baseball calendar, over the years the time from early July to the middle of August, summer's most sultry stretch, has generally been regarded as dog days. For the players, it is kind of like "the wall" experienced by marathon runners. While it might be a matter of pushing through, for teams contending for a pennant, more is required. For them, it is imperative somehow to find a second wind and continue playing well. Contenders cannot be satisfied with mere survival.

Pittsburgh found that second wind as the dog days of 1960 began in a most favorable manner for the Pirates, with an 18-game home stand. They split their first two games in August and then reeled off seven wins in a row. Pittsburgh starting pitchers allowed only four runs in the opening four games of the month and pitched complete games in five of the first six.

Four men comprised the team's starting rotation and started 124 of the Pirates' 155 games in 1960. Bob Friend made 37 starts, Vernon Law 35, Harvey Haddix 29, and Vinegar Bend Mizell 23. The quartet logged 875⅓ of the team's 1,399⅔ innings, 62.5 percent. Pittsburgh's rotation turned in authentic "quality starts." When rainouts and/or days off provided the necessary rest, Danny Murtaugh would use Friend or Law out of sequence, even though it might have been Haddix's or Mizell's turn. The Bucs skipper wanted his two aces on the mound as many times as possible.

On August 2, the Continental League ended without having played

"Had 'Em All the Way"

a game. A year after its formation, what was to be the third major baseball league agreed to disband. The eight teams tentatively listed to comprise the Continental League unanimously accepted an arrangement which would allow four of its franchises to be absorbed into the existing structures of the National League and the American League, expanding both from eight to 10 teams. Expansion was targeted for 1961 and would take place no later than 1962.[1]

Law pitched a five-hit shutout against Los Angeles, while Friend lost despite giving up just six hits in a game shortened to seven innings by rain. The Pirates took the series as George "Red" Witt got his first win in two years, pitching six innings of six-hit baseball and getting three shutout innings of relief from Elroy Face.

That same day, August 4, there was extracurricular activity at Wrigley Field. More action than fans, as fewer than 5,000 showed up to watch the Cubs take on the Reds. Chicago rookie Jim Brewer threw a pitch close to the head of Cincinnati's Billy Martin. The former New York Yankees second baseman took exception, and on the next pitch, he intentionally swung and missed, letting the bat fly toward the mound. It landed between the mound and first base. When Martin walked out to retrieve the bat, he and Brewer tangled. One of Martin's punches broke Brewer's cheekbone, and he was hospitalized for two months, suffering blurred vision. Martin was suspended for five days.[2] Brewer went on to become a very effective relief pitcher. The left-hander averaged 20 saves over a five-year period, made an All-Star team, and pitched in three World Series with the Los Angeles Dodgers.

The Pirates continued to get fine pitching. On August 5, Mizell blanked the Giants on five hits, the game's only run scoring in bizarre fashion. Bill Virdon led off the bottom of the eighth inning with a walk and was bunted to second by Dick Groat. Losing pitcher Sam Jones fielded the bunt and threw it over the head of second baseman Don Blasingame, who was covering first. When Groat and Blasingame collided, Virdon was able to score.

The Pirates got a big scare in the seventh inning when Roberto Clemente, running full speed, crashed into the Forbes Field right field brick wall while making a sensational catch of a blast by Willie Mays. Danny Murtaugh said it was the best catch he ever saw.[3] Clemente suf-

Thirteen. Dog Days and Doubleheaders

fered a deep cut to his chin and required five stitches. He was replaced by Gino Cimoli, whose catch ended the inning. Clemente was taken to a hospital for X-rays which proved negative. He missed the next six games, but his teammates didn't miss a beat. In what by then had become typical fashion for the Bucs, they rallied for three runs in the 10th to nip the Giants. Law went the distance and appeared headed for a loss.

First, he saw victory slip away when ex–Pirate Dale Long clouted a two-run pinch homer in the ninth inning. Long was most remembered for two things. In 1957, as Pittsburgh's everyday first baseman, he set a major league record when he homered in eight consecutive games. (The record has since been equaled by Don Mattingly and Ken Griffey, Jr.) Traded to the Cubs, in 1958 Long became the first left-handed throwing catcher in the majors since 1902.

Orlando Cepeda hit a two-run home run in the 10th to give San Francisco a 7–5 lead. The Pirates stormed back behind four singles, the last of those the game-winner by Dick Groat, to win it. Law's 15th victory was tops in the majors.

Pittsburgh swept a Sunday doubleheader and the four-game series from the Giants. Friend pitched nine innings to win for the 12th time. In the nightcap, Face helped himself with a bunt single and threw three scoreless innings for the victory as the Bucs turned three double plays. The Bucs had yet another hero as Joe Christopher, playing in the outfield because Clemente was hurt, cracked a three-run homer.

The Pirates won both games of a short series with the Cubs to extend their streak to seven. Stinginess by the pitching staff continued to be the norm as Mizell allowed five hits and Law four, both in complete-game performances.

Solly Hemus always was a spunky guy. He put together a solid big league career as an infielder who knew how to get on base and do the little things that helped win ball games. Hemus batted .273 with a .390 on-base percentage in 11 seasons, most of them with the St. Louis Cardinals. At the age of 37, he was in his second year as the Cards' manager. It was a job that would end midway through the 1961 season. The Cardinals trailed the Pirates by five games as they prepared to begin a series in Pittsburgh that would include five games in four days and could have a lot to say about the National League pennant.

"Had 'Em All the Way"

Waiting around in the afternoon before an August 11 night game that would kick off the series, Hemus had plenty to say about the upcoming games, even sounding a warning of sorts.

> Just tell Murtaugh to be ready for us. We are due to have a good series here, and there's no time better than the present. We are 1–4 against the Pirates here and that's bad. Maybe all will be changed when we leave here Sunday night. I know the Pirates are tough, but my Cards didn't come here only to fulfill a schedule commitment. We are in town to flatten them like a rug. And if we can take this series, we will be that much harder to handle.[4]

St. Louis, which had passed Milwaukee in the standings and was in second place, made its skipper look good by taking the first two games at Forbes Field. The Cardinals had a seven-game winning streak and had won 14 of their last 16. Stan Musial's two-run homer in the 12th inning stopped the Pirates' seven-game win streak. Both starting pitchers, Ernie Broglio and Bob Friend, threw complete games. Musial knocked in two more runs the next night to help Bob Gibson even his record at 3–3.

The Pirates' lead over the Cards had been reduced to just three games. Milwaukee had faded into a third-place tie with the Dodgers, six games out of first. And then, as it often happens in adventure novels and movies, someone saved the day—in this case, he prevented negative momentum from building for the Pirates. That someone was Roberto Clemente, who was turning into an all-around star.

Clemente was back. Really back. After going hitless in his August 12 return to the lineup following a six-game absence, he had three hits and drove in all four Pittsburgh runs the next day. Clemente singled in a run in the first inning, smacked a two-run home run in the third, and added an RBI single in the fourth. Dick Groat went 4-for-4. That was plenty of offense for Harvey Haddix, who slowed the Cardinals express by allowing one run in nine innings.

When Law survived 12 hits—including a cycle by St. Louis first baseman Bill White—to win in the opener of a Sunday doubleheader, it was the Pirates' 10th complete game in a dozen August outings. (The major league team leader in complete games for the entire 2013 season was Tampa Bay with nine.) Rocky Nelson's three-run homer and three hits by Bill Virdon helped Law to his big-league-leading 17th win.

Thirteen. Dog Days and Doubleheaders

Five scoreless innings by the bullpen lifted the Bucs to an 11-inning victory in the nightcap and provided them with their largest lead in the standings all season. That was such big news that it made headlines on the front page of the *Pittsburgh Post-Gazette*. Don Hoak singled in the decisive run as Forbes' second-largest crowd of the year, 36,775, watched. In two days, Pittsburgh had doubled its lead to a comfortable six games, while the Cardinals were in danger of falling into third place. St. Louis committed seven errors in the twin bill, while the Pirates pulled off five double plays.

On August 14, the same day the Bucs were wrapping up their important series win over St. Louis, one of their all-time greats died. Fred Clarke, a member of the Hall of Fame, was 87. Clarke, who played in the major leagues for 21 years, was a big league manager for 16 years, all with Pittsburgh. He took the Pirates to four National League pennants and one World Series title.

Danny Murtaugh's patience and refusal to panic were in strong evidence when it came to Bill Virdon. At the season's outset, the Pirates manager had platooned the left-handed-batting center fielder with Gino Cimoli, who batted from the right side. When Cimoli was hitting and Virdon wasn't, Cimoli played more, even getting an appreciable number of at-bats against right-handed pitchers.

When Virdon continued to struggle, there were trade rumblings, but Murtaugh did not address them except to say they were rumors and nothing more. He expressed confidence in Virdon, insisting that he would eventually hit and would play a big part in the Bucs having a very successful season. On June 9, Virdon's batting average dipped to .183 and still hadn't climbed above .200 by the middle of the month. When questioned about Virdon, the Pittsburgh skipper simply said, "Just wait. You'll see." Meanwhile, whenever he played, Virdon was outstanding in center field. He was contributing defensively as he made several fine plays that prevented runs and stopped opposing teams' rallies.

"Virdon was as good as anybody," Pirates utility infielder Dick Schofield said. "He could be counted on to get to the ball, and then he was going to catch it. He was smart ... knew how to play the hitters and what they were liable to do with a particular pitch."[5] Those things helped Virdon get two "jumps" on the ball, according to Bob Friend. The first was before the ball was hit, a positioning jump which had him in the area of center field where the ball was likely to be hit. The second was when the ball was hit, as he possessed an almost instinctive ability to take off in the right direction on impact. The combination allowed him to make routine catches on balls many outfielders either would not reach or would have to make a spectacular play to make the catch.[6]

Virdon was a great outfielder, the most dependable Schofield ever saw, even though most people didn't realize it because he made everything look easy out there. The Bucs' center fielder never did anything to hurt the team, Schofield said, was an excellent base runner and was as sound fundamentally as they came. He might not get a hit, but he didn't take the Pirates out of an inning with a base running blunder. And he didn't throw to the wrong base or miss his cutoff man.[7]

By August, Bill Virdon was hitting the ball hard as well as catching it. His improvement had been gradual. He used four two-hit games to get his average up to .238 by the end of June. In July, he batted .337 and hit five home runs, twice in back-to-back games. One of the homers was a pinch-hit two-run shot off of St. Louis's Bob Gibson that made the difference in a 5–4 win. Virdon's three hits against the Cardinals on August 14 boosted his batting average to .286. A Virdon home run and another from Hoak weren't enough to prevent a loss to Philadelphia, but the Pirates won the last three games of the series and took the first of four with Cincinnati to give them seven wins in eight games.

Clemente played key roles in both ends of a Forbes Field Tuesday doubleheader, sparking Pittsburgh to a sweep of the Phillies. He and Bob Skinner had three hits and three RBI apiece in an opening game blowout. The Bucs produced the winning run in an unusual way in the second game. In the bottom of the eighth inning, Groat, Skinner, and Rocky Nelson all bunted for base hits. Robin Roberts walked Clemente to plate Groat.

It was announced that Pittsburgh had signed Clem Labine as a free agent. The long-time anchor of the Dodgers bullpen had more recently been with the Detroit Tigers, who released the 34-year-old right-hander one day before the Pirates picked him up. Murtaugh wasted no time in putting Labine to work. In the final game of the series, when the Phils chased Harvey Haddix with three singles in the sixth inning, Labine got

Thirteen. Dog Days and Doubleheaders

the call with one out. He walked a batter, induced a ground ball which scored a run when the Pirates were unable to turn a double play and had to settle for a forceout, and struck out Tony Curry. Labine was brilliant the rest of the way, giving up no hits, striking out five more, and getting three groundball outs. He definitely saved the day with three and two-thirds innings of hitless work.

That concluded a 14–4 home stand for Pittsburgh. Meanwhile, the Cardinals had gone into a tailspin. After trimming their deficit to three games, they had lost six in a row, dropping them nine games behind the first-place Pirates and one and a half back of Milwaukee, which had leap-frogged St. Louis into the second spot.

In mid–August, *The Sporting News* named Ted Williams as its "Player of the Decade" for the 1950s. From 1950 to 1959, Williams batted .336 with 227 home runs and 729 RBI. Two years of military service, along with various ailments and injuries, limited him to 995 games during that period, magnifying his tremendous production.

The Pirates started a 14-game road trip in Cincinnati on August 18. Law allowed a first-inning run and left, trailing 1–0. Dick Stuart batted for him in the top of the eighth and blasted a three-run pinch-hit homer off Cal McLish. Elroy Face finished off Law's 18th victory. The game took only an hour and 49 minutes. Stuart hit two more home runs in the series finale, with the Bucs and Reds splitting four games.

Pittsburgh struck for more of its patented late lightning at Wrigley Field, scoring all eight of its runs in the last three innings to beat the Cubs on August 23. The next day, the Bucs scored four runs in the ninth inning in a 10–6 win, back-to-back home runs by Stuart and Clemente keying the rally. Virdon had four hits and was batting .280 with six home runs, 13 doubles, and six triples. As the Bucs' leadoff man, he was getting on and then getting around to score. The Cubs salvaged a win by handing Pittsburgh its 16th one-run loss of the season. Danny Murtaugh was tossed out of the game for arguing a call in the ninth inning.

Baseball fans in St. Louis have always been among the most rabid and most knowledgeable in the game. The sea of red that blankets the stands at Busch Stadium symbolizes the terrific support the Cardinals receive. And it was strongly in evidence when the Pirates paid a visit in late August. The Cardinals swept the three-game series from the Bucs as Stan "The Man" Musial played the villain, slugging game-deciding home runs in the first two games. His 13th homer of the season was a two-run shot in the seventh inning that proved the difference in a 3–1 St. Louis win. The blast came off Friend, the third time the Cardinals great had homered off the right-hander in 1960.

The following night, Musial's home run was even more dramatic. He came to bat in the bottom of the ninth with two outs in a 4–4 game and deposited an Elroy Face pitch over the right field wall. The Bucs had rallied for four runs in the seventh to tie the score. Busch attendance for the three games was 83,727, pushing the Cards' attendance for the year to nearly 942,000, well past that of the previous year.

A four-game skid had whittled Pittsburgh's National League lead to five and a half games over both the Cardinals and the Braves.

Official major league statistics showed that Los Angeles first baseman Norm Larker was leading the National League in hitting with a .346 average. He had more than one hundred fewer at-bats than the next four players in the batting race, but enough to qualify. Willie Mays was second at .325, followed by Dick Groat (.320), Roberto Clemente (.317), and Cubs center fielder Richie Ashburn (.307). Only three other hitters in the league had averages of .300 or higher. Vernon Law had the most wins in the majors with 18, two more than Warren Spahn and the Cardinals' Ernie Broglio.

The Pirates were not known as a power-hitting team, but they used the long ball to get out of their losing rut and win all four games of a West Coast swing.

They stopped the slide on August 29 by pounding the Dodgers behind a 16-hit assault that included three-run homers by Hal Smith and Don Hoak. Law, who pitched a complete game for his 19th win, even got into the act. Los Angeles reliever Ed Palmquist knocked the Deacon down with a fastball, and on the next pitch, Law hit his only home run of the season. Hoak and Bill Mazeroski each contributed three hits. It was the fifth time Law had beaten the Dodgers for the season.

The next day, Dick Groat hit his second home run of the season and Roberto Clemente hit his 11th, both off Sandy Koufax, who lasted into the fifth inning. Bob Friend was the beneficiary, winning his 14th. It was more of the same in Candlestick Park. Clemente connected again.

THIRTEEN. *Dog Days and Doubleheaders*

The Giants were up, 3–0, when he smashed a Billy O'Dell pitch over the right field wall with Groat aboard. Bill Mazeroski also drove in a pair of runs. The Pittsburgh bullpen picked up an ineffective Vinegar Bend Mizell by holding San Francisco to a run on four hits over the last five innings. Face saved his 20th game.

The Pirates concluded August with a 21–10 record, a winning percentage of .677 that was the team's best in any full month of 1960. (Pittsburgh had a .786 percentage but in only 14 April games.)

The Bucs began September with their fourth win in a row. Clemente continued his power surge, smacking a three-run homer in the first inning at Candlestick Park. That gave him a home run in three straight games and 13 for the season along with 86 RBI. He rapped out three hits for the second straight day, raising his batting average to .323, the same as Dick Groat's. With a month left in the season, Larker remained the league batting leader, but the gap was decreasing. His average was .339 and Mays' was .326, with Clemente and Groat tied for third place. Harvey Haddix won his 10th despite getting battered a bit. He allowed 10 hits in less than six innings, but only one run. Clem Labine impressed in his second long-relief outing by throwing three and a third scoreless innings.

The Pirates activated coach Mickey Vernon that day, giving him the distinction of playing in the major leagues in four decades. Vernon, 42, played 20 years in the majors. Most of Vernon's career was spent with the lowly Washington Senators. He was a smooth-fielding first baseman and won two batting titles, hitting .353 in 1946 and .337 in 1953. He had 490 career doubles. Vernon played in the Pirates' first game after they added him to their roster. Pinch-hitting in the ninth inning against Philadelphia's Art Mahaffey, he grounded out.

So did 11 other Bucs as Mahaffey struck out just one batter in nine innings. The rookie right-hander improved to 5–0. Law lost for the first time since July 17, having won eight successive decisions.

A column by Jack Hernon appeared in the *Pittsburgh Post Gazette*. He discussed the Pirates' candidates for the National League Most Valuable Player Award, saying Dick Groat, Don Hoak, Vernon Law, Elroy Face, and Roberto Clemente were all deserving of consideration. Hernon pointed out that hardly anyone in the national press corps mentioned Clemente. Bucs backup first baseman Rocky Nelson also wondered why not.

"Had 'Em All the Way"

> One thing I can't understand. I've read many stories about who is the most valuable player on the Pirates, but I never see the name of Roberto mentioned. I don't know how he can be overlooked when you talk about players on this club. Actually, there is no one player that can be classed as the most valuable in my opinion. There are about five fellows on this team we couldn't get along without. I mean individually. There's Groat and Hoak and the Deacon and Elroy and Clemente, but he doesn't get a call.[8]

A Pittsburgh sportswriter who covered the Pirates regularly had campaigned openly against Clemente as a viable Most Valuable Player candidate, saying he was not deserving. While Nelson did not say the right-fielder was a clear-cut choice for the award, he noted that he was certainly deserving of strong consideration.

> Roberto has been consistently around .320 all season. He has hit more home runs than ever. He just might be the only player here to drive in 100 runs. And certainly he is the best right fielder in the league. Sure, those others are valuable to this team. But no more valuable than Clemente. He's won games for us with his bat, with his arm, and with his speed on the bases. What more can you ask a player to do to be recognized? If Roberto beefs about not being mentioned, I wouldn't blame him. He's done as much as any other player on this team to keep us in first place.[9]

"The more you think the situation over," Hernon wrote, "the more the Rock's observation deserves a bit of mention."[10]

Hernon added that during the first part of the season, Clemente was the Mr. Clutch of the ball club and that he led the league in hitting and RBI at one time. Dick Groat mentioned at the time, "Boy, you should see how Roberto's eyes light up when he comes to the plate with men on base. He actually drools when he sees someone in scoring position. That the other teams recognized this lies in the fact he has been the target of the brushback and knockdown pitch in recent weeks."

Don Hoak said,

> I have talked to Roberto about this. I explained to him that he has to expect this kind of treatment on a first-place ball team. I guess I was knocked down as much or more than anyone on the club last year. I told Robby that when I was with Brooklyn, the hitter who was doing the damage to a certain club was decked pretty often. But they would bounce right up and rip into the ball.
>
> This is the first time he has gone through anything like this. But it has to be expected. He's leading the team in runs batted in, so those other guys are trying to keep him loose at the plate.[11]

THIRTEEN. Dog Days and Doubleheaders

Labine did it again on September 4. He pitched more than three innings of scoreless relief for the third time since signing on with the Bucs less than three weeks earlier. He allowed one hit and struck out five to save Vinegar Bend's 10th victory. Clemente and Hoak hit home runs. It was the 14th for both.

Hoak homered again the next day, and so did Dick Stuart. Their blasts sparked a seven-run fourth inning that allowed the Bucs to outlast Milwaukee, 9–7. Bob Buhl cooled Pittsburgh bats in the second game of the doubleheader.

September 6 was a dark day for the Pirates. They won their game with the Braves, but lost their shortstop. Dick Groat was hit by a Lew Burdette pitch in the first inning on his left wrist. After getting hit, Groat stayed in the game until the third inning. He caught a throw from pitcher Joe Gibbon, who had fielded a comebacker, for a force out in the top of the third, and the wrist began to swell. He was unable to continue in the bottom of the inning and was taken to a Pittsburgh hospital.

Dick "Ducky" Schofield, the backup infielder who could play second base, shortstop, or third very capably, pinch-hit for Groat. Schofield singled and scored the game's first run on Bob Skinner's 29th double of the season. Schofield made a dandy defensive play in the top of the sixth. Trailing, 2–0, the Braves got a leadoff single from Billy Bru-

"Tiger" was a fitting nickname for Don Hoak, who played all 155 games for the 1960 Pirates despite injuries. He had enough left in the tank to bat .347 and drive in 15 runs in the final month. For the season, the third baseman led the team in runs scored and on-base percentage, was second in extra-base hits, and fourth in RBI.

ton. Del Crandall followed with what looked like another single, a hard-hit groundball toward left field. But Schofield ranged into the hole, speared the ball backhanded, and fired a perfect throw to Mazeroski at second. Mazeroski made a slick pivot and quick relay as usual to complete the double play. Instead of having the tying runs on base with no outs and slugger Eddie Mathews at the plate, the Braves had two outs and no one on. Mathews flied to center to end the inning.

Milwaukee scored three times in the eighth, getting five successive singles after two were out to take a 3–2 lead, and ruining what had been a lovely evening for Joe Gibbon. The Pirates rallied for three runs in the eighth, once again demonstrating their ability to come from behind late in games. Warren Spahn relieved Burdette and failed to get an out. Stuart and Clemente doubled for one run, and Smoky Burgess singled in another. Ron Piche replaced Spahn and got a couple of ground-ball outs. The Old Pro, Mickey Vernon, lined a pinch single to right, scoring Joe Christopher, who had gone in to run for Burgess. Elroy Face pitched a scoreless ninth to nail it down.

After the game, it was reported that hospital X-rays showed a fracture in Groat's left wrist. Pittsburgh general manager Joe L. Brown said the shortstop would be out four weeks. That meant Schofield would be the club's everyday shortstop. The switch-hitter was a terrific fielder who could make all the plays, and he had a strong, accurate arm. He didn't hit much, which was the reason he wasn't somebody's starting shortstop. Before he took over for Groat, Schofield was batting .200 for the 1960 season, with a career average of .195 over parts of eight big league seasons. The most at-bats he had in one year was 145 in 1959, when he batted .234 for Pittsburgh.

There was no question "Ducky" could do the job in the field. The hope among the Pirates was that he might find a way to get on base—a walk here, a base hit there—and lay down some bunts, something else at which he was very adept. The game he went in for Groat, Schofield had three singles in three trips to the plate. He had at least one hit in the next five games and never really cooled off. He turned what most people thought would be a definite offensive liability into an asset. Clemente went 3-for-4 with a pair of doubles and an RBI.

Although Groat's injury was tough for the Bucs, they couldn't com-

Thirteen. Dog Days and Doubleheaders

plain because the team had enjoyed remarkably good health all season. The shortstop's lengthy absence was the club's first. At the time, Groat was riding an 11-game hitting streak and was batting .325, second in the National League and six points behind leader Norm Larker.

Ernie Broglio beat the Bucs for the fourth time during the season without a loss, outdueling Law in a 2–1 St. Louis win. It was a one-night stand, the Cardinals stopping off in Pittsburgh to make up a rainout.

Mizell came within an out of a complete game on September 9, and Face got that out on one pitch. Schofield's two-run triple was the big blow as the Pirates nipped the Cubs and ended a six-game losing streak in one-run games. Another day, another key hit by Dick Schofield. An RBI double this time that helped Friend win his 15th. The Cubs got nine hits but just one run as the Pirates infield turned five double plays. Bill Mazeroski was involved in all five.

The Pirates split two-game series with San Francisco and Los Angeles, and they had trouble making contact in the two losses. Pittsburgh's lead was seven and a half games with 17 left to play after downing the Giants. Harvey Haddix went the distance and allowed just a ninth-inning run. Stuart singled, tripled, and smacked his 20th home run to lead the Bucs' 16-hit attack. It was the second straight game he had three hits that included a homer.

The loss eliminated the Giants from the National League pennant race. They had been picked by the majority of pre-season prognosticators to win the title. On September 13, lefty Mike McCormick struck out 13 Pirates and allowed 13 base runners, while winning his 13th game of the season. Clemente's 15th home run was wasted.

The Dodgers' Stan Williams fanned 13 Bucs the next evening as Vernon Law failed for the third time in his attempt to win his 20th game. Law lasted only five innings. Pittsburgh's loss, combined with the Cardinals' win over the Reds, reduced the Pirates' lead to five and a half games with a little over two weeks remaining in the season.

The pennant race would not get any closer.

Gino Cimoli, who was playing center field most of the time against left-handed pitching, led off the first inning on September 15 with a single. Bob Skinner followed with his 15th home run. Friend made those two runs stand up for his 16th win. He beat the Dodgers in going the distance and allowing one run. Friend twice got into trouble, and the infield bailed him out with double plays both times.

Dick Groat was only three points behind National League batting leader Norm Larker, whose average had fallen to .328. Willie Mays went 5-for-6 and improved to .325 for a share of the second spot.

Thirty-nine-year-old Warren Spahn pitched the first no-hitter of his illustrious career. He struck out 15 in beating the Phillies, 4–0. With two outs in the ninth, Bobby Malkmus lined a ball off Spahn's glove. It caromed to Milwaukee shortstop Johnny Logan, who threw to Joe Adcock at first to end the game. The win was Spahn's 20th, the 11th time he had reached that plateau. It was the second time Philadelphia had been no-hit by a Braves pitcher in 1960. Lew Burdette did it a month earlier in a 1–0 victory. A hit batter spoiled what would have been a perfect game. Burdette also shut out the Giants in his start before the no-no and blanked the Dodgers in his next start after the no-hitter.

A little-known outfielder named Carroll Hardy made some history in Baltimore as the Orioles and Boston Red Sox played. When Ted Williams fouled a ball off his ankle and had to leave the game, Hardy was sent to the plate to finish the at-bat. He became the only player to pinch-hit for Williams. Later in his career, Hardy batted for Carl Yastrzemski, becoming the only player to pinch-bat for the two Red Sox Hall of Famers. Hardy also hit his first major league home run in 1958 while pinch-hitting for Roger Maris when they played for the Cleveland Indians.[12]

Doubleheaders were once as much a Sunday afternoon ball park staple as straw hats and hot dogs. Now, two games are seldom played on the same day, and doubleheaders, with rare exceptions, do not appear on a season's original schedule. Ernie Banks' cry of "It's a beautiful day for a ball game, let's play two" was echoed by fans in every big league city. Seeing two games for the price of one was a treat, and with games requiring much less time to play back then, a person could take in both ends of a twin bill and be home for supper.

The truth is that doubleheaders have always made for a long day for the players, despite what Banks might have said. As well as a possibly tortuous day for relief pitchers and for managers trying to navigate 18 innings without severely affecting the bullpen for days to come. So it

Thirteen. Dog Days and Doubleheaders

was that the Pittsburgh Pirates played three doubleheaders in five days of September in 1960, two of them on the road.

Author Jim Brosnan nailed down Jim O'Toole's win over the Bucs in Cincinnati. Haddix had one of his worst outings of the season, walking two and giving up three hits and three runs in two innings. Face allowed the deciding run in the seventh as the Reds won, 4–3, in a Thursday night contest.

The next day, September 17, was a rainout. That meant the Pirates and Reds would play two games on Sunday, the 18th.

Law won his 20th in the first game, 5–3, as Don Hoak and Dick Stuart both doubled, homered, and drove in a pair of runs. Law became just the fourth 20-game winner for the Bucs since 1930. Bob Friend had done it two years earlier, Murry Dickson in 1951 and Rip Sewell in 1943 and 1944. Law pitched a complete game, and so did Mizell as the Pirates took both ends of the doubleheader. Mizell threw a three-hitter for his third shutout. Schofield was on base seven times in the two games, with four hits and three walks. The shortstop also had a hand in three double plays.

The only run of the nightcap came in the seventh inning when Hoak led off with a double, moved to third when Bill Mazeroski grounded out to the right side, and scored on Schofield's double to right field. Vada Pinson's bunt single was the only hit off of Mizell over the last four innings. Willie "Puddin' Head" Jones twice grounded into Schofield-to-Mazeroski-to-Stuart double plays.

A graphic on the front page of the *Pittsburgh Post-Gazette* showed a drawn thermometer with the mercury on the number seven. Moving to the top, the numbers grew smaller, representing the shrinking magic number for the Pirates' clinching the pennant.[13]

September 19 was a day off for the Pirates, who were set for another doubleheader the following day at Connie Mack Stadium in Philadelphia. Two games were played because, back in late June, Pittsburgh player representative Bob Friend had told the National League his teammates had voted against playing two games on July 10. He said the Bucs' night game on July 9 made a twin bill the next afternoon too strenuous. National League officials agreed, scheduling the makeup of the Bucs-Phillies June 4 rainout for September 20.[14]

"Had 'Em All the Way"

Pittsburgh pitching was magnificent in both games, allowing a total of three runs. Friend's complete-game performance earned him victory number 17, the Phils' only run coming on Jim Woods' first career homer. Bill Virdon had a single, double, his eighth home run, and three RBI.

Friend struck out six, giving him 178, breaking the single-season franchise record which had stood for 48 years. Claude Hendrix had fanned 176 batters for the 1912 Pirates.

Harvey Haddix gave up an earned run in six innings of the second game, and Clem Labine picked up the win with three shutout innings. Four errors cost the Bucs only one unearned run. Two RBI from Bob Skinner and one from Schofield gave Pittsburgh its 90th win. The Pirates' National League lead was six games over St. Louis with nine games left to play.

There was more good news that day for the Pirates. They learned that their shortstop, Dick Groat, might be able to return for the last few games of the season. He had his cast removed, and X-rays taken showed new bone forming, with the possibility of enough healing in the next week to permit Groat to play. Groat had gained another point in the batting race. Larker was hitting .327, Groat .325, Mays .320, and Clemente .316.

"Teddy Ballgame" closed out his astounding 19-season batting display in dramatic style. Williams, 42, blasted a home run off of Baltimore's Jack Fisher in the final at-bat of his career. Fittingly, it came in Fenway Park.

The Bucs had another day off on September 21, then still another doubleheader the following day. The Cubs would fly from Chicago to Pittsburgh for a make-up doubleheader on September 22, then fly immediately back to Chicago for another make-up doubleheader with St. Louis on September 23.

Law pitched nine innings once again in the first game, but left with the score 2–2. Face threw two shutout innings and got his 10th win when seldom used Gene Baker singled with the bases loaded. The win was Pittsburgh's 11th in 15 extra-inning games. In the nightcap, Mizell pitched a six-hitter for his eighth complete game. He allowed one run in lowering his earned run average to 3.41 and improving his record to 13–8. Hoak had two hits and drove in three runs, extending his hitting streak to

Thirteen. Dog Days and Doubleheaders

nine games. During that period, he batted .444 with five extra-base hits and six RBI.

The sweep by the Pirates, giving them six wins in five days, eliminated idle Milwaukee from the National League pennant race. The lead paragraph in the *Pittsburgh Post-Gazette* story on the race said, "The Braves is dead." St. Louis, which was also idle, was in second place, seven and a half games back. Pittsburgh's magic number for winning the title was two, meaning any combination of Bucs wins and Cardinals losses totaling two would send the Pirates to the World Series. Six of Pittsburgh's remaining seven games were with the Braves, three at County Stadium and three at Forbes Field sandwiched around a single-game visit by the Cubs. All 10 of the Cardinals' games were on the road, including four in Chicago, three in Los Angeles, and three in San Francisco.

There was a bit of drama for a couple of days. Bob Buhl stopped the Pirates' six-game winning streak with a five-hitter, while St. Louis won a doubleheader at Wrigley Field. The Braves also won the next two games to sweep the series. Pittsburgh pounded out 11 hits off of Lew Burdette, but scored their only runs on solo homers by Roberto Clemente and Dick Stuart. Warren Spahn allowed four hits in eight innings, with Milwaukee winning on Eddie Mathews' two-out, two-run home run off Face in the bottom of the 10th.

Despite their third straight loss, the Pirates celebrated in the locker room on Sunday afternoon, September 25. That's because an hour before their game ended, the Cubs had defeated the Cardinals, eliminating them from the race. Here is the way things played out that day: If the Cubs or Pirates won, Pittsburgh would be the National League champion. Bill Mazeroski's 11th home run gave the Bucs a 1–0 lead over Warren Spahn and the Braves. The scoreboard showed the Cubs leading St. Louis, 5–0, in the eighth inning.

"I can't take it any longer," Groat told Virdon. Both ran into the clubhouse to join Burgess, Gene Baker, and some of the pitchers listening to the Cards-Cubs game on WGN. At 4:46 p.m. Pittsburgh time, Glenn Hobbie finished beating St. Louis, 5–0, and the Pirates were champions![15] The players broke for the dugout. "We're in," Groat yelled. "It's all over," Virdon hollered. Somebody grabbed the phone and called the bullpen, saying, "Wake up, you freeloaders. It's all over." Clemente stepped out of the batter's box and asked Dick Stuart, who was kneeling in the on-deck circle, "Did we win it?" The public address announcer barked, "The Cubs defeated the Cardinals, and the Pirates have clinched the National League pennant."[16]

Corks popped and champagne flowed as the Pirates whooped it up and toasted their first pennant in 33 years.

Their World Series opponent would be the New York Yankees, who nipped Boston to clinch the American League pennant the same day Pittsburgh was wrapping up the National League title. The flag was the 10th in 12 years for the Yankees under Casey Stengel. In what would prove to be irony, the hero of the Yanks' clinching win over Boston was a tall right-handed pitcher named Ralph Terry, who got his 10th victory and doubled in the deciding run. Stengel talked about how Terry's pitching could prove to be a big boost to his club in the World Series.

The front page of the September 26 *Pittsburgh Post-Gazette* ran triple-banner headlines at the top: "Bucs Clinch Flag, First in 33 Years"; under that was, in all-caps, "NOW BRING ON THE YANKS"; and under that—"100,000 Welcome Champions Home." The lead story reported that "police officials estimated the crowd as great or greater than the downtown throngs that gathered for VE or VJ Day victory celebrations or the crowds that have greeted Presidential visitors."[17] The Yankees' celebration was understandably more subdued. After all, winning pennants was old hat for the Pinstripes.

The Bucs closed the season with four home games. They nipped the Reds in 16 innings on Dick Schofield's run-scoring single before taking two out of three from the Braves. Dick Groat, who was expected to miss four weeks, returned sooner. In his first action in three weeks, he went in to run for Bob Oldis. The number three catcher, Oldis had caught the entire game with Cincinnati and had singled in the 16th inning. The next night, on the last day of September, in Pittsburgh's fourth straight loss to Milwaukee, Groat pinch-hit and grounded out. Bob Buhl five-hit the Pirates for the second time in a week. Vernon Law was shelled for 10 hits and eight runs, all of them earned, in less than three innings by the Braves. The worst news, however, was the apparent reason for those bloated numbers.

It was revealed that Law had injured his right ankle when he slipped

THIRTEEN. *Dog Days and Doubleheaders*

on the wet floor during the Pirates' locker room celebration a week earlier. The diagnosis was a pulled tendon. The pitcher seemed to be favoring the ankle, and he said after his bad outing that it bothered him when he pushed off the pitching rubber. Pirates trainer Danny Whelan said there was no swelling in Law's ankle and that it only hurt when he twisted it a certain way.[18]

Danny Murtaugh said he could not, at that point, say whether Law's injury would force a change in pitching plans for the Bucs. Those plans had Law penciled in as Pittsburgh's starter for the opening game of the World Series. The manager said if that did not work out, Bob Friend would get the ball instead.[19]

Groat was back in the lineup playing shortstop and batting second when the Pirates downed Spahn and the Braves, 7–3. Friend won his 18th game, and Face finished up with two shutout innings. Groat had two hits and drove in two runs, and so did Dick Stuart. The victory was the Bucs' 12th in 21 games against Milwaukee and allowed them to prevail in the season series with the Braves for the first time since 1945. After managing just 24 hits in four straight losses to the Braves, the Pirates broke loose for 13, then came back with 15 more hits on the last day of the season. Rocky Nelson, Don Hoak, and Dick Schofield had three hits apiece to fuel Mizell to his 14th win. Schofield played second base to give Mazeroski a rest.

Groat had a single in four trips to the plate to end 1960 with a batting average of .3246, rounded to .325. That was good for the National League batting title as Dodgers first baseman Norm Larker finished at .3227, or .323, after a 1-for-4 day. Groat was only the third shortstop to lead the National League in hitting. The others also played for the Pittsburgh Pirates. Honus Wagner did it eight times from 1900 to 1911, and Arky Vaughan in 1935.

Ernie Banks of the Cubs led the league with 41 home runs, the Braves' Hank Aaron was the RBI leader with 126, and Maury Wills of the Dodgers was tops in stolen bases with 50. Milwaukee's Warren Spahn and Ernie Broglio of St. Louis both had 21 wins to lead in that category. San Francisco's Mike McCormick posted the lowest earned run average, 2.70, and Don Drysdale of Los Angeles led the NL with 246 strikeouts.

The American League batting crown was won by Boston's Pete Runnels, with a .320 average. New York's Mickey Mantle led in home runs with 40, his teammate Roger Maris in RBI with 112, and Luis Aparicio of the Chicago White Sox swiped 51 bases. Baltimore's Chuck Estrada and Cleveland's Jim Perry were tops in wins with 18, Frank Baumann of the White Sox had the lowest ERA of 2.67, and Detroit's Jim Bunning led the AL with 201 strikeouts.

All of the games for the 1960 season had been played. All of the races, both team and individual, had been decided. It was Sunday, October 2. The World Series between the Pirates and the Yankees would begin on Wednesday, October 5, at Forbes Field.

Fourteen
Bucs' Bench Just Ducky

Coming off the bench is a difficult job in any sport. In baseball, the task can be monumental when it involves going up to the plate cold and facing a pitcher who has been on fire, or having to make a difficult play on defense right away. One at-bat or a few innings, and it's normally back to the pines until the next call comes from the manager. That may be a day or two, or a week. And that's tough. So is being called upon to replace a regular position player who is injured. While everyone yearns for the chance to play every day, the circumstances surrounding that opportunity can be quite imposing.

Take Dick Schofield in 1960, for example.

He was the Pittsburgh Pirates' utility infielder, and a darn good one. Primarily a shortstop, he could play second base and third equally well. He had outstanding range, a strong arm, and good feet, and he could make the pivot on the double play from short or second. He could make all the plays.

Hitting, or a lack of it for most of his time in the majors, was another story, the main reason Schofield was not somebody's everyday shortstop. Which he was for a few of his big league seasons. A switch-hitter who was five-foot-nine and weighed around 160 pounds, he was good bunter who tried to put the ball in play, advance runners, and just get on base.

On September 6, when Dick Groat had his wrist broken by a Lew Burdette pitch, the Pirates' shortstop job was Schofield's. While there weren't any rah-rahs or go-get-'ems from his teammates, they knew the man called Ducky was more than adequate with the glove. "Ducky" was a nickname Schofield inherited from his dad, who was affectionately called that by folks in the town of Marcus Hook—near Chester, Pennsylvania—where he grew up. Some of Schofield's teammates heard him

"Had 'Em All the Way"

call his dad Ducky and started calling him the same thing. So the moniker fit right in with the Dogie and Quail served up by Pirates broadcaster Bob Prince, but it wasn't his idea.

Schofield slid comfortably into the eighth spot in the Pittsburgh batting order and into the left side of the infield, with Don Hoak on one side of him and Bill Mazeroski on the other. He entered the lineup as a pinch-hitter for Groat, who was unable to continue after his right wrist had swollen. It was the bottom of the third inning, there was one out, no one was on base, and the game with Milwaukee was scoreless. Hitting .200 for the season, Schofield singled to right field and promptly scored on a double by Bob Skinner. The Bucs went on to win, 5–3, as Schofield went 3-for-3 and started a double play in the field. He got a hit in the next game and the one after that, eventually hitting in his first six games after taking over for the Pirates' captain. After a couple of hitless games, Schofield put together an eight-game hitting streak.

Following is a detailed game-by-game account of his amazing three weeks as Pittsburgh's shortstop and definite man on the spot (plus one game at the close of the season when he spelled Mazeroski).

September 6—3-for-3, run, started double play, one assist

7—1-for-3, three putouts, three assists

9—1-for-3, triple, two RBI, seven assists

10—1-for-3, double, RBI, middle of two double plays, four putouts, three assists

12—2-for-4, started double play, four putouts, three assists

Super sub Dick "Ducky" Schofield was an excellent utility infielder. In the final month of the 1960 season, he was pressed into service as a regular. He responded, not only with his usual fine play in the field, but with outstanding hitting. His play was critical, coming as it did in the Pirates' stretch run to the National League pennant.

FOURTEEN. *Bucs' Bench Just Ducky*

13—2-for-4, two putouts, three assists
14—0-for-3, walk, three putouts, one assist
15—0-for-3, middle of double play, unassisted double play, three putouts, two assists
16—1-for-3, walk, run, middle of double play, two putouts, three assists
18—2-for-2, double, two walks, three putouts, three assists
18—2-for-3, double, walk, RBI, started two double plays, four assists
20—1-for-4, run, RBI, middle of double play, four putouts, one assist
20—2-for-3, double, walk, run, started double play, one putout, three assists
22—1-for-3, walk, sacrifice, middle of three double plays, six putouts, five assists
22—2-for-4, RBI, two putouts, one assist
23—1-for-3, two putouts, error
24—0-for-3, two putouts, five assists
25—1-for-4, started double play, error, one putout, seven assists
27—1-for-2, RBI, one assist
30—0-for-3, walk, two putouts, two assists
October 2—3-for-4, two RBI, three putouts, one assist

In this stretch of 21 games, Schofield had one or more hits in 17 of them, went 27-for-67 for a .403 batting average, scored four runs, and batted in nine. He had four doubles and a triple, drew eight walks, and had a .467 on-base percentage. He handled 105 chances with two errors for a .981 fielding percentage and was in on 15 double plays.

"It was a fantastic time," Schofield said. "Things worked out pretty well. We lost a really good player and a leader when Dick went down. Nobody likes to see someone get hurt, especially one of your key players when you're in a pennant race. But it was an opportunity for me to play. I don't remember thinking I was on the spot or anything like that. I know Murtaugh and the players never gave me the feeling that there was pressure on me to do certain things."

Schofield knew the team needed him to play well. But really, everyone needed to play well. That's the way it is for a contending team. Especially when that team doesn't have one or two big guns. Like Groat and so many other Pirates said, Schofield pointed out that what the club did in 1960 was a team thing in every sense. Different guys coming through

"Had 'Em All the Way"

every day. Rather than count heavily on one player, the Bucs counted on a whole bunch of guys. That is why, Schofield felt, even though Groat was having a great year and was a key player, there wasn't a burden on a backup infielder to do what Groat had been doing. The main thing, as a shortstop, was to make the plays, the routine plays. And Schofield knew he could do that. He was always confident in his ability to catch and throw the ball. He could field, and he had a good arm. As for the hitting, Schofield smiled, knowing he surprised some people. He said he would never say he could have kept it up over an entire season, that only Ted Williams could do that.

Batting eighth is a tough job, one Bill Mazeroski had done until Schofield was inserted into the lineup. The eighth-place hitter can often help a club by driving in a few runs and also by keeping an inning alive so that at the very least, the top of the order would be up the next inning. Schofield thought he did both of those things fairly consistently. Even though it felt good to help win some big games down the stretch, Schofield said that was his job, and there wasn't a lot said about it in the clubhouse. He was just doing his job, after all, like everyone else on the team. He was more proud of being one of a great bunch of men than he was of himself.[1]

Schofield signed with the St. Louis Cardinals in 1953. Because of his "bonus baby" status, the Cards were required to keep him on their 25-man roster for two full seasons. Schofield got 39 at-bats as an 18-year-old in 1953 and seven at-bats in 1954. The next two years were spent, except for short call-ups, with Omaha, St. Louis' Triple-A farm team. He batted .273 and .295. He didn't play much or hit much for the Cardinals in 1957 and the early part of 1958, before being traded to Pittsburgh. Among his teammates in St. Louis were Bill Virdon, Harvey Haddix, and Vinegar Bend Mizell.

Groat said he has always felt Dick Schofield was the finest utility man ever to play baseball, and that he did a fantastic job coming in and playing like he did.[2]

According to the stats sheet, Gino Cimoli was the Pirates' fourth outfielder in 1960. In reality, he was the co–center fielder for much of the season, sharing the position with Bill Virdon. Cimoli also filled in at the other two outfield spots. Cimoli had certainly paid his dues. A

Fourteen. Bucs' Bench Just Ducky

high school star in San Francisco, he signed with Brooklyn at the age of 19, and it would be seven years before he wore a big league uniform. He spent his first professional season, 1949, with Nashua (New Hampshire) in the Class B New England League. In the next six years, he played mainly for Montreal and Saint Paul (Minnesota), both Triple-A Dodgers affiliates. The Montreal manager during most of Cimoli's time with the club was Walter Alston. Cimoli was never called up during his trek through the minors. Of course, the Dodgers had right fielder Carl Furillo and center fielder Duke Snider all of that time, with Andy Pafko and Sandy Amoros playing in left.

Finally, after batting .306 with 85 RBI for Montreal in 1955, the 26-year-old Cimoli was promoted to the majors He got into 73 games with Brooklyn in 1956, but batted just 36 times. The next year, as a regular, he had a good year, hitting .293 with 10 home runs.

Cimoli made history on April 15, 1958, when he went to the plate as the leadoff man for the Los Angeles Dodgers. The game was against the Giants in Seals Stadium and was special for Cimoli since he had grown up in San Francisco. He became the first major league batter on the West Coast, following the Dodgers' and Giants' move from New York after the 1957 season.

After batting .246, Cimoli was traded to St. Louis, where he hit .279 with 72 RBI as the everyday center fielder in 1959. It was a fine season, but the Cards had Curt Flood, who was young and loaded with potential, for center. They wanted to move Bill White from the outfield to first base, where he was much better defensively, and they planned to play Stan Musial in left field rather than at first. Plus, they had obtained Leon Wagner in mid–December of 1959 from the Giants to provide power off the bench, and he was an outfielder. There was no longer any room in St. Louis for Cimoli, so a week after the Wagner trade, he became part of a package that was shipped off to Pittsburgh.

Hal Smith was another player who, although usually listed as a backup, contributed like a starter. He did frequently start as the other half of Pittsburgh's two-catcher platoon. The right-handed hitter, to go with the lefty-hitting Smoky Burgess, played a little third base and first base during his career. But his defensive position was almost always behind the plate, and that was solely the case with the 1960 Pirates.

"Had 'Em All the Way"

Smith signed with the New York Yankees in 1949, an irony which did not materialize until 11 years later in October. In November of 1954, he was included in one of the most bizarre trades ever. It was huge in many ways. Trying to keep up with the players involved practically required a program. There were 17 of them. The New York Yankees and the Baltimore Orioles made the swap, and their general managers needed the better part of two weeks to sort things out and complete the deal. None of the 17 names that swapped rosters were big ones at the time, but two pitchers who joined the Yankees went on to become World Series heroes. They were Don Larsen and Bob Turley, the most notable players to change uniforms. The right-handers were among seven players acquired by the Yankees, while the Orioles got 10.

Hal W. Smith (the middle initial is necessary because the St. Louis Cardinals also had a catcher at the same time named Hal Smith, with the middle initial R.) made his major league debut with the Orioles in 1955. Smith played in 135 games that season and batted .271. Midway through the 1956 season, Baltimore dealt him to Kansas City for another catcher, Joe Ginsberg. Smith finished that year and played three more with the Athletics, establishing career highs with a .303 batting average and 13 home runs in 1957. He played quite a bit of third base and some at first in addition to his work behind the plate.

After hitting .288 for Kansas City in 1959, he was traded on December 9 to the Pirates.

Rocky Nelson was a minor league legend and, for the most part, a major league bust. Prior to joining Pittsburgh for the second time in 1959, he had not had even a decent year in parts of six big league seasons. Primarily a first baseman, Nelson was what was referred to as a journeyman player, one who bounced around from team to team, good enough to reach the majors but not productive enough to stick.

The story had it that Glenn Richard Nelson was dubbed "Rocky" when a baseball hit him in the head one day during batting practice. Not realizing he had been hit, he was called Rockhead by his teammates, who later shortened that to Rocky.

Signed by the St. Louis Cardinals in 1942, Nelson played that year with Johnson City in the Appalachian League. A left-hander, he played first base and pitched. He spent three years in military service, then bat-

Fourteen. Bucs' Bench Just Ducky

ted .371 for Lynchburg to lead the Piedmont League and .303 with Rochester in the International League.

The Cards gave him a shot at winning the first base job in 1949 and again in 1950, but he could not hit as high as .250, and he totaled five home runs in nearly 500 at-bats for the two seasons. A couple weeks into the 1951 season, St. Louis traded him to Pittsburgh, and the Chicago White Sox claimed him on waivers in September. The Chisox swapped him to Brooklyn in December. Nelson missed much of the next year with a broken ankle. Then, from 1953 to 1955, he simply tore up the International League. Playing for the Montreal Royals, he hit 34 home runs and drove in a league-leading 136 runs. He led the Cuban Winter League for the 1953–1954 season with a .352 batting average.

Meanwhile, he had been traded in October of 1953 from the Dodgers to Cleveland. In May of 1954, the Indians sold him back to Brooklyn. Nelson got a handful of at-bats for the Dodgers in 1952 but only four for Cleveland in 1954. Nelson's minor league exploits continued. He hit 31 homers for Montreal in 1954 and .364 the following year when he had 37 home runs and 130 RBI to win the International League Triple Crown.

When he jumped off to a tremendous start in 1956, the Dodgers called him up. But he did not do well, hitting four homers before being placed on waivers. Selected by the Cardinals, he had three more home runs, batting .217 overall for the season. St. Louis sold Nelson to Toronto in March of 1957, and he hit like gangbusters once more. He put together an outstanding season for the Maple Leafs, then a great one in 1958 when his .326 average, 43 home runs, and 120 RBI earned another International League Triple Crown. He twice was named the league's Most Valuable Player.

Pittsburgh drafted Nelson from Toronto in December, and although he never approached the numbers he stacked up in the minor leagues, the first two of his three seasons with the Pirates were the most productive of his big league years. A two-time member of three different major league teams, he had a .237 lifetime batting average and 13 home runs in parts of six big league seasons when general manager Joe Brown grabbed him for the Pirates.

Gene Baker did not sign his first contract until he was almost 25 years old, and he was 28 when the Cubs brought him up in 1953. He was their regular second baseman from 1954 to 1956, hitting 36 home runs during that time while averaging 143 games per season. He was switched to third base and played 12 games there in 1957 before being dealt to the Pirates. Baker played second, third, and short for the Bucs, appearing in 111 games that season. He suffered a serious knee injury in June of 1958, tearing tendons and ligaments. He missed the rest of that season and all of 1959, as he was released by Pittsburgh in May. He worked hard to come back, and he was re-signed by Pittsburgh before the 1960 season.

Joe Christopher, a backup outfielder for the Pirates, was born in the Virgin Islands. He was 18 when he represented his homeland in the National Baseball Congress tournament in Wichita, Kansas, in 1954. Playing shortstop, Christopher hit well and attracted the attention of Pittsburgh scout Howie Haak, who signed him early in 1955. Christopher, who was moved to the outfield, batted .366 for Phoenix of the Class C Arizona-Mexico League. He was promoted to Class-A Lincoln of the Western League in his first season and then to Williamsport in the Eastern League. He was back at Williamsport in 1956 and then Mexico City the year after that. He led the Double-A league in stolen bases, with 24 in 64 games. In 1958, he played with Triple-A Salt Lake City, where he hit .327 and swiped 16 bases.

Christopher was called up to the Pirates in May of 1959 when Roberto Clemente was injured. He became the club's reserve outfielder when Roman Mejias played right in place of Clemente. Christopher got a couple of starts and a handful of plate appearances. One of them came when he replaced Mejias in right field during the game in which Harvey Haddix pitched 12 perfect innings against the Braves.

Bob Oldis was the least used member of the Bucs' 1960 roster, at least, among players who were with the club all season. He was an outstanding defensive catcher, but his bat was far too weak to get at-bats ahead of either Burgess or Smith. Oldis signed with the Washington Senators in 1949. It took him four years to reach the majors, and when he did, he accumulated fewer than 50 at-bats in three seasons. Sent back to the minors, he stayed there five more years until Pittsburgh drafted him from the New York Yankees, who had purchased his contract from Washington.

Fifteen
Character and Characters

Smoky Burgess was a man with character, while Dick Stuart and Don Hoak *were* characters ... very interesting characters.

Stuart was known for his powerful bat and stiff glove, the latter leading to ongoing jokes which he could take with a sense of humor and even re-tell. He was a cocky guy, but in a likeable way. In fact, in spite of his bragging, he was always well liked by his teammates. The six-foot-four first baseman wasn't at all bothered by his "Dr. Strangeglove" nickname or the jokes about his poor fielding. He lived for the home run, the chance to hit one and the satisfaction of celebrating one.

Dr. Strangelove came out in 1964, a comedy directed by Stanley Kubrick and starring Peter Sellers. Stuart's reputation for being a terrible fielder made the takeoff on the movie title a natural for a nickname.

Stuart signed with Pittsburgh in 1951 and received a $10,000 bonus. Eighteen years old at the time, he reported to Class C Modesto and played in the outfield. He batted .229 with four home runs in 66 games. In 1952, with Class C Billings, he hit .313, slammed 31 homers, and drove in 121 runs, while leading the Pioneer League in hits, runs, and total bases. Following two years in the military, Stuart quickly wore out his welcome at Class A New Orleans. He reportedly demanded that only clean baseballs be pitched to him in batting practice, and he was shipped to Mexico City, where he batted .148 in 27 at-bats. Pittsburgh sent Stuart back to Billings, and he again had a big season, belting 32 home runs with 104 RBI and batting over .300 in 101 games.

He then made his mark by bashing 66 home runs and knocking in 171 runs for Lincoln of the Class A Western League in 1956. With typical brashness, Stuart told reporters that he would have hit 90 home runs if the pitching was better, adding that he had to chase a lot of bad balls to hit 66. After that season, he wrote "66" along with his name every time he signed an autograph.

Stuart was promoted to Hollywood and moved to first base in 1957. But when he struck out 63 times in 46 games at Hollywood and Atlanta, he was sent back down to Lincoln. He continued to average more than a strikeout per game, but hit 31 homers. That gave him 45 in his three minor league stops for the year. When the Pirates acquired slugging first baseman Ted Kluszewski in December of 1957, Stuart, undaunted, predicted that Pittsburgh would have to trade Big Klu to make room for Big Stu.

In 1958, Stuart smacked 31 home runs and had 82 RBI in 80 games for Class AAA Salt Lake City. With Kluszewski experiencing back problems that severely diminished his power production, Pittsburgh called up Stuart to share first base duties. His first error came in his first game, a July contest at Wrigley Field. Appropriately, he also hit his first big league home run in the ninth inning. He finished the season with 16 homers in 67 games. The next year, Stuart ended up winning the Bucs' first base job as well as seeing his prediction come true. After hitting only six home runs in 160 games for Pittsburgh, Kluszewski was swapped to the Chicago White Sox in August. As a starting first baseman, Stuart would go on to lead his league in errors seven years in a row (sometimes sharing the dubious honor). During that period, he hit 192 home runs.

Showing his sense of humor, he said that one of his most memorable days as a Pittsburgh Pirate was when a Forbes Field crowd of 30,000 gave him a standing ovation for grabbing a windblown hot dog wrapper. A writer called him "The Ancient Mariner" from the classic poem in which the title character was said to "stoppeth one in three." After he had a terrible game in a 6–3 loss to the Giants, striking out three times, missing a ground ball that was ruled a hit, and dropping a throw to let two runs score, he said, "The score should have read Stuart 6, Pirates 3."[1]

Getting 397 at-bats in 1959, Stuart clouted 27 home runs and batted in 78 runs to go with a .297 average. One of the home runs traveled an estimated 500 feet, soaring out of Forbes at the 457-foot mark. Some people, including Danny Murtaugh and Pie Traynor, who had been

FIFTEEN. Character and Characters

around Pirates baseball a long time, said it was the longest ball ever hit at Forbes Field.

While playing for the Pirates, Stuart had an unusual relationship with their fans. It wasn't exactly love-hate, because the Pittsburgh faithful did not dislike him. They did, however, grow irritated with his shoddy fielding, and they let him know with cascades of boos. Still, he remained lovable, and it only took one of his long blasts into the seats to get him back in the fans' good graces. In truth, even the boos were not vicious. He was well liked by the Bucs' fans and his teammates.

"Tiger" was the ideal nickname for Don Hoak. He was always a fighter who would not take anything from anyone and who never quit. The former Marine and pro boxer paid his own way to the Brooklyn Dodgers' minor league camp at High Point, North Carolina. He had boxed as a middleweight, winning 28 of his 39 fights. His largest purse was $220. "I didn't like it," he said. "I got a little tired of being flattened. When I saw how hard it was to go anywhere as a fighter, I gave it up."[2]

A Brooklyn Dodgers scout who had seen Hoak play baseball while in the Marines told him he should give the game a try, so he did. He signed with the Dodgers as a catcher in 1947, at the age of 19. It took him seven years to make it to the major leagues.

Hoak was assigned to Class D Valdosta, Georgia. In the middle of the season, the team lost its third baseman, and he switched to the hot corner. He batted .295, then moved to Class B Nashua, New Hampshire, in 1948, and to Greenville, South Carolina, in the Class A Sally League the following year. His .280 at Double A Fort Worth, Texas, finally got him within a step of the major leagues. But it was a long step as Hoak spent three years at the Triple-A level. First stop was Saint Paul, Minnesota, in the American Association in 1951. He was elevated to the Dodgers' higher Triple-A team at Montreal for two games at the end of the year. Hoak stayed with the International League farm club for two years, hitting .293 with 70 RBI the first season. He dropped in every category the next year, but still was promoted to the big team for the 1954 season.

He batted .245 his rookie year and .240 in 1955, when Brooklyn beat the Yankees in the World Series. Hoak managed one hit in three Series at-bats, with two walks.

"Had 'Em All the Way"

Two months later, the Dodgers traded him to the Chicago Cubs with pitcher Russ Meyer and outfielder Walt Moryn for pitcher Don Elston and third baseman Randy Jackson. Hoak stayed with the Cubs only one season, batting .215 in 121 games, before getting traded again. Chicago sent him to the Cincinnati Reds with pitcher Warren Hacker and outfielder Pete Whisenant for third baseman Ray Jablonski and pitcher Elmer Singleton.

Hoak enjoyed a breakout season with the Reds in 1957. He played 149 games, batted .293, hit 19 home runs, and led the league with 39 doubles. He was voted to the National League All-Star team for the only time in his career. His fine season earned an 11th-place finish in the league's Most Valuable Player balloting.

He fell to .261 the next year and was swapped to Pittsburgh. He rebounded to hit .294 with 65 RBI, while playing in 155 games for the first of two successive seasons. In Hoak, the Pirates acquired a fine fielding third baseman and a clutch hitter, and just as important, a fiery player who could inspire teammates and spark a team. Clem Labine, who joined the Bucs late in the 1960 season, hung the "Tiger" nickname on Hoak. He had his nose broken nine times, once when kneeling in the on-deck circle. The bat slipped out of the batter's hands when he swung and missed, hitting Hoak in the face.

He was hit in the face many times, in and out of a boxing ring. Never one to back away from a fight, he was one of the first to pile into brawls on baseball fields. He had a temper, and it sometimes didn't take much to light a fire under him. While with the Dodgers, they were having a big inning against Cincinnati and had the bases loaded with Hoak coming to the plate. Reds manager Birdie Tebbetts went to the mound, pulled his pitcher, and then yelled for Frank Smith, who was in the dugout. Smith had not even warmed up, and Hoak took that as an insult. He lit into Tebbetts, cursing him and calling him some choice names. He then smacked the ball over the fence for a grand slam.[3]

Forrest Harrill Burgess was one of the more popular players on the Pirates, not only in 1960 but throughout his five-and-one-half-year stay in Pittsburgh. In fact, the little round man known as Smoky was a favorite wherever he played. His nickname was a hand-me-down from

Fifteen. Character and Characters

his dad, his talent for hitting a baseball a gift from God. Standing five-foot-eight and weighing close to 200 pounds (before putting on more weight late in his career), he made hitting look easy.

Burgess did not chew or smoke tobacco or drink alcohol. He was a devout Christian who was committed to living his faith. He could always hit a baseball and hit it well.

Burgess, tagged "Shake, Rattle and Roll" by Bob Prince, was one of those players of whom it was said, "He could get out of bed on Christmas morning and hit a line drive." His left-handed stance was so comfortable that he looked like he might be sitting in a rocking chair with a bat in his hands. Perhaps it was his temperament or maybe it was just his ability to hit a baseball—probably a combination of the two—that made him a fantastic pinch-hitter. One of the best ever in the big leagues.

In his younger years, Burgess was a fine defensive catcher ... no Johnny Bench, but more than adequate. He moved around well behind the plate, blocking pitches in the dirt, and had a good arm. While he was not a fast runner, he did move quickly, and his quickness was a tremendous asset as a catcher. Burgess was selected to the National League All-Star team six times, including four as a member of the Pirates. He started behind the plate for the 1961 NL All-Stars.

The native of Caroleen in western North Carolina signed with the Chicago Cubs as a 17-year-old in 1944. It didn't take long to show that hitter was his most natural, and best, position. In his seven-year minor-league journey to the majors, Burgess led his league in batting in back-to-back

Smoky Burgess could always hit. In 1960, he was half of a platoon that gave the Pirates tremendous production at the catcher's position. He could hit for power and he was tough in the clutch. Nicknamed "Shake, Rattle and Roll" because of his portly stature, Burgess was one of major league baseball's all-time great pinch-hitters.

years. His .387 average for Fayetteville, North Carolina, topped the Tri-State Class B League in 1947. The next year, he hit .386 for Nashville, Tennessee, to lead the Double-A Southern Association.

Starting at Class D Lockport, New York, of the PONY (Pennsylvania–Ontario–New York) League in 1944, Burgess played with Portsmouth, Virginia, in the Class B Piedmont League; Macon, Georgia, in the Class A Sally League; the Los Angeles Angels of the Triple-A Pacific Coast League; and Springfield, Illinois, of the Triple-A International League, in addition to Fayetteville and Nashville.

He was called up by the Cubs in 1949, batting .268 in 46 games, and was back in the minors the following year. In 1951, he was in the major leagues for good. After his rookie season, Burgess was traded twice in two months. On October 4, the day of the first game of the World Series between the New York Yankees and New York Giants, the Cubs sent him and outfielder Bob Borkowski to Cincinnati for catcher Johnny Pramesa and outfielder Bob Usher. On December 10, the Reds swapped Burgess, pitcher Howie Fox, and infielder Connie Ryan to Philadelphia for two members of the Phillies' 1950 Whiz Kids starting lineup—catcher Andy Seminick and left fielder Dick Sisler—along with infielder Eddie Pellagrini and pitcher Niles Jordan.

Burgess played three full seasons with the Phils and a few games of a fourth. He played in more than 100 games from 1952 to 1954, hitting .296 and .292 before batting .368, but he did not have enough plate appearances to qualify for the 1954 batting title. A week into the 1955 season, Philadelphia packaged him with outfielder Stan Palys and pitcher Steve Ridzik and shipped the trio to Cincinnati for Seminick and outfielders Jim Greengrass and Glen Gorbous. On July 29, against Pittsburgh at Crosley Field, Burgess smashed three home runs and knocked in nine runs. He hit a pair of two-run homers, one of them off future Pirates batterymate Vernon Law, and a grand slam, and he added an RBI single. Burgess, who was chosen to the All-Star team that year, finished 1955 with 20 home runs, 77 RBI, and a .306 batting average.

On the next-to-last day of the 1956 season, he hit a pinch home run that was historic. Batting for pitcher Tom Acker in the eighth inning, Burgess slammed a pitch from the Cubs' Sam Jones out of Wrigley Field. It was home run number 221 for the Reds that year, the last one they

Fifteen. Character and Characters

would hit in 1956, allowing them to tie the single-season major league record then held by the 1947 New York Giants.

Burgess dropped to .275 the next year and then had back-to-back .283 seasons, totaling 33 home runs from 1956 to 1958. His drop in production figured in Cincinnati including him in a seven-player trade with Pittsburgh in January of 1959. In the ensuing season, Burgess batted .297 in 114 games and again made the All-Star team. He was also behind the plate for Harvey Haddix's marvelous 12 innings of perfection against the Milwaukee Braves in 1959.

His addition was the foundation of a one-two punch that gave the Pirates the best catching in the National League in 1960, at least offensively. Burgess formed a potent catching platoon with Hal Smith and provided an excellent left-handed bat off the bench, his pinch-hitting prowess equaled only by George Crowe of the St. Louis Cardinals. Burgess eventually made pinch-hitting practically an art form with his consistent ability to get clutch hits and drive in key runs despite entering the game cold.

He always liked talking with people, and he did a lot of that when he was behind the plate. Batters didn't always enjoy the conversations as much as Burgess, who was being as much a distraction as he was a conversationalist. Richie Ashburn of the Phillies was so agitated by the constant bantering that he asked umpires to put a stop to it, once threatening that if they didn't, he might hit Burgess over the head with his bat.[4]

That did not happen, but Smoky never stopped talking to batters, either.

The zaniest character on the Pirates did not wear a uniform. No one would argue, though, that Bob Prince was as much a part of the team as the pitching staff and position players. He was just a great guy, Dick Groat said, one everybody liked. He was so close to the players. The fans felt close to him, too, because he would stop and talk with them after a game, in the parking lot or at a restaurant. The personable broadcaster was as popular as any of the players. He did so much for the community. He was a very special part of the Pirates.[5]

Prince broadcast the Bucs' games on KDKA radio for 28 years, the last 21 as the number one play-by-play man. He was the Voice of the

"Had 'Em All the Way"

Pittsburgh Pirates. It was a voice that was colorful, knowledgeable, articulate, creative, humorous, and descriptive. And candid. Prince spoke his mind. He was an unabashed fan of the Battling Bucs, but he did not tint his broadcasts with partiality. He was accurate and complete in telling listeners what was happening. Prince told everyone exactly what happened along the way if the Pirates were trailing on the scoreboard. Then he would blatantly cheer for them to rally, calling for "a bloop and a blast" to wipe out a two-run deficit or waving a Green Weenie (a hot dog painted green) from the broadcast booth, aiming it toward the opposing pitcher to jinx him.

In college, he was a member of the University of Pittsburgh swim team, and he was an accomplished diver. Prince once bet Dick Stuart that he could dive from a balcony of the Chase Hotel in St. Louis into the swimming pool. Stuart took the bet and lost.[6]

Wild, bright sport coats were one of Prince's trademarks. Another was his rapid-fire delivery, which earned him the nickname "Gunner." He was a gifted storyteller who could entertain audiences on nights when the Pirates were getting pounded. His quick wit made him fun for fellow broadcasters who joined him at the microphone over the years, and surely for listeners.

He had a tremendous following and was as recognizable in and around Pittsburgh as the most famous Pirates players. The players liked him, too. Prince did not second-guess or criticize them, unless it was for failing to hustle. He supported them, openly pulled for them, and defended them when others sometimes took cheap shots. Something he did not do. Prince was a fine on-the-air reporter, and he knew what "off the record" meant and did not abuse the privilege of having players share things with him in confidence. He never showed them up in order to make himself look good with a scoop. He truly was part of the Pirates' team.

He loved giving players nicknames and came up with a number of phrases that became popular. His home run call was "You can kiss it goodbye," and he referred to a double play as a "Hoover." Best known of all was "we had 'em all the way." It started out as a way of underlining a comeback victory for the Pirates. If they trailed most of the game, then mounted a dramatic comeback to win, Prince would end the broadcast

Fifteen. Character and Characters

with "We had 'em all the way," really saying, "we never had 'em." By the end of the season, he was using it as a sign-off to any game the Pirates won.

It was the perfect end stamp to the 1960 World Series, too, as a proud and joyous Bob Prince put the finishing touch on what his beloved Buccos had accomplished.

Prince died in 1975 at the age of 68.

Prince's sidekick in the booth that memorable season, and for 11 others, was Jim Woods. Better known as "the Possum," he was color commentator for Pirates radio broadcasts from 1958 to 1969. Woods' voice was deep, his delivery smooth. Like his partner, he possessed a wonderful sense of humor, and he joined Prince to make a terrific team.

He went on to call games for the St. Louis Cardinals and Oakland A's, but never enjoyed his work as he did in Pittsburgh. Late in his life, he said his time with Prince doing the Pirates games was the highlight of his career.

Woods died in 1988 at the age of 71.

Sixteen
World Series Mismatch

The 1960 Pittsburgh Pirates were a great story. The Bucs were playing the World Series for the first time in 33 years. Pittsburgh had made a leap from worst to first in just three years, having tied for last place with the Chicago Cubs in the 1957 National League standings.

And, then, there were those damn Yankees. It was their 10th trip to the World Series in 12 years. They had captured seven world championships in those nine previous Series. They used a tremendous home stretch to reclaim the pennant they felt was rightfully theirs. And what a home stretch. Although they clinched the pennant on the same day as the Pirates nailed down the National League flag, the Yankees did it with gusto. They won their last 15 games of the 1960 season.

Talk about momentum.

New York's record (97–57) was only two games better than Pittsburgh's (95–59), and the Pirates had a much easier time winning their league. But the teams' October matchup still looked like a mismatch. Probably because of the names of the Yankees' headline players … Mantle, Maris, Skowron, Berra. Even more likely because of the numbers accompanying those names … Mantle, 40 home runs and 94 RBI; Maris, 39 and 112; Skowron, 26 and 91; and Berra, 15 and 62.

New York scored just a dozen more runs than Pittsburgh for the season, but it was the way the Yanks scored them. They slammed an American League–record 193 home runs, 73 more than the Pirates. WHAM! BAM! That was the sound of the Mighty Yankees scoring runs. They scored loud runs. The Yankees always made noise, and, yes, mighty was practically part of the team's nickname.

The Battling Bucs? They hit and ran, moved runners along, and registered doubles and triples as their long balls. They had to scrape for

Sixteen. World Series Mismatch

their runs. Why else would they make battling part of their nickname? While the media and general fandom digested this kind of stuff as baseball gospel, predicated on holy statistics, the Pirates weren't buying it. Some of them didn't even read it, and those who did figured they hitched up their Louisville Sluggers just like the next man.

The Yankees' power was the obvious reason for favoring them. Possibly a more important factor, however, was their pitching. Particularly their World Series pitching experience. Whitey Ford, who would set some Series records before he was finished, had 12 starts, a 5–4 record and a 3.08 earned run average in Fall Classics. Bullet Bob Turley was 3–3 with a 2.86 ERA and 46 strikeouts in 44⅓ innings.

Pittsburgh, on the other hand, had no one in its starting rotation with World Series experience. The only member of the pitching staff to toe the rubber on the October stage was Clem Labine, and he had shined. Labine had pitched for the Dodgers in 10 World Series games, all but one against the Yankees. He even shut them out in his lone Series starting assignment. Labine was one of four Pittsburgh players with World Series experience, all with the Dodgers.

Third baseman Don Hoak had one hit in three at-bats for the 1955 Dodgers, who beat the Yankees. Those at-bats came in the decisive Game Seven when he started at third base, handling two chances flawlessly and getting a single and a walk. Hoak also pinch-ran in the first game and drew a pinch-hit walk in the second. Outfielder Gino Cimoli was a late-inning defensive replacement for Brooklyn in its Game Two win over the Yankees in 1956, and he caught a fly ball. First baseman Rocky Nelson pinch-hit four times in the Dodgers' seven-game loss to the Yankees in 1952. He did not get a hit, striking out twice and walking once.

The Yankees, on the other hand, had tons of World Series experience. Yogi Berra had 223 at-bats, Gil McDougald 172, and Mickey Mantle 135. Mantle had hit 11 Series home runs, Berra 10, McDougald seven, and Moose Skowron four, including a grand slam. Berra had driven in 28 runs in the Fall Classic, McDougald 24, and Mantle 20. Of course, the New York Yankees of the fifties and early sixties were synonymous with the World Series. October was normally the extension of their season, with bonus dollars for playing the extra week or so.

People often say, "It's just another game" when responding to the added pressure of a World Series or Super Bowl. But the Yankees meant it. For most of them, it really was just another game ... over and over again. It is easy for fans and writers to use that "just another game" phrase—players, too. The difference is, whether they admit it or not, the players know better. They realize how much the peripherals can become factors when the big game begins. For the Yankees—collectively, of course, since some of them might also be experiencing a first—they had been there and done that. So frequently that it was just another (World Series) game. Old hat. A regular autumn occurrence. So, in addition to the mystique of the striped uniform topped off by the deep navy cap with the white NY, the boys from New York boasted impressive numbers. High-grade performances enhanced by nearly habitual basking under baseball's October spotlight.

Two days before the opening game, the *Pittsburgh Post-Gazette* ran this headline across the top of page one of its sports section: "Yankees Are 13–10 Series Pick Over Pirates." The story dropping down the left column pointed out that "The power-minded Yanks were favored to defeat pitching-studded Pittsburgh in the fifty-seventh annual World Series."[1] The boys in Las Vegas made the Yankees 7–5 favorites by the day of the first pitch.

Vernon Law and Bob Friend anchored the Pirates' pitching staff, combining for 38 wins and 34 complete games. The right-handers were balanced by a pair of lefties, Harvey Haddix and Vinegar Bend Mizell, who had 24 victories between them. The Yankees' staff totaled 35 complete games, but that didn't have as much to do with their pitchers' durability as it did their manager's quick trigger finger. All it took was for a couple of batters to reach base, and Casey Stengel would be pointing that finger toward his bullpen.

"Old Case" was playing his usual games with the press. This time it was a bit of peek-a-boo regarding his choice of a starting pitcher for Game One. Ford, the wily southpaw, was everybody's logical pick since he was World Series tested and known to be a terrific big-game pitcher. Plus, he was New York's best, and it stood to reason that any manager would want to start out with his best.

The Perfessor, of course, wasn't just any manager. He liked theatrics, and he liked being called a genius. He loved to go against the obvious,

Sixteen. World Series Mismatch

even if it sometimes meant out-managing himself. In retrospect, many observers felt he did just that in the 1960 World Series. Much of that feeling would focus on the decision not to start Ford in the opening game. Stengel ended up naming Art Ditmar as his Game One pitcher, explaining that he would go with right-handers at Forbes Field, then come back with Ford when the Series moved to Yankee Stadium with its short porch in right field.

The immediate question, however, was why would Stengel decrease the number of starts he could get out of his ace pitcher? Location had not been a factor in the past in giving the ball to Ford for Game One. He got it in 1955, 1956, 1957, and 1958, whether the first game was at Brooklyn's Ebbets Field, Milwaukee's County Stadium, or New York's Yankee Stadium. "The only thing I didn't understand then, and still don't to this day," Yankees second baseman Bobby Richardson said, "is why Whitey Ford wasn't the starting pitcher in Game One. He was the Chairman of the Board, the pitcher you always called on in a tough situation. Whitey had been our big pitcher for years."[2]

Ditmar had pitched three times in relief against Milwaukee in the 1957 and 1958 World Series, totaling nine and a third shutout innings. His 1960 record was 15–9 with a 3.06 earned run average, and he led the Yankees with 200 innings pitched. None of New York's hurlers was overworked. Ford, the only lefty among the team's starters, threw 192⅔ innings, going 12–9 (3.08 ERA). He and Ditmar had eight complete games apiece. Jim Coates, splitting time between starter and reliever, won 13 games, Ralph Terry 10, and Bob Turley nine. None of them pitched more than 173 innings.

Vern Law was the man all along to start Game One for Pittsburgh manager Danny Murtaugh. The 20-game winner acknowledged that his right ankle was sore, but insisted that it would not affect his pitching. Trainer Danny Whelan said that Law's ankle had not swollen and that it bothered him only when it twisted a certain way. Whelan said it would not affect Law's normal delivery.[3] Bob Friend, himself an 18-game winner and the most prolific strikeout pitcher on either team with 183, would go for the Pirates in the second game.

Murtaugh had his mound assignments mapped out nicely, with left-handers Haddix and Mizell penciled in to start Games Three and

"Had 'Em All the Way"

Four in Yankee Stadium, where left-handed pull hitters would have a shorter distance to reach the seats.

Elroy Face, the Baron of the Bullpen, gave Pittsburgh a decided edge in the relief pitching department. He had pitched 114⅔ innings in 68 appearances, finishing 62, with a 10–8 record, 24 "saves," and a 2.90 ERA.

Murtaugh said Bill Virdon would play center field no matter who was pitching because of his outstanding defense. Early in the season, the lefty-batting Virdon and right-handed-hitting Gino Cimoli had platooned in center. Now, Murtaugh said Cimoli would be platooned in left field with Bob Skinner. The same plan would apply behind the plate, with Smoky Burgess catching when New York started a right-hander and Hal Smith facing lefties. Otherwise, nothing would change. Virdon would be joined in the lineup by Dick Stuart at first base, Bill Mazeroski at second, Don Hoak at third, Dick Groat at shortstop, and Roberto Clemente in right field.

Elroy Face was an old-school relief pitcher. He was a finisher. The "Baron of the Bullpen" pitched as long as necessary to wrap up a victory, frequently two innings or more. Many of his escapes were done the Houdini way, as he often entered close games with runners on base. Face was a good fielder and possessed a fine pickoff move he used to help get out of trouble. He saved three World Series games, all by working at least two innings.

Elston Howard was the only key player on either team likely to miss World Series time with an injury. The Yankees' regular catcher suffered a ligament sprain to the ring finger of his right hand when hit by a foul tip while behind the plate on September 28. Doctors said Howard, although unable to throw for a game or maybe two, would be available for pinch-hitting duties and that he should be able to get behind the plate when the Series moved to New York.

SIXTEEN. *World Series Mismatch*

Facing Berra instead did not make Murtaugh any more comfortable. "The Yankees are certainly dangerous," he said, "and I guess Yogi is the most dangerous of them all. Didn't [Baltimore Orioles manager] Paul Richards say Yogi was the most dangerous man in baseball in the last three innings of a game?"[4] Stengel said Howard's injury did not change anything, noting that he was already planning to have Berra do the catching in Pittsburgh. The Yankees manager teased writers by promising to divulge the rest of his lineup on the day of the opening game. There was not a lot of mystery in that regard, however, with Mantle set for center field, Maris for right, Skowron for first base, Bobby Richardson for second, Clete Boyer for third base, and Tony Kubek for short. The only question involved Hector Lopez in left field. There was a good chance he would take a seat and be replaced by Berra when Howard did the catching.

One dilemma facing Stengel was how to get Gil McDougald some at-bats. The 32-year-old infielder had played regularly for the Yanks at second base, third base, and shortstop over the years. Now he was relegated to the role of utility man. McDougald had played in 47 games over seven World Series with a batting average of just .232. But seven home runs and 24 RBI were evidence of the damage he had done in October.

A crowd of 38,000 was expected at Forbes Field for Game One, scheduled for one o'clock on the afternoon of October 5. Those were the days when television did not rule professional sports and when all World Series games were played in the daylight, when fans could call into work sick and youngsters could skip school in order to listen to every pitch on the radio. Or take in a game if they lived close enough.

NBC Television would be showing the games, with play-by-play announcers Bob Prince of Pittsburgh and Mel Allen of New York sharing the microphone. The primary sponsor was Gillette, with its familiar jingle, "Look Sharp, Feel Sharp, Be Sharp."

Luis Arroyo was one of the better stories leading up to the Series. The stocky Yankees left-hander had found his niche coming out of the bullpen in the late stages of close ball games. Making him even more newsworthy for this World Series was the fact that he had spent one season and part of another with the Pirates. He won 11 games for the St.

"Had 'Em All the Way"

Louis Cardinals as a 28-year-old rookie in 1955, while starting 24 times. Just after the 1956 season began, the Cards traded him to Pittsburgh for veteran right-hander Max Surkont. The Pirates sent Arroyo to the minors, where he pitched for Hollywood and Omaha before being called up. He appeared in 18 games, then threw in 54 1959 games for the Bucs, going 3–11 with a 4.68 ERA.

Pittsburgh sent him to Cincinnati, and the Reds sent him to Havana, where he relieved for the Sugar Kings of the Triple-A International League. In late July of 1960, the Yankees purchased his contract from the Reds and summoned him from Jersey City, where the club had moved from Havana. Arroyo was like clockwork the rest of the season. He pitched in 29 games, all out of the bullpen, and had a 5–1 record, and a 2.88 earned run average and saved seven games. He credited the screwball, and learning to throw it for strikes anywhere in the count, for his new-found success as an end-of-game specialist. He replaced Ryne Duren in that job. The man with the thick glasses, overpowering fastball, and erratic control had walked himself down the ladder of the Yanks' pitching staff. In 49 innings, Duren struck out 67 but walked 49.

One Yankee had once been a prominent Pirate. Dale Long was Pittsburgh's everyday first baseman for two years. He had 13 triples and 16 home runs in 1955 and hit 27 homers and drove in 91 runs in 1956. The Yanks bought Long from the San Francisco Giants in August to give them some left-handed pop off the bench. Virdon and Smith of the Bucs also had connections with New York, which had signed both to their first pro contracts.

Thumbing way back into baseball's history book revealed that the Pirates had played in four World Series, winning two. Their most recent championship had come in 1925, when the Bucs batted .307 as a team. Kiki Cuyler hit .357, Max Carey .343, Pie Traynor .320, and four others in the lineup were over .300. The eighth hit a mere .298.

More recently, the Pirates had been the worst team of the 1950s. This dubious honor was decided by record, not vote. Pittsburgh's winning percentage for the fifties was an awful .408, and that was with the club being 16 games over .500 for the last two years of the decade.

All the while, the Yankees were steamrolling along, playing in 21 Fall Classics from 1926 to 1959 and taking 17 of the huge trophies back

Sixteen. *World Series Mismatch*

to Gotham, winning more than 80 percent of the time, no less. It was simply the Yankees being the Yankees.

Three days before Game One, the *Pittsburgh Post-Gazette* reported that scalpers were asking as much as $50 for a ticket, and that police were making arrests accordingly. Major League Baseball announced record attendance figures for the 1960 season. More than 10,684,000 had taken in National League games during the regular season, the most ever. The American League gate was over 9,226,500. Pittsburgh set a Forbes Field attendance record with 1,705,828. Yankee Stadium drew 1,627,349 fans. The Los Angeles Dodgers set the National League record with 2,253,887, surpassing the previous high recorded by the 1957 Milwaukee Braves.

Seventeen

Six Games of Sparring

Game One

Wednesday, October 5, became a holiday in the Golden Triangle, Pittsburgh's downtown area generally regarded as the central business district. Stores were closed, courts shut down early, and businessmen walked the streets wearing black derby hats with gold bands. Storefronts for blocks and blocks displayed signs that read "Beat 'Em, Bucs!" City officials urged fans to leave their cars at home and take a streetcar to the ball park. Railways made special preparations. Ninety minutes before game time, 150 buses and trolley cars rolled from downtown.

More than 400 plainclothes police officers, male and female, mingled with the crowds entering Forbes Field, watching for pickpockets. The official attendance was 36,676, and many of them started pushing through the turnstiles at 10:30 a.m., two and a half hours before the scheduled first pitch.[1]

When the Pirates played their 1960 home opener on April 14, there was a sellout crowd on hand at Forbes Field. As the gates opened at 11 o'clock in the morning, fans were greeted by a ragtime band, Benny Benack and the Iron City Six, who had anointed themselves the team's musical mascots. For the first time, Pirates fans would hear a tune that would become the season's baseball anthem. It went like this: "Oh, the Bucs are going all the way, all the way, all the way. Oh, the Bucs are going all the way, all the way this year. Beat 'em, Bucs! Beat 'em, Bucs!" "Beat 'em Bucs" soon became the Pirates' slogan and rallying cry. It appeared on posters that popped up all over Forbes Field, as well as all over the city of Pittsburgh, throughout the season. Now, with the World Series about to begin in Pittsburgh, local radio stations blared out the Pirates' theme song.[2]

SEVENTEEN. *Six Games of Sparring*

It was a perfect autumn day. The upper deck of Forbes Field was draped with red, white, and blue bunting. In the box seats behind third base sat Hall of Famer Joe Cronin, the American League president. Pointing to the screen behind first base, Cronin said he was responsible for it, that the screen was installed after he made so many wild throws into the stands as a rookie shortstop for the Pirates in 1926.[3]

These were the starting lineups for the opening game of the 1960 World Series:

NEW YORK	PITTSBURGH
Tony Kubek, shortstop	Bill Virdon, center field
Hector Lopez, left field	Dick Groat, shortstop
Roger Maris, right field	Bob Skinner, left field
Mickey Mantle, center field	Dick Stuart, first base
Yogi Berra, catcher	Roberto Clemente, right field
Bill Skowron, first base	Smoky Burgess, catcher
Clete Boyer, third base	Don Hoak, third base
Bobby Richardson, second base	Bill Mazeroski, second base
Art Ditmar, pitcher	Vernon Law, pitcher

The Pirates were strong up the middle in the opening game of the 1960 World Series, and that was the main factor in their 6–4 win over the Yankees. Center fielder Bill Virdon and second baseman Bill Mazeroski provided heroics with their bats and gloves, while Vernon Law shrugged off tenderness in his famous right ankle to pitch seven outstanding innings. Mazeroski had a hand in three double plays, two of them helping Law out of trouble, the other aiding Elroy Face, who pitched the final two innings. Virdon reminded the front office and scouts of the Yankees why they had signed him 10 years earlier. He was on base twice, made a key steal of second base, and ran down a drive that could have changed the game's outcome.

There was action right off the bat in this one. Tony Kubek led off with a grounder that hit third base and popped into the air. Kubek got a single off Law, but was erased when Hector Lopez bounced into a double play. Mazeroski fielded the ball as he moved toward second base, stepped on the bag, and flipped to Dick Stuart at first. When Roger Maris followed with a towering drive into Forbes Field's boxes in the second

"Had 'Em All the Way"

deck of right field, Law had to take consolation that the damage could have been worse.

Virdon drew a walk from Art Ditmar to give Pittsburgh a good start. With Dick Groat at the plate, expectations of a hit-and-run were high, both from the Yankees and the fans. Indeed, Virdon did take off for second base, but his attempt was delayed. Yogi Berra's throw was on target, except that there was no target. Neither second baseman Bobby Richardson nor shortstop Tony Kubek covered second. The ball sailed into center field, with Virdon scurrying to third as the Yankees catcher was charged with an error. After the game, there was all kinds of explaining. Virdon said there was no steal signal given and that he had run on his own. Kubek said he was supposed to have covered second, so the official scorer gave him an error instead of Berra.[4]

Groat doubled into the right-field corner, driving in Virdon with the tying run. Bob Skinner followed with an RBI single, and he, too, swiped second base. Dick Stuart flied to right for the first out. Roberto Clemente sent a ball bounding up the middle and into center field for a run-scoring base hit that put Pittsburgh in front, 3–1.

Casey Stengel had seen enough. Never one to hesitate when it came to removing pitchers, he went to the mound and returned to the dugout with Ditmar. The right-hander, on whom Stengel had bestowed so much praise and confidence, was done. His first World Series start had lasted five batters and 18 pitches.

On came another righty, six-foot-four Jim Coates, New York's long man out of the bullpen. It was his mission to stop the bleeding and then hold the fort, eating some innings while his power-laden offense heated up. Coates had been effective in this role all season. Actually, he had been effective in whatever role he was used. He had started 18 games and relieved in 17 others, with six complete games. He got out of the first inning on a couple of groundballs by Smoky Burgess and Don Hoak. Two more groundouts and a strikeout got him through the next inning. Groat and Stuart singled in the third, but Hector Lopez's arm prevented trouble as he cut down Groat trying to make third base on Stuart's hit.

Yogi Berra wasn't having his best day. His first throw to second base ended up in center field, and his second—on Skinner's steal—was terrible and could have been an error if not for Kubek's backup of Richardson.

SEVENTEEN. *Six Games of Sparring*

Berra singled to start New York's second inning. Bill "Moose" Skowron singled him to second. Dale Long flied to Clemente in right, and Richardson lined the ball hard to left. Skinner came in to make the catch, giving him momentum on his throw. When Berra ventured too far off of second base, Skinner fired a strike to Mazeroski as Berra did a belly-flop into the dirt. It was Pittsburgh's second double play in two innings. Not good base running by Berra.

Long's appearance at the plate shocked everyone because he pinch-hit for Clete Boyer. In the second inning. The Yankees third baseman was not taken ill, and he wasn't injured. The move was just one of those bizarre things Stengel occasionally did on a whim.

The World Series was the first for Boyer, who had hit .242 in the regular season but flashed some power with 14 home runs. He was denied his first at-bat while being embarrassed at the same time. Old Case was viewed by the general public and almost all of the press corps as "beloved," but it was this sort of antic that former players would recall with a totally different emotion. The emotions from Boyer were total surprise, humiliation, and anger. As he headed to the plate, he was called back to the dugout. He first believed Stengel had words for him on what to look for from the pitcher, Law, but the Yankees manager's only words were for Boyer to take a seat on the bench. The third baseman was livid.

The M&M Boys reached base to begin the fourth inning, Maris on a single and Mantle with a walk. The stage was set—for one of the best World Series clutch hitters of all time and for the Yankees to put together a big inning. Berra connected. His drive to right-center field looked like extra bases. Virdon was on the move to his left, but he had acres of ground to cover. Clemente closed in from right field. Virdon leaped and made the catch as he neared the wall, and even though he and Clemente bumped, the Bucs center fielder held on for the first out.

Virdon and Clemente had both called for the ball, but they could not hear one another because of the tremendous roar of the crowd. Virdon's spikes cut the back of Clemente's right shoe, but the right fielder was not hurt. Writers who had not seen Virdon field were stunned. Danny Murtaugh in the dugout, Law on the mound, and regular observers of the Pirates were elated but not the least surprised. They considered Virdon the nearest thing to Willie Mays in center, perhaps even his equal in terms of going and getting the ball, and with Clemente patrolling beside him, any ball hit to center or right figured to be caught if it stayed in the park.[5]

Skowron's single to left plated Maris and brought New York within a run. Law avoided further trouble by retiring Gil McDougald, who had replaced Boyer at third base, on a foul pop-up and Richardson on a fly to center.

Vernon Law was a 22-game winner for the 1960 Pirates. He won 20 during the regular season and a pair in the World Series. "The Deacon" was dependable, always taking his turn and consistently pitching into the late innings. The Cy Young Award winner was tough, too, proving it by making three starts and throwing 18 innings in the Series despite a tender right ankle. A good hitting pitcher, he came up with a key RBI double against the Yankees.

In the bottom of the fourth, the Pirates spoiled what had been a nice day for Coates. He began his own demise with a one-out walk to Hoak. Mazeroski made Coates pay by blasting a home run high and far over the left-field scoreboard and into the trees in Schenley Park.

In the fifth, Skinner reached second on an error by Richardson. The second baseman fielded Skinner's ground ball but threw it away. When Clemente hit a chopper to Kubek at short, Skinner got caught in a rundown and was tagged out at third. Skinner slid awkwardly into the bag and jammed his thumb. He stayed in the game until he was hit in the arm by a Ryne Duren fastball in the seventh inning. Gino Cimoli ran for him and remained in the game to play left field in the eighth.

The score was 5–2, Pirates, and it remained that way until the bottom of the sixth when Pittsburgh added an insurance run off Duke Maas. Mazeroski singled, was sacrificed to second by Law, and scored on Virdon's double. The Yankees

Seventeen. Six Games of Sparring

made some noise in the eighth as Lopez and Maris singled. Murtaugh brought in Elroy Face to pitch, and he took care of business on 10 pitches. Mantle took a called strike three, Berra skied to Clemente in right, and Skowron fanned. When the game was over, Law admitted that the pain in his ankle had become "awful" late in the game and that he was glad Face was ready to do the job.

No one ever expects the New York Yankees to go down easily. Coming from behind, rallying in the late innings, and never feeling beaten are who they are. Forbes Field faithful must have been thinking along the lines of "Here they go" when McDougald led off the ninth inning with a single to right. Richardson grounded to Mazeroski, who tossed to Groat for a forceout. Face needed two more outs. Elston Howard batted for Duren, who threw two scoreless innings. Howard belted a Face pitch deep to right, and the ball barely cleared the screen as Clemente helplessly watched. Kubek singled for his third hit of the game, and Lopez walked to the plate representing the tying run. With Maris and Mantle coming up behind him, two outs were looking very hard for the Pirates to get.

Not hard at all, as it turned out, and they got them quickly. Lopez grounded sharply to second, and Pittsburgh doubled up, Mazeroski to Groat to Stuart. Ball game over. Afterward, Virdon talked about his catch, saying, "I've made a lot better catches, but this one was the most pleasing."[6]

Richardson, responding to questions about the failure of him or Kubek to cover second base on Virdon's first-inning steal, said that they had hit-and-run on their minds. "We had heard that Groat very seldom missed a swing, always got a piece of the ball when they hit-and-ran," Richardson said. "Neither of us thought to cover the bag until Yogi threw the ball, and then we both went for it. Tony and I were both holding our ground so we didn't give Groat a big hole to hit through. Turned out the hit-and-run wasn't even on."[7]

Years later, Groat would offer more on the situation. "I didn't say anything at the time. I just went along with the idea that Billy surprised the Yankees with a delayed steal. The truth, though, is that I messed it up. Billy ran because he missed my sign or because I gave the sign too late. I think the latter is probably the case." The Pirates' captain explained that everybody knew that he usually gave his own signal for the hit-and-run. He said Virdon got the signal, but then he (Groat) noticed Richardson and Kubek holding a conference around second base. He knew what they were meeting about. They knew he liked to work the hit-and-run in a situation like that. Groat, however, decided to cross them up, so he flashed the sign to take off the hit-and-run. He was more surprised than anybody when Virdon ran on the next pitch. It was high and outside, and Groat let it go by. He was positive Virdon never got his second signal.

There was talk that Richardson and Kubek were confused about who would cover the bag, said Groat, who added that he didn't think that was the case at all. He believed they had just decided that Groat would hit the first pitch, and they decided not to leave their position because he might hit the ball through the open spot. Groat insisted that it wasn't Virdon's fault, that he had messed everything up. As it turned out, he guessed it was a good thing he did.[8]

Hoak revealed that he had played in pain. In a daily column he was writing for the *Pittsburgh Post-Gazette*, the third baseman said, "Last Friday night, when we were playing Milwaukee, I slipped rounding second base and pulled my groin muscle. The field was loose from rain. It was hard to keep your footing. The pulled groin pained me badly, and it was no fun playing nine innings, but I'll be playing the second game and the third game and the fourth game—and I hope that's all we'll need."[9]

Everyone looks for edges, or reasons to give edges to teams, and one of the standard assumptions is that the first-game winner of any series has an advantage. Not just in terms of being up, 1–0, but psychologically. Hoak disagreed, saying, "I don't feel we gained any psychological edge on the Yankees by winning the first game. I just don't buy that psychology yak-yak because the Yankees aren't a bunch of neurotics who are going to fold."[10] The Pittsburgh third baseman made a brief visit to the mound in the ninth inning when the Yankees had two men on base and one out. Hoak elaborated on the conversation with Face, his roommate, "I said, 'Come on, Roomie. Get that double play and let's get the blazes out of here.'"[11]

Summary: Berra, Virdon, and Mazeroski were right in the middle of

SEVENTEEN. *Six Games of Sparring*

several key moments. For Berra, it was all bad: His errant throw; his long, potentially damaging clout that was caught; and his careless base running. Virdon made the catch that robbed Yogi; he stole second base to ignite the Pirates' offense in the first inning; and he doubled in a run. Mazeroski scored on that double; he hit a two-run homer, those runs proving to be the winning runs; and he helped in three double plays.

Game Two

The Yankees really put on a show while taking batting practice at Forbes Field. Unfortunately for the Pirates, New York continued batting practice when Game Two began, teeing off on one Pittsburgh pitcher after another.

The Bronx Bombers lived up to their nickname, pounding out 19 hits in trouncing Pittsburgh, 16–3, to even the World Series at a win apiece. Mickey Mantle hit nearly 900 feet of home runs—two of them—and drove in five runs. Tony Kubek had three hits for the second straight day, and Bobby Richardson had three as well, with a double. Everybody in New York's starting lineup had at least one hit. That lineup included Elston Howard behind the plate, with Yogi Berra making his first-ever World Series start in left field.

Right-hander Bob Turley went eight and one-third innings despite allowing 13 hits and walking three. "Bullet Bob," who threw 141 pitches, did not strike out a batter. Strangely, Casey Stengel didn't remove him until the ninth.

The left-handed hitting Kubek led off the game by slapping an opposite-field single. He was cut down attempting to swipe second base as Smoky Burgess's throw was right on the money, Bill Mazeroski making the tag. That likely saved a run because Roger Maris singled. Bob Friend looked strong as he struck out four in two innings, while Turley worked around a Roberto Clemente single and a double by Mazeroski. Friend triggered his own undoing by walking Richardson to start the third. Turley bunted Richardson to second, and he scored on another Kubek base hit. Kubek came all the way around from first on a double by Gil McDougald, playing third base in place of Clete Boyer. It was 2–0

"Had 'Em All the Way"

Yankees, and they added a run in the fourth inning on a Richardson single, a passed ball, and an RBI hit by Turley.

The Pirates showed some life by beginning the bottom of the fourth with three straight hits. Gino Cimoli and Smoky Burgess singled, Cimoli scoring on a Don Hoak double. But Bill Mazeroski lined out to third, Gene Baker batted for Friend and popped to second, and Virdon grounded to second to end what had been a promising inning. Pittsburgh had closed within two, 3–1. As it turned out, that would be the Bucs' best chance all day of catching up to the Yankees.

Lefty Fred Green replaced Friend in the fifth and walked McDougald, the first batter he faced. Maris bounced into a forceout, bringing to the plate Mantle, who was hitless in four Series at-bats thus far with three strikeouts. Batting right-handed, Mantle caught hold of a Green fastball and sent it the opposite way, some 400 feet into the lower grandstand in right field, making it 5–1, Yankees.

The roof caved in on the Pirates the next inning, the sixth, when New York sent 12 men to the plate. Nine of them reached base, seven on hits, one on a walk, and one on an error by Bucs shortstop Dick Groat. Elston Howard had a single and a triple in the inning, Richardson a single and a double. Green, Clem Labine, and George "Red" Witt all were hit hard during the seven-run uprising. It was 12–1.

Joe Gibbon, another left-hander, took a turn in the seventh as the Yankees tacked on three more runs. They came on Mantle's second blast of the game, this one traveling even farther than the first. The ball landed in an area over the right-center field vines that had been reached previously only by left-handed sluggers Stan Musial, Duke Snider, and Dale Long. A city policeman standing near where the ball landed helped estimate its distance at 478 feet.[12] The Yankees were pouring it on, 15–1.

The Pirates were getting men on base, but could not bring them home. They had a base runner in eight of the nine innings and six times had more than one. Only in the ninth did they mount much of a threat, but by then it was much too late. When Turley hit pinch-hitter Joe Christopher and gave up consecutive one-out singles to Rocky Nelson, Gino Cimoli, and Burgess, allowing two runs to score, Old Case tromped to the mound. Little Bobby Shantz made fast work of it from there. He fielded Hoak's bouncer and started a game-ending double play.

SEVENTEEN. *Six Games of Sparring*

Turley paid no attention to what today is considered a high pitch count. "I once threw 200 pitches in a game and won," he said, "so I wasn't tired. Well, I wasn't exhausted, let's say. "The danger spot for me was in the fourth inning when Gino Cimoli and Smoky Burgess singled and Hoak doubled. Casey came out and told me to try to get my pitches lower. Bill Mazeroski and Gene Baker were the two big outs of the game for me."[13]

A popular second-guess was questioning Danny Murtaugh for removing 18-game winner Friend with the Bucs trailing by just two runs in the fourth inning. The five pitchers who followed him gave up 13 runs, turning what had been a close game into a romp. Friend was not among the second-guessers. "I don't blame Danny for taking me out," he said. "Danny did the right thing."[14]

The Pirates were 4-for-15 with runners in scoring position. They left 13 runners on base. They had received bad news long before the game even began, learning that left fielder Bob Skinner would be out for an undetermined time with his thumb injury. As it turned out, he did not return until Game Seven.

The only real suspense took place before the first pitch as there was some concern whether the game would start on time or even be played at all. Rain had fallen heavily all night in Pittsburgh, had slowed to a drizzle in the early hours, but had continued throughout the morning. It stopped long enough for both teams to take batting practice before resuming and forcing the ground crew to cover the infield again. Then the skies cleared, the sun shined brightly, and the first pitch was made at one minute after one.

Historians and statisticians turned pages and found that the teams' combined total of 32 hits was a World Series record and that New York's seven-run inning matched its own record set in 1936 and repeated in 1937. One story in the *New York Times* ended with this sentence: "There remains the question of how well the battered Bucs can recover from the psychological blow of the second-game rout."[15]

Summary: Nineteen hits, 16 runs—it was classic Bronx Bombers. Mantle, like so many times, took over the spotlight with his raw power. He left the Forbes Field crowd and the Pirates buzzing about his two long home runs. Richardson and Howard had two hits apiece in the seven-run sixth that salted away victory for the Yankees.

"Had 'Em All the Way"

Game Three

The location was different, but New York's hitting assault was the same: relentless. The Yankees rapped out 16 hits in handing Pittsburgh its second straight thrashing, 10–0.

The Fall Classic had moved to Yankee Stadium, and a crowd of 70,001 was treated not only to another Yankee offensive show, but also to a classic Whitey Ford pitching performance. The Yanks' ace threw a four-hitter, making everyone wonder again why in the World Series the left-hander had not started Game One.

Mickey Mantle hit his third home run in two games and had three other hits, but the Yankees' hitting star this day was second baseman Bobby Richardson. Never acclaimed as much of a hitter, Richardson belted a grand slam and knocked in six runs. The Pirates needed three pitchers to get out of the first inning and six to finish the game. Vinegar Bend Mizell lasted just one-third of an inning, Clem Labine the same. Red Witt, Tom Cheney, and Joe Gibbon did a nice job of mopping up with zeroes over the last four innings. The joke in the press box was that by the time that trio pitched, New York batters were too tuckered out to put much into their swings.

Casey Stengel might have been a baseball traditionalist in many ways, but he did not allow superstition to override the inklings and instincts which drove his decisions. So it was that, despite the Yankees' steamroller display in the previous game, the Perfessor changed his lineup. Changed it quite a bit. Tony Kubek, who had six hits in the first two games of the Series, was dropped from leadoff to the eighth spot. Bob Cerv, who hit in the middle of batting orders most of his career, batted first. He played left field in place of Yogi Berra. Both of those moves were in response to Pittsburgh starting a southpaw pitcher, Mizell. Stengel also dropped Gil McDougald from second to fifth in the order, while pushing five others higher: Roger Maris from third to second, Mickey Mantle from fourth to third, Moose Skowron from sixth to fourth, Elston Howard from seventh to sixth, and Richardson from eighth to seventh.

Everybody in the lineup except Maris had at least one hit, including Ford, who pitched a complete game with three strikeouts and one walk.

SEVENTEEN. *Six Games of Sparring*

He dominated with finesse, getting 14 outs on ground balls, 15 counting one bouncer turned into a double play.

The first inning was a bad dream for the Pirates. After they went down one-two-three, Cerv singled to center to start things for New York. Maris lined out to Clemente, Mantle singled Cerv to third, and Skowron singled him home. When Mizell walked McDougald, he was finished for the day. On came Labine, who got Howard to hit a little nubber to third, but it went for an infield hit and another run. Richardson tried to bunt once and fouled the ball. On a three-two pitch from Labine, Richardson hit the ball like a rocket down the left field line, depositing it into the lower left field seats. It was the seventh grand slam home run in World Series history.

Kubek singled and already had his seventh hit of the Series. Ford hit into a forceout, and Cerv smacked his second single of the inning, sending Labine to the showers and bringing on Fred Green. When he got Maris on a foul pop-out, the half-inning had taken more than a half-hour. The Yanks sent 11 men to the plate and were up, 6–0.

Richardson singled in another pair of runs in the Yankees' four-run fourth inning, giving him six RBI to set a single-game Series record. Mantle smashed a two-run homer off Green that landed in the upper deck in left. All three of Mantle's home runs in the Series had come from the right side. New York's 25-year-old second baseman was the unlikeliest of hitting stars. Batting .252 for regular season, Richardson had hit one home run in 507 plate appearances. That gave him three homers in more than 1,500 trips to the plate in his brief big league career. He had been used sparingly in the 1957 and 1958 World Series against Milwaukee, going 0-for-5.

Ford set down the first nine batters he faced, was nicked for a lead-off double by Bill Virdon in the fourth inning, and retired the next six Pirates. Only twice did two Bucs reach base in the same inning. In the seventh, with one out, Dick Stuart singled, and Gino Cimoli walked. Hal Smith bounced a comebacker to Ford, who threw to Richardson, who relayed to Skowron for an inning-ending double play. After two were out in the ninth, Clemente singled, and Kubek booted Stuart's grounder. Ford stuck out Cimoli to end the game. He faced just 31 batters all day.

"Had 'Em All the Way"

I-told-you-so's were on the lips of hundreds of sportswriters in view of two-game totals that saw the Yankees amass 35 hits and 26 runs. Pittsburgh scored a meager three times in the two massacres. It was a lousy birthday for Murtaugh, who turned 43 that day.

Hoak, in his column, wrote, "If you quit on the Pirates now, there's a very good chance you'll have to eat your words in a few days."[16] The Pinstripers had to be feeling fine. Up two-one, with the next two games to be played in that grand house that Ruth built.

Summary: More bombing from the men in pinstripes, the littlest one of them providing the noisiest fireworks. Richardson, the light-hitting second sacker, belted a grand slam and drove in six runs. Mantle homered for the third time in two games and had four of the Yankees' 16 hits. Looking very much like a Game One pitcher, Ford tossed a four-hit shutout.

Game Four

Facing the possibility of getting slugged right out of the World Series, Pittsburgh's Danny Murtaugh dialed up the same combination that produced a victory in Game One, and he got the same result. Vernon Law, once again receiving tremendous supporting performances from Bill Virdon and Elroy Face, beat the Yankees to even the Series at two wins apiece. The Pirates nipped New York, 3–2, in front of a Yankee Stadium crowd of 67,812.

Not only were the Bucs even, they were assured of returning home to Forbes Field.

Law quieted the Yankees' bats that had boomed for 35 hits in a two-game, 26–3 blitz. He also doubled in a run and scored one in the Pirates' three-run fifth inning. Virdon singled in a pair of runs and made another terrific catch. Face escaped a major jam and pitched two and two-thirds hitless, scoreless innings to save his second game of the Series, both preserving victories for Law. "As I've told you all along," Murtaugh said, "this club does not discourage easily. We don't waste any time thinking about what happened yesterday. They counted us out a dozen times this season, and we always bounced back. We're resilient."[17]

Law was in trouble right away. Bob Cerv led off the bottom of the

Seventeen. Six Games of Sparring

first inning with a single to center, and when Tony Kubek went the other way and doubled to left, the Yankees appeared to be in business with two runners in scoring position, nobody out, and the heart of the batting order coming to the plate. Roger Maris lifted a fly ball to medium right field, but it was not deep enough for New York third-base coach Frankie Crosetti to risk sending the slow-running Cerv home. Not with Roberto Clemente and his rifle right arm in right. Mickey Mantle was walked intentionally, setting up a double play. And that's just what Pittsburgh pulled off, at least, according to first-base umpire Dusty Boggess. Yogi Berra, one of the best clutch hitters in World Series history, barely put wood on a Law pitch and topped the ball toward the bag at third. Don Hoak easily gloved the roller, stepped on the base, and fired to first. Boggess said the ball smacked into Pittsburgh first baseman Dick Stuart's mitt before Berra's foot came down on the first-base bag. The ump's out signal completed the double play, the Yankees' threat, and the inning.

Questioned later about the immediate mess he encountered, Law said, "When you're in trouble, you just have to keep your head and have a good idea of where to throw the ball."[18] Law and Ralph Terry matched zeroes for three innings, the Yankees right-hander no-hitting the Pirates through four. New York scored first, Moose Skowron lining a home run into the lower right-field stands in the bottom of the fourth.

Left-fielder Gino Cimoli singled to right for the Bucs' first hit to lead off the fifth inning. Smoky Burgess grounded weakly to first, and Skowron, eager to cut down the lead runner, gunned a throw to Kubek covering second base. Cimoli was called safe, umpire John Stevens saying he beat the throw. Kubek was upset, feeling the only way he didn't get the out would have been if his foot was off the bag.

Hoak and Bill Mazeroski both popped out, and with the pitcher up next, it looked as though Terry was about to wriggle off the hook. But Law lined a double down the left-field line, driving in Cimoli with the tying run and sending Burgess to third. Virdon looped a single to center, and with two outs, both runners were on the move at the crack of the bat. Burgess and Law scored easily, and the Pirates had a 3–1 lead.

Bobby Richardson singled to start the Yankees' fifth, but never advanced as Law struck out the side, getting Terry, Cerv, and Kubek. Two ground balls and a fly out in the sixth, and Law had set down six in a row. Skowron continued his hot hitting against Law, bouncing a ground-rule double into the bleachers in right field. That gave the Yankees first baseman four hits in six Series at-bats vs. Pittsburgh's 20-game winner.

Gil McDougald singled to right, Crosetti holding Skowron at third. "Crow," as he was affectionately known among the Yankees, was again showing respect for Clemente's arm but also playing it smart. New York had the potential tying runners on base with no outs. To the plate walked Richardson, the hottest hitter in this Fall Classic. He was 2-for-2 so far on the day, with a double and single, raising his batting average to .467 with eight RBI in the Series. This time, Richardson tapped a grounder to Mazeroski, who stepped on second base to force McDougald while Skowron crossed the plate. The score was 3–2, Pirates.

Stengel called on Johnny Blanchard to bat for Shantz, who had gotten the last two outs in Pittsburgh's half of the seventh in relief of Terry. Blanchard was a left-handed pull hitter with power. New York's third catcher and an occasional outfielder, he would hit 50 home runs in the next three seasons as a part-time player. If he could reach the Stadium's short right-field porch, the Yankees would have the lead. He did not do that, but the pinch-hitter did line a base hit to right field, Richardson stopping at second. Infielder Joe DeMaestri ran for Blanchard.

Murtaugh headed for the mound, and Law knew he was done for the day. Face was up in the bullpen, and he needed only six or seven tosses to be ready. The Baron of the Bullpen thrived on challenges, and if he felt any pressure or tension, he never showed it. His expression never changed.

There was one out and two on, Richardson representing the tying run and in scoring position. The first batter Face saw was Cerv, who was enjoying a fine Series. Cerv was 35 years old and in the second of what would be three stints with the Yankees, who had signed him back in 1950. They sent him to their "farm club," the Kansas City A's, after the 1956 season. In 1958, Cerv hit 38 home runs, knocked in 104 runs, and batted .305. He placed fourth in the American League MVP balloting. The Yankees "promoted" him early in the 1960 season. They traded third baseman Andy Carey to K.C. in May, acquiring Cerv to add bench strength and a right-handed power bat. (From 1955 to 1960, the New

SEVENTEEN. Six Games of Sparring

York Yankees made 16 deals with the Kansas City Athletics. Many of those deals involved money, with the rich Yankees either purchasing players from the A's or supplementing trades with cash. On occasion, New York would send a player to K.C. and get him back sometime down the road.)

Cerv stepped in, with four hits in nine trips to the plate in the Series. He was starting in left field and batting leadoff for the second straight game. Face threw Cerv a forkball that didn't fork. It rode high instead of dipping violently like most of the Baron's pitches. Cerv swung and connected solidly, smashing a long drive toward the 407-foot sign in right-center. Virdon, as he almost always did, got a great jump and dashed gracefully from straightaway center field. Just before the ball reached the fence, Virdon leaped high, crashed into the wall, and came down with the ball in his glove.

Richardson tagged and made it to third, but that was the extent of the damage. What for moments looked like extra bases for Cerv and a one-run lead for the Yankees became simply an out. Well, not simply, because Virdon's catch was spectacular. It was the play of the World Series to that point, nudging his own first-game grab to second place in the rating of defensive gems. Asked if he was worried when the ball left Cerv's bat, Face said, "Not really. I knew if it stayed in the ball park, Bill would get it."[19]

"Now you know why I decided to play Virdon every day in this Series," Murtaugh said after the game.[20]

Kubek grounded meekly back to the mound to end the seventh inning. That would be the Yankees' best chance against Face. He retired all eight batters he faced. In the eighth, Maris skied to center, Mantle struck out, and Berra grounded to third. There was a hard-hit ball in the ninth, but good positioning turned what might have been trouble into a loud out. Skowron was looking for his third hit of the game when he led off the ninth inning. He had a home run in the Series, and if he could go deep again, the score would be tied. And Skowron did go deep. Always known for his power to the opposite field, the right-handed Moose ripped a shot toward the corner in right. There was no doubt that it had home run distance; the question was whether the ball would stay fair. It did not. It sliced to the right of the foul pole.

"Had 'Em All the Way"

Asked after the game if he heaved a sigh of relief when Skowron's drive went foul, Face shrugged. "I never worry much about fouls," he said. "They don't count, so I didn't think much about it one way or another."[21] Of course, it is hard to believe any pitcher in that situation would not at least flinch internally at such a close call.

Face's forte was getting batters to hit the ball into the dirt, and he came back to do that. Skowron again hit the ball hard, though, a smash at the third-base bag that would normally have become a double. However, Pittsburgh third baseman Hoak was stationed close to the bag and was able to make a terrific play. He backhanded the scorcher and threw across the diamond to Stuart for the first out. Skowron reflected on his ninth-inning at-bat and his two near-misses. "The ball I hit to right just went foul at the last second. Then Hoak made a backhand grab and threw me out. I don't know why he was playing me so far over toward the line," Skowron said of the Bucs' third baseman. "I don't usually pull the ball that good."[22]

With Skowron out of the way, Face made quick work of the final two Yankees. McDougald lined to shortstop Dick Groat. Stengel, no doubt hoping for a long ball that could tie it up, pinch-hit Dale Long for the .438-hitting Richardson. The former Pirate flied to Clemente to end the ball game.

Virdon, who had a scrape on his left elbow from colliding with the wall, wanted to talk more about his two-run single than his great catch. "After all, I got the hit that won the game. I'll put hits over catches any time—maybe because I make more catches than hits."[23]

"You saw a typical Pirate ball game today," Murtaugh said. "Good pitching and good defense. Those have been our trademarks all season."[24]

Summary: After getting floored twice, the Pirates used the Law-Face-Virdon combo to win Round Four. Law, doubling in a run for good measure, was superb until Face Time rolled around. The little Baron slammed the door on the Yankees' foot just when they were getting it in the door. Virdon knocked in the two deciding runs and made another of the great catches New York writers were starting to think he had patented.

SEVENTEEN. *Six Games of Sparring*

Game Five

The accepted storyline of the 1960 World Series was that the New York Yankees hammered the Pittsburgh Pirates with haymakers, but the Bucs won the match on a split decision. There was a more subtle subplot. It suggested that Danny Murtaugh outmanaged Casey Stengel, perhaps mostly by not overmanaging. Old Case was his own public relations man, and a very good one. He frequently reminded the press that his brains made the Yankees' brawn triumphant. And Stengel was a genius, a tremendous card player who could shuffle jacks and queens into outstanding support for his aces and kings. He was a superior handler of personnel. But he operated on instinct as much as guile, and sometimes his hunches fizzled. Not just in terms of the immediate results, but also in terms of the whiplash effect on his players. He loved playing chess on newspapers' sports pages. The pawns were not always amused.

Game Five had Stengel second-guessing himself for second-guessing himself. Following New York's Game Four loss to the Pirates, he had told writers that he would probably go with rookie Bill Stafford as his starting pitcher for the next game. "Unless I decide to start Ditmar," he added. And Art Ditmar it was. Stengel, as usual, went with experience in big games. The right-hander who lasted one-third of an inning in the Series' opening game pitched exactly one inning longer this time. One and a third innings, three hits, three runs, one earned run.

Stafford pitched five innings of three-hit shutout relief, but Harvey Haddix and Elroy Face held the Yankees to five hits in a 5–2 Pittsburgh win for a 3–2 Series edge. A 21-year-old righty, Stafford began the 1960 season with Triple-A Richmond. The Yanks called him up in August after he went 11–7 with a 2.06 earned run average. Stafford was 3–1 with New York, starting eight times and pitching 60 innings, with one shutout and a 2.25 ERA.

Ditmar set the Pirates down one-two-three in the first inning. Gil McDougald became the third Yankee to lead off in the Series, Tony Kubek having done it the first two games and Bob Cerv the next two. McDougald tried bunting for a base hit and was thrown out by third baseman Hoak. Roger Maris grounded out to second. Cerv topped a roller toward third that Hoak picked up and threw away. Cerv was

"Had 'Em All the Way"

credited with an infield hit, Hoak with an error allowing him to go to second base. Haddix walked Mickey Mantle intentionally and then struck out Bill Skowron.

Dick Stuart singled to left field to start the Bucs' second inning. Gino Cimoli hit a bouncer to second baseman Bobby Richardson, who raced to the bag to force Stuart. It was the last out Ditmar would get. Smoky Burgess belted a double into the right-field corner, with Cimoli stopping at third base. Hoak grounded to Kubek, and the shortstop tossed to McDougald in an effort to cut down Burgess, while Cimoli scored. McDougald dropped the ball, Burgess safe at third and Hoak winding up at second. Mazeroski hit a chopper toward third. The ball took a kangaroo hop and bounded over the head of McDougald down the left-field line for a double that knocked in Burgess and Hoak.

Ditmar was done. In came Luis Arroyo, a screwballing left-hander, and he did a nice job of damage control by striking out Haddix and getting Bill Virdon on a pop foul to McDougald. Pirates 3, Yankees 0.

New York got a run back in the bottom of the second on an Elston Howard double to right and a couple of groundouts, Kubek's good for an RBI. Dick Groat smashed a double to left to start the fourth inning. Roberto Clemente singled to drive in Groat and make the score 4–1. That gave Clemente at least one hit in all five Series games. Stafford replaced Arroyo and retired the Bucs. He continued to mow them down until getting into two-out trouble in the seventh and then escaping without a run.

Maris boomed a home run into the upper deck in right in the New York third, and Mantle was walked for the second time. He was left stranded when Skowron lofted a routine fly to Clemente. Pirates 4, Yankees 2.

Haddix got in a pickle again, the fourth time in as many innings, when Groat bobbled Howard's ground ball. Richardson then hit the ball right on the nose—what Hall of Fame pitcher turned broadcaster Dizzy Dean called a "blue darter"—that Hoak stabbed and threw to Stuart to double off Howard.

After Richardson again lined to third to begin the seventh inning, Kubek singled to center and pinch-hitter Hector Lopez singled to right. With the tying runs on base and one out, Murtaugh waved in Elroy Face

SEVENTEEN. *Six Games of Sparring*

from the bullpen. Face had pitched two and two-thirds innings a day earlier. That didn't seem to matter. He induced a ground ball to short from McDougald, Groat flipping to Mazeroski to force Lopez. Face struck out Maris on a forkball that fell off the table to end the threat. A fly ball, ground ball, and pop-up sandwiched around a walk to Mantle took care of the Yankees in the eighth. It was the third time in the game that Mantle had drawn a bases on balls.

Pittsburgh added some insurance in the ninth against Ryne Duren, with some sloppy play by New York thrown in. Burgess singled and continued to second on Cerv's bobble in left. Joe Christopher ran for Burgess and moved to third on Duren's wild pitch. Hoak's single plated Christopher.

Face made it look easy in polishing off the Yankees, with a bounce out, pop out, and fly out. The Baron had pitched a total of five and a third innings of hitless relief in two days, one walk blotting two otherwise perfect appearances. "I'm tickled we snapped back and showed the baseball we're capable of," Murtaugh said. "I don't mind telling you the bad press we received after those two big Yankee wins hurt our pride—not that we warranted any better treatment. We do have a pretty good ball club, you know. I think we proved it again today."[25]

Summary: Face turned out a carbon copy of his seventh-inning Houdini act from the previous day after Haddix kept the Yanks off balance. The bottom part of the Pirates' batting order did the big damage, with Hoak and Mazeroski, the seventh and eighth hitters, each driving in two runs. Clemente got a hit for the fifth straight game and had the other RBI.

Game Six

Now it was the Yankees who were in a must-win situation on the road. Any casually interested baseball fan would have quickly told you that New York's starting pitcher had to be Whitey Ford. Casey Stengel tried to turn his decision into a mystery, even a game. "I asked my players if they wanted Ford to start," he said, "and they all did except six or eight; they was the other pitchers which wanted to start themselves."[26] Saying he was torn between Ford and Bob Turley, Stengel made up his mind the morning of the game. His splendid southpaw proved the decision a wise one. Pitching after three days rest, Ford was his usual stellar big-game self. He threw his second shutout, scattering seven hits, walking one, and striking out five as the Yankees cruised, 12–0. Their third pounding of the Pirates forced a seventh game.

This massacre began innocently enough, with Ford driving in a run with an infield single in the second inning. The most significant thing to happen in that inning, however, was Elston Howard getting hit by a Bob Friend pitch. Howard suffered a broken finger on his right hand and left for pinch-runner Eli Grba, a pitcher. The injury would keep Howard, who was batting .462 for the Series, out of Game Seven.

The Yanks, as they had in his previous start, gave Ford a large early lead. They piled on five runs in the third inning, sending Friend to his second fast exit in the Series. Friend hit Tony Kubek with a pitch to start the inning. Roger Maris lined a double to right, putting runners at second and third with no outs. The game before, Pittsburgh had pitched around Mantle, walking him three times. This time, with a base open, Friend pitched to the Yankees' center fielder, and he singled in two runs. Berra singled Mantle to third. Friend was gone, having pitched two innings and failing to get anyone out in the third. Tom Cheney came on and got Bill Skowron on a sacrifice fly, scoring Mantle. Johnny Blanchard, who had replaced Howard behind the plate, singled. Richardson tripled in two runs.

New York scored two runs in the sixth, seventh, and eighth innings, four of those runs coming off Clem Labine. Blanchard, Maris, and Berra, again playing left field, each had three of the Yankees' 17 hits. Richardson's three RBI gave him 12 for the Series, setting a record that still stands.

Danny Murtaugh was far from crushed after his club absorbed yet another battering. "The last time I checked," he said, "they were still setting the World Series on games won and lost, not on total runs. The record shows the Yankees have been beaten three times, just like us."[27]

Don Hoak tried to be optimistic. "All three of our defeats have been shellackings, but that doesn't hurt our pride one bit," he said. "When you've had the tar kicked out of you, you don't lose sleep replaying the game."[28] Bill Virdon smiled and offered this consolation: "We had a lot

SEVENTEEN. *Six Games of Sparring*

of good exercise chasing those balls in the outfield today. It will loosen us up for tomorrow. There is one good thing to be thankful for. You don't take a game like this home with you. There are no might-have-beens about it."[29]

Summary: Another Ford masterpiece, with nine more zeroes and seven scattered hits allowed. Richardson continued to be an RBI machine, adding three to set a World Series record. The Yankees pounded out 17 hits in another skunking.

Eighteen
The Game

Game Sevens are supposed to go down to the wire. A shot at the buzzer. A game-winning hit in the bottom of the ninth. At least, that's the hope of the purist fan, one who dreams of witnessing the ultimate deciding game decided by the ultimate finish.

When that happens, it is amazing.

But what happened at Forbes Field in Pittsburgh on October 13, 1960, was beyond amazing. The ending that was both dramatic and thrilling was a first for major league baseball. People are still talking about it and watching replays of it today. "It" has immortalized the letters M-A-Z.

October 13 was a Thursday. Temperatures in Pittsburgh were in the low seventies. A bit of a haze hung over old Forbes Field, not at all ominous but more illusory, like a picture from another place and time.

Back in Gotham, New Yorkers were fully expecting their Yankees to bring home another World Series trophy. Almost everyone who followed baseball expected it, too. Early-morning newspaper readers were raising their eyebrows over what had happened at the United Nations building the previous day. Russian leader Nikita Khrushchev had thrown a temper tantrum, taking off his shoe and banging it on a table. Cold War talks had heated up.

As had been his custom throughout the Series, Casey Stengel tried to keep everyone—perhaps including himself—guessing about his starting pitcher. Bob Turley, a veteran and the winner in Game Two, was the obvious choice. The Perfessor, though, said he was considering rookie Bill Stafford, who had been so effective out of the bullpen in Game Five. It was Turley. He found out, not from his manager but by way of an old baseball custom. Frankie Crosetti, the Yankees' third-base coach and

Eighteen. The *Game*

Stengel's "lieutenant," left a brand-new baseball in one of Turley's shoes. It was nothing new. In fact, it was the same method used by Stengel to inform Don Larsen he would get the start in Game Five of the 1956 World Series. That day, Larsen pitched his perfect game.

There was no such suspense from Danny Murtaugh and the Pirates. They had known since Vernon Law started Game Four that he would also be the starter if there was a seventh game. And he was.

The official attendance for Game Seven of the 1960 World Series was 36,683. No doubt the number of those saying they witnessed that classic would be thousands higher. It was certainly one of those ball games folks feel privileged to see.

Before the 1960 World Series started, Pittsburgh shortstop and captain Dick Groat had predicted it would be like a boxing match. A match that pitted the strategic boxer against the brutal slugger, one dancing, bobbing, and throwing jabs, while the other went for the knockout as he swung from the heels. In this game, however, the boxer would resort to the same tactics as the slugger. The two of them stood toe to toe and traded blows, throwing their best punches, both landing some doozies, each taking the other's best shots.

Everyone knew the numbers through six games. The Yankees had scored 46 runs on 78 hits, reaching double figures in runs scored in all three of their wins and getting 13 or more hits four times. The Pirates had scored 17 runs on 49 hits. Their largest run total was six. New York had out-homered Pittsburgh, eight to one.

Stengel wrote out his seventh different lineup in seven games. Bobby Richardson became the fifth Yankee to lead off. The game before, it had been Clete Boyer. Richardson was batting first after being in the eighth slot four times and the seventh spot twice. Shortstop Tony Kubek was hitting second for the second day in a row after leading off twice, batting eighth twice and being in the number two slot one other time. Johnny Blanchard got his first start in the Series as he was behind the plate in place of the injured Elston Howard. Richardson, lining out hard to Don Hoak at third base for the third time in the Series, Kubek, and Roger Maris went down in order against Law to start the game.

Murtaugh's lineup had changed very little over six games. Hal Smith had caught both games that Whitey Ford pitched, Smoky Burgess going

"Had 'Em All the Way"

behind the plate against New York's right-handed starting pitchers. Rocky Nelson played first base and batted cleanup in Game Two, Dick Stuart in those spots for the other five games. With Turley back on the mound, it made sense for Nelson to be back in the lineup. And he was, but not by design. Nelson had gone 2-for-5 against Turley. Considering that success and that he would give the Bucs another left-handed bat in the lineup, Nelson was a logical choice to play first base. But his manager intended to start Stuart and have Nelson available for power off the bench.

Murtaugh made out two lineup cards before the game. One had Stuart at first base, the other had Nelson at first. As captain, Groat always carried the lineup to home plate before game. This time, he took the wrong one by mistake. Nelson was officially in the game. To replace him would have meant he was finished for the day, a wasted player.[1] Bob Skinner returned from a thumb injury to play left field and bat third. That dropped Roberto Clemente to the fifth spot.

Encouraging for the Bucs was that their largest hit total in the Series, 13, had come against Turley. He had walked three and hit a batter, so Pittsburgh had 17 base runners and left 13 of them stranded, while managing four hits in 15 at-bats with runners in scoring position. The Pirates had to feel they could get to Turley. And they did, almost immediately. With two outs, Skinner coaxed a base on balls. On a two-and-one pitch, Nelson lifted a fly ball to right field that sailed over the 350-foot sign and barely cleared the 30-foot screen. Fate—the mistaken lineup card—played a part, and Nelson did his, Pittsburgh profiting with a 2–0 lead.

Law used two ground balls and an easy fly to get the Yankees one-two-three again in the second. The Pirates added another pair of runs. Burgess singled, and Stengel dismissed Turley, whose day concluded after 20 pitches. In came Stafford, who walked Hoak. Bill Mazeroski, attempting to sacrifice, laid down a bunt and beat it out for a hit to load the bases with nobody out. Law bounced back to Stafford, who threw to Blanchard, who threw to Skowron for a double play. Just like that, Stafford and the Yanks were on the brink of getting out of a full-blown mess without allowing a run. Virdon, however, spoiled that hope with a two-run single to right field, giving the Pirates a 4–0 lead.

Eighteen. *The Game*

Law got two outs, making it eight straight batters he had set down, before Hector Lopez pinch-hit for Stafford and singled. Richardson hit a lazy fly to Skinner in left. Bobby Shantz came in to pitch for the Yankees. At 34, he was strictly a reliever after being a premier starter for the Philadelphia Athletics early in his career. He won 18 games in 1951 and topped that the next season when his 24–7 record and 2.48 earned run average won him the American League Most Valuable Player Award.

The A's moved to Kansas City, and like so many others who stood out for K.C. in the 1950s, Shantz was traded to the Yankees in 1957. The five-foot-six lefty gave his club exactly what it needed this day. He shut the Pirates out over the next five innings, while Yankees teammates finally got the best of Law. Moose Skowron put them on the board with a home run in the fifth as the right-hander showed signs of tiring. Then, in the sixth, after Richardson singled and Kubek walked, Murtaugh went out and took the ball from Law. It was early even for Elroy Face, but with no more games for six months, there was no reason to rest.

The Baron of the Bullpen had pitched in 68 games during the regular season, working 114⅔ innings. His record was 10–8 and he saved 24 games. This was long before the day when the closer almost always enters a game in the ninth inning with no one on base. Face often inherited serious jams, with the tying and possibly winning runners on base. He frequently entered games in the eighth or even seventh inning. In 1960, he pitched more than an inning to save 11 games, and seven of those were two or more innings. All 10 of his wins came after working two or more innings.

Face already had pitched in three Series games—at least two innings in each—saving all three, working a total of seven and a third innings. He had given up three hits, two runs, and one walk, and had struck out four. He had thrown two and two-thirds innings on back-to-back days. As the old saying goes, Murtaugh went to the well with Face one too many times. He retired Maris on a foul pop to third baseman Hoak. Mantle singled to center, scoring Richardson and sending Kubek to third. Yogi Berra fouled off a pitch before lifting a high fly ball down the right-field line. The sign at the base of the foul pole there said 300 feet, so it wasn't a long blast. It was high, dropping into the upper deck not too far from that foul pole. The three-run shot was Berra's 11th World Series home run.

The Yankees led, 5–4. Law's chance at a third Series victory was ended, and so was Face's spell over the boys in pinstripes. And they weren't done with him. Face blanked New York in the seventh inning and retired the first two batters in the eighth before walking Berra. Skowron trickled a ball to third that Hoak fielded but too late to make a throw. Blanchard singled in Berra, and Boyer's double down the line in left plated Skowron. The Yankees were up, 7–4, and Shantz was sailing along, having allowed a mere single while sticking five zeroes on Pittsburgh's side of the scoreboard. It was looking like the Yankees' dynasty would add another notch to its gun. But destiny—or fate, or luck, or the baseball gods—had other ideas.

Gino Cimoli, back on the bench with the return of Skinner, batted for Face. Shantz jammed him, but Cimoli was able to fist the ball into right field for a hit. Next came the most talked-about routine ground ball in World Series history. Except, of course, that it didn't turn out to be routine. Virdon beat the ball into the dirt, right at Yanks shortstop Kubek. It looked every bit like a double play. But the ball hit something—maybe a pebble—and bounced wildly. The ball bounded over Kubek's glove and hit him in the throat. He went down, the ball rolling to his side. Cimoli made it safely to second, Virdon to first with a bad-hop single. Kubek begged to stay in the game, but everyone could see that wasn't going to happen. He was taken to a hospital. Little-used Joe DeMaestri, known as a slick fielder, took over at shortstop.

Groat came to the plate, batting .185 for the Series. He singled to left to drive in Cimoli and reduce the Bucs' deficit to two runs. Stengel removed Shantz and brought in Jim Coates, a right-hander. Shantz, who said later that he was not tired, had pitched five brilliant innings of relief and had made two out pitches in his sixth inning, only to see both become hits.

Coates first faced Skinner, who sacrificed Virdon to third and Groat to second. Nelson hit a fly to right, but it was not deep, and with Maris possessing a strong arm, there was no point in taking a chance. Not when the potential tying run was on second and not third. The runners held. It looked as though Coates had done a masterful job of escaping,

Eighteen. The *Game*

when Clemente tapped a roller to the pitcher's left. Skowron fielded the ball easily, but Coates was slow to cover first base, and Clemente beat the play for an infield single and an RBI as Cimoli scored.

The score was 7–6, Yankees. Hal Smith batted next, his first trip to the plate. Normally, he didn't face many right-handers. He was in the game because starting catcher Smoky Burgess had been lifted for a pinch-runner. Smith hit 11 home runs and batted .295 in 258 at-bats during regular season. He had two singles in seven trips to the plate in the Series when he stepped in against Coates. Smith clouted a Coates pitch over the left-field wall for a three-run homer that put Pittsburgh ahead, 9–7. Ralph Terry relieved for the Yanks and got the final out in the eighth.

The Pirates had a two-run lead with three outs to get, but they had already used their trusted closer. Murtaugh called upon Bob Friend to get those last three outs. The right-hander, whose rise to prominence personified the rise of his team, wanted badly to atone for what had been a terrible World Series. As he toed the rubber and readied to face Richardson, Friend had a 10.50 earned run average after two starts that were little more than cameo appearances.

The other half of a potent catching platoon, Hal Smith made the best of his opportunities. He averaged an extra-base hit for every 8.3 at-bats and had the highest slugging percentage on the 1960 Pirates. He made Mazeroski's Series-winning home run possible by slugging a pressure-packed home run one inning earlier.

This outing was no better. Richardson singled. So did Dale Long, who was pinch-hitting for DeMaestri. Friend was finished, replaced by Game Five starter and winner Harvey Haddix. The little lefty, known as "the Kitten," got Maris on a foul pop to the catcher, Smith. Mantle singled home Richardson. Long reached third and was replaced by Gil McDougald as Stengel looked for additional speed in the potential tying run.

"Had 'Em All the Way"

The way it scored was bizarre. Berra hit the ball hard on the ground, and Nelson fielded it a step from first base. He stepped on the bag, thus removing the force on Mantle meaning Mantle now had the right to re-occupy first base. Which is what he did. To the dismay of everyone at Forbes Field, Mantle scampered back to first, and Nelson, frozen in surprise for an instant, tried to tag him. He was too late, though, and Mantle was safe.

While all that was taking place, McDougald crossed the plate with the Yankees' ninth run. The tying run. Skowron hit a grounder to Groat's right. The shortstop backhanded the ball and threw wide of second, Mazeroski making a heck of a play to keep his foot on the base and force Mantle for the third out.

Mazeroski was the first batter up for Pittsburgh in the ninth. Dick Stuart loosened up in the on-deck circle to pinch-hit for Haddix. It was up to Terry to carry the Yankees into extra innings and give them a chance to add one more Series prize to their already overcrowded trophy case. The 24-year-old right-hander threw two pitches. The first was a ball. The second was a long ball.

Mazeroski swung at a high fastball from Terry and connected, sending a drive over the 18-foot wall in left-center field. Berra watched helplessly as the blast cleared the 406-foot sign.

It was 3:37 in the afternoon when time stood still in Pittsburgh, Pennsylvania. Thirty-five years had passed since the Pirates last won a World Series. To win one at all was unbelievable. To win one like this was storybook stuff. Mazeroski fairly danced around the bases. As he rounded second base, he held his batting helmet aloft and waved it over his head. Later, he would recall that his feet didn't seem to touch the ground; it was as if he was floating. His victory lap was Peter Pan–like.

Historic too. Never before had a World Series ended this way, signing off with a home run.

The money paid out to the Pirates and Yankees would make today's players laugh. They might think it was meal money. Each winner's share was $8,417.94; the loser's was $5,214.64 each.

The 24-year-old second baseman with the lightning-quick double-play release will always be remembered as the hero of the 1960 World Series. Even if the other second baseman drove home the Corvette presented to the MVP. Maz was The Man.

Eighteen. The *Game*

Roberto Clemente had at least one hit in each of the seven games. Vernon Law and Harvey Haddix both had two wins. Elroy Face saved three games. Bill Virdon, the most unsung of the heroes, made spectacular catches and came up with crucial RBI. Hal Smith hit the home run that led to THE home run.

Pittsburgh's World Series triumph was accomplished the same way the National League pennant was captured. Lots of Pirates took turns making big pitches, getting big hits, and making big plays. It was totally a team effort.

While the Battling Bucs celebrated in their locker room, the proud New York Yankees mourned in theirs. Almost to a man, they were in a state of shock and a state of denial. Several of them declared that the best team did not win this World Series. Some simply could not believe what had happened. If they had thought numbers do not lie, they found out otherwise. What they could not accept was that only one number mattered.

Four.

Berra, in one of the Yogi-isms that have become so beloved, and at times downright philosophical, muttered that "We made too many wrong mistakes."

The Yankees were left shaking their heads. Mickey Mantle was not the only one to weep, the tears apparently shed as much over of what they perceived to be the unfairness of the defeat as over the defeat itself. Dale Long seemed somehow bewildered that Hal Smith, of all people, had hit such a clutch home run. Bobby Richardson, although he credited the Pirates for doing the little things required to win the World Series, admitted in a book he wrote and had published in 2012, that he still had not gotten over the Yankees' loss to Pittsburgh.

> The outcome shows that they had the better team for the Series, though I still firmly believe that we had the better team that season. Contributing to our feelings was the fact that we had absolutely dominated the three games we'd won.
>
> Yet they had won the close games, and won one more time than we did. That goes to show how important it is in tight games to do the little things. That's what Pittsburgh was doing in the close games in that Series, and that's why they won the championship.[2]

"Had 'Em All the Way"

Arthur Daley of the *New York Times* called the Pirates "Destiny's Darlings." He wrote about how a double-play ball was spitefully steered by Dame Fortune so that it struck a pebble and leaped at the throat of Tony Kubek.[3]

While it is true that the Yankees overwhelmed the Pirates on the seven-game scoreboard and in the scorebook, it is also a fact that Pittsburgh did not play its best baseball in the World Series. Not many people mentioned that. Since New York's dominance on paper was so well documented, it is only fair to say that the Bucs' numbers were not an accurate barometer of the way they had played for 155 games. Most of them did not have a good Series, yet they still found a way to win more games than the Yankees. Mazeroski was the most productive Pirate, batting .320 with two doubles, two home runs, and five RBI. Virdon matched him for the team lead in runs driven in and had three doubles, while batting .241. Clemente hit safely in all seven games and had nine hits in all, but every one of them was a single. He knocked in three runs, the same as Hoak, who batted .217. Groat managed to hit just .214. Stuart, the club's main power source, did not have an extra-base hit and batted .150 without even one RBI. The catchers did not contribute much until the final game, when Burgess had two hits and Smith came off the bench to launch his tremendously clutch pinch three-run homer.

In the end, the Pittsburgh Pirates won the 1960 World Series because they found a way. It included a fairy tale home run by a second baseman always known for his defense; stout-hearted performances from two pitchers, one a starter and the other a reliever; and the belief by everyone wearing white vests and black sleeves that they just couldn't be defeated.

There is an old saying that it isn't so much how you reach a destination, it's just that you get there. The Pirates were a prime example.

Bob Prince kept saying all season of his beloved Buccos, "We had 'em all the way."

It turned out he was right.

Nineteen
How It All Happened

The Pittsburgh Pirates won the 1960 National League pennant with a 95–59 record, a .617 winning percentage, that left them seven games ahead of the second-place Milwaukee Braves and nine in front of the St. Louis Cardinals, who finished third.

The Pirates never suffered through an extended losing streak. Their longest was four—twice—and they dropped three in a row five times. They had 13 winning streaks of three or more games. Their longest was nine games, starting in late April and going through the first day of May. They won seven straight once, six in a row twice, five straight twice, and four in a row five times.

The Pirates never seemed to be out of a ball game. They started a trend of coming from behind early in the season and kept it up. Thirty-three of Pittsburgh's wins came after it trailed or was tied in the seventh inning or later. The Bucs won with timely hitting, not with power or speed. Their .276 team batting average was the best in the league, their 120 home runs placed them sixth in that category, and the 34 stolen bases they mustered were dead last. They posted the National League's highest on-base percentage of .336 and struck out the fewest times, 747. In the all-important runs scored department, Pittsburgh led the league with 734, 10 more than power-laden Milwaukee.

The Pirates certainly did it with pitching and defense. Their staff 3.49 earned run average was third in the league, their 2.5 walks per nine innings ranked first, and their 47 complete games were third-most in the NL.

Pittsburgh, with Bill "No Touch" Mazeroski in the middle of most of them, turned the most double plays in the league, 163. The team tied for the highest fielding percentage of .979 with Los Angeles and Cincinnati.

"Had 'Em All the Way"

Pittsburgh's record at home was 52–25; on the road it was 43–34. The Pirates were 26–22 in one-run games and 12–5 in extra-inning games. They went 11–3 in April, 16–11 in May, 15–11 in June, 15–14 in July, 21–10 in August, 15–10 in September, and 2–0 in October. Pittsburgh's record against each club: Chicago, 15–7; Cincinnati, 16–6; Los Angeles, 11–11; Milwaukee, 13–9; Philadelphia, 15–7; St. Louis, 11–11; San Francisco, 14–8. The Pirates swept 16 series, lost 12, split eight, and got swept four times.

Four of their seven everyday players played 140 or more games, led by third baseman Don Hoak, who played all 155. Second baseman Mazeroski played 151, left fielder Bob Skinner 145, and right fielder Roberto Clemente 144. Shortstop Dick Groat, despite missing three weeks with a broken bone in his wrist, played 138. The eighth position, catcher, was shared by Smoky Burgess, who played in 110 games, and Hal Smith, who played 77.

Groat led Pittsburgh and the National League with a .325 batting average. He topped his team with 186 hits. Skinner led the team in extra-base hits with 54, including a team-leading 33 doubles. Hoak had 49 extra-base hits, first baseman Dick Stuart 45, and Clemente 44. Stuart led the Bucs in home runs with 23. Clemente led in RBI with 94, Skinner had 86, Stuart 83, and Hoak 79. Bill Virdon and Hoak shared the triples lead with nine. Hoak led in runs scored with 97, Clemente had 89, and Groat 85.

Vernon Law won the Cy Young Award. (Only one was given each year in the major leagues until 1967.) His 20–9 record, 3.08 ERA, and 18 complete games in 271⅔ innings also helped him to be named *The Sporting News* "Pitcher of the Year."

Bob Friend, who was 18–12, led Pittsburgh with 275⅔ innings pitched, 183 strikeouts, and four shutouts. He threw 16 complete games. Elroy Face led the National League in appearances with 68 and saved 24 games, second in the league.

Several Pirates improved considerably over their 1959 seasons. Friend was named National League "Comeback Player of the Year" after raising his win total by 10 and his strikeouts by 79, while lowering his ERA by almost a whole run. Clemente, staying healthy, played 39 more games than the year before, while driving in 44 more runs and lifting

NINETEEN. How It All Happened

his batting average by 18 points. Groat raised his batting average by 50 points and Mazeroski increased his by 32. Skinner knocked in 25 more runs, Hoak 14.

Here is a look at Pittsburgh pitchers' records against each National League team:

Law (20–9)—Chicago 1–1, Cincinnati 4–1, Los Angeles 5–1, Milwaukee 0–1, Philadelphia 4–2, St. Louis 5–2, San Francisco 1–1.

Friend (18–12)—Chicago 3–3, Cincinnati 2–2, Los Angeles 2–1, Milwaukee 3–1, Philadelphia 4–1, St. Louis 2–2, San Francisco 2–2.

Haddix (11–10)—Chicago 1–1, Cincinnati 0–1, Los Angeles 0–0, Milwaukee 4–2, Philadelphia 2–2, St. Louis 1–3, San Francisco 3–1.

Mizell (13–5)—Chicago 6–1, Cincinnati 2–1, Los Angeles 0–1, Milwaukee 1–0, Philadelphia 1–0, St. Louis 0–1, San Francisco 3–1.

Face (10–8)—Chicago 2–0, Cincinnati 2–0, Los Angeles 2–2, Milwaukee 1–3, Philadelphia 1–1, St. Louis 0–2, San Francisco 2–0.

Green (8–4)—Chicago 1–0, Cincinnati 1–0, Los Angeles 1–1, Philadelphia 2–1, St. Louis 2–1, San Francisco 1–1.

Gibbon (4–2)—Cincinnati 1–0, Los Angeles 0–1, Milwaukee 1–0, St. Louis 1–0, San Francisco 1–1.

Labine (3–0)—Milwaukee 1–0, Philadelphia 1–0, San Francisco 1–0.

Giel (2–0)—Chicago 1–0, Milwaukee 1–0.

Cheney (2–2)—Cincinnati 2–0, Los Angeles 0–1, San Francisco 0–1.

Witt (1–2)—Los Angeles 1–0, Milwaukee 0–1, St. Louis 0–1.

Harvey Haddix beat second-place Milwaukee four times in 1960. The little left-hander won 11 games during the regular season and posted two more victories in the World Series. "The Kitten" was an outstanding fielder and a good-hitting pitcher who helped himself in a lot of ways.

Francis (1–0)—Cincinnati 1–0.

Umbricht (1–2)—Cincinnati 0–1, Los Angeles 0–1, Philadelphia 1–0.

Daniels (1–3)—Cincinnati 1–0, Los Angeles 0–2, Milwaukee 0–1.

Breaks—some call it luck—always play a part in winning and losing. It might be a bad bounce, a close call by an umpire, weather that helps or hampers, or any number of things. It could even be the schedule. Over the final two months of the 1960 season, the "Dog Days," the Pirates were fortunate to play 36 games at home. That might have provided a lift down the stretch. Perhaps it was one of the reasons Pittsburgh won 42 of its last 64 games.

Normally, Most Valuable Player awards are based on stats, with a team's success weighed heavily in the mix. The theory is that enormous numbers for a player on a last-place or second-division team don't mean as much as lesser numbers that helped win a pennant. (The saying that comes to mind is, "We could have finished last without you.") In the 1960 MVP voting, intangibles probably played as big a part as tangibles. Groat was a terrific leader; no player was smarter in terms of positioning. At shortstop, he did what managers hope all players will do: make the routine plays consistently. He could handle the bat like nobody's business. He was Mr. Hit-and-Run. A look at Groat's offensive statistics does not inspire immediate MVP thoughts—.325 batting average, 50 RBI, .371 on-base percentage, .394 slugging percentage, 26 doubles, four triples, two home runs. Groat garnered 276 points in the voting done by the Baseball Writers' Association of America before the World Series began. Hoak was a distant second with 162 points, followed by Willie Mays, Ernie Banks, and St. Louis reliever Lindy McDaniel. Ken Boyer and Law tied for sixth place, and Clemente was eighth with 62 points.

When Clemente voiced his displeasure over the voting, it was widely interpreted that he felt he should have been the National League's MVP. He never said that. His complaint was in receiving so few points and placing so far down in the balloting. Groat was deserving of the MVP, Clemente said years after the World Series, adding that he never said he was more worthy. What Clemente always said was that he thought he should have received more votes for what he did for the

Nineteen. How It All Happened

Pirates. "Dick, Don [Hoak], Vernon [Law] ... they all had great years and were big reasons Pittsburgh won the National League title and then the Series," the right fielder said, but "so was I." He just wanted the writers to notice that was true. He wanted to be recognized for the player he was.[1]

It was hard then, and is hard now, to disagree with Clemente. He batted .314, hit 16 home runs, and, most importantly, drove in 94 runs. Early in the season, he gathered clutch RBI in bunches, getting the crucial hit for Pittsburgh time after time. Not all of Clemente's weapons were offensive. His rifle arm cut down 19 runners, and there is no telling how many others were discouraged from trying to score or advance. They dared not risk being shot down. His speed enabled him to get to drives headed for gaps or walls. He often made sensational catches that turned runs into outs and potentially big innings into dismissed threats. The argument is not with Groat being the MVP. But Clemente certainly warranted more respect in the voting than what he received. It was a personal affront that one of the beat writers for a Pittsburgh newspaper openly campaigned against Clemente, saying that he did not warrant MVP consideration.

When taking a second look at the MVP voting, it should be noted that Groat's selection was representative of his team in a way, a vote for the Pirates' playing style, the manner in which they won all season. And in the World Series. As Bobby Richardson pointed out in discussing the Bucs' World Series triumph, they did the little things and did them well, and they did them consistently.

Groat said the same. "There is something unique about winning ball clubs. We all had roommates, yet we all palled around together. You could go out and have a beer after a game with anyone on the team. There were no cliques. We were a very, very close-knit team, which helped us win, and winning made us even closer. We'd stay close for the rest of our lives."

Groat said Pittsburgh wasn't a big drinking team or a heavy card-playing club. Forget poker. That was a no-no. Murtaugh had a cut-and-dried rule against poker; he said gambling made for hard feelings. So the Pirates played a lot of hearts and gin, but not for high stakes. Groat played bridge with Elroy Face. The shortstop said players knew the guys who were going to be goofy and kept tabs on them. Sometimes two or three players would get in a cab and go get them out of trouble, before somebody had them drawn and quartered. Those things would happen, and that was part of being a team.

Ballplayers were targets, Groat said, especially if they were well known, so they had to be very, very careful. He believed they had to set good examples for kids. Kids could have done worse, he said, than looking up to guys like Bill Mazeroski and Bill Virdon and others on that team.[2]

Looking back at the 1960 Pirates more than 50 years later, Groat said, "It was a very unique ball club. We were friends ... good friends." Several of them—Bill Mazeroski, Roy Face, Bob Friend, Vernon Law, Bill Virdon, and Bob Skinner—get together now. They liked each other. Many times, they would go out to dinner, and there would be 10 or 12 of them.

When you go through a pennant race together, Groat said, it makes you closer, and the Bucs were already pretty close. But, he added, those times when you are trying to hold on and win a pennant and you go through some tough times, maybe a losing streak or two, those times bond you closer together, and you never forget those times. There wasn't any question, Groat said, that Clemente was the most talented player on the team. And he had a big year. But everybody on that team did things that contributed to Pittsburgh winning the National League pennant. Players picked each other up. Two or three might be in a slump, and there would be a guy coming off the bench with a big hit or driving in big runs. Or somebody who had not been hitting much got hot when others weren't.

The 1960 Pirates knew how to play baseball, said Groat, who stressed that they knew how to produce a run; they could scramble. They did all the little things. Somebody would hit a ground ball to the right side and move a runner over to third. Then they would get a fly ball, and there ... they had a run.

One thing people didn't realize was that the Pirates were an excellent base running team. They did not have a lot of speed and didn't steal a lot of bases, Groat conceded, adding that there is so much more to base running and that the Bucs seldom made a base running blunder.

NINETEEN. *How It All Happened*

They went from first to third on a single, took good leads so they could do that and so they could score from second base on a hit. They could bunt, Groat said, and the team had hitters who used the whole field rather than trying to pull the ball all the time and thinking about home runs.[3]

Guys on the 1960 team actually liked each other, Dick Schofield said, and enjoyed being around each other. But the personalities of the individuals—and the personality that gave the team—made the relationships special. The infielder stressed that there were some fantastic people on that club. Not just fantastic ballplayers, but terrific people. He said everyone wants to play, and sometimes those who don't play as much as they think they should can cause problems and that jealousy can rip a team apart. He didn't think the Pirates had that. He knew guys on the bench would like to be out there every day, but there was no resentment. Everyone on the team appreciated everybody else. Schofield said the guys in the regular lineup appreciated the players who came off the bench and appreciated hits or plays they made in taking the place of the starters, whether for a day or a week. He said the 1960 Pirates were just a special team.[4]

The Bucs had guys who came in and made a contribution, Bob Friend said. There would be somebody different getting the big hit almost every day. He said it was funny how that works, almost like it's contagious. Someone would replace a regular in the lineup because of an injury or something, and that guy would get a clutch hit or make a play in the field that saved some runs. It was just one of those seasons where everything seemed to fall into place.[5] When a team is winning like the Pirates were, players can't wait to get to the ball park, Friend said. Every day was fun. After winning early in the season and rallying for victories became almost a habit, the Bucs expected to win.

Everyone knows frame of mind plays a very large role in sports, providing a foundation for success or failure. The Pirates' frame of mind was excellent. "We would wonder, how the hell are we going to win it tonight?" Friend said. "What doggone thing are we going to do to win this one?"[6] The Pirates came from behind to win so often that it got to where they expected it, said Friend, who pointed to Easter Sunday as

"Had 'Em All the Way"

the building block. Winning the second game the way Pittsburgh did to sweep that doubleheader from Cincinnati set the stage for the whole season.[7]

There were probably two key days for the Pirates during that 1960 season. One was the Easter Sunday to which Friend referred. The Bucs had won the first game of the April 17 doubleheader at Forbes Field behind Friend's four-hit shutout. They trailed, 5–0, in the second game going into the ninth inning. After one out, the Pirates put together three hits, and a Hal Smith pinch-hit home run brought them within a run. After the second out, there was another base hit before Skinner unloaded a two-run, game-winning blast. It wasn't just a miraculous win, though it was surely that; it was a mental boost, showing the team that just about anything was possible. Again and again, the Pittsburgh players would use the memory of that tremendous rally to stage more comebacks.

The second key day for the Pirates came on July 25. The previous day, they had fallen out of first place—though only by percentage points behind Milwaukee—for the first time in eight weeks. The Bucs responded with a four-game winning streak that put three games between them and the Braves. Pittsburgh was in first place to stay.

Memories of 1960 are happy ones. Seeing a city caught up in the euphoria of remaining in the thick of a pennant race for six months can be a thrill for players as well as fans. "The city of Pittsburgh was cranked up almost from the start of the season," Schofield said. Big crowds came out to Forbes Field to see the Pirates play, and there was an excitement in the air the whole summer. At the ball park and downtown. It's always fun going to the ball park when you're winning, but when the fans add to that excitement, players can't wait for the next game. Especially the home games. All of that made for a wonderful summer and a wonderful season, according to Schofield. He said that what the Pittsburgh Pirates accomplished was amazing and they did it as a team; they were truly a team in every sense.[8]

There are times that teams put together extraordinary seasons, and afterward it is said that many of the team's players had "career years." That wasn't the case with the Pittsburgh Pirates in 1960. While a few enjoyed seasons that were not again matched, there was a larger number

Nineteen. How It All Happened

of the Bucs who had good, but not great years. It was more that they came up with big games, or at-bats, or catches, or throws, or pitches, when they were most needed. A bunch of players having a good year made for a great season.

And that is how it all happened.

Twenty

What Next?

Danny Murtaugh was named National League "Manager of the Year" late in 1960. Casey Stengel was fired.

Stengel met with the press and uttered his famous response to being let go by the Yankees, coldly dismissed after leading New York to 10 American League pennants and seven World Series championships in a 12-year period. "I'll never make the mistake of being seventy again," said the Old Perfessor, who had his 70th birthday during the 1960 season.[1]

Murtaugh quietly looked forward to more good times with a Pittsburgh club he felt would only get better. The Pirates were young, their eight regular position players averaging under 30 years of age and their starting rotation just 31.

Things change, though. Injuries, off years, and another team's turn in the sun. One of the Bucs' biggest positives in 1960 was one of their biggest negatives in 1961. Vernon Law, the incumbent ace of the staff, experienced shoulder problems that limited him to 59⅓ innings. He was 3–4 with a 4.70 earned run average. Dick Groat's batting average fell 50 points from the year before. Bob Skinner hit just three home runs and drove in less than half as many runs as in 1960. Once reliable bench players, Rocky Nelson and Dick Schofield both batted under .200. Hal Smith contributed only three homers and 26 RBI.

Roberto Clemente blossomed, winning his first National League batting title with a .351 average, with 201 hits, including 23 home runs, and scoring 100 runs. Dick Stuart enjoyed his best season as a Pirate. Don Hoak, Bill Mazeroski, and Smoky Burgess all had solid seasons.

However, the Bucs' pitching fell apart. Bob Friend sank to 14–19, Vinegar Bend Mizell to 7–10 with a bloated ERA of 5.04, and Elroy Face

Twenty. What Next?

went 6–12. Earl Francis tried to take up some of the slack, but had a 2–8 record in 15 starts. Lefty Joe Gibbon was a bright spot, going 13–10 with a 3.32 ERA in 29 starts.

The 1961 Pirates' record was 75–79. They finished in sixth place in the National League, 18 games behind pennant-winning Cincinnati. Just three years after winning the World Series, the Pirates ended the 1963 season in eighth place, with only expansion teams New York and Houston below them in the standings. By 1965, only eight players were left on the Bucs roster from 1960. Pittsburgh would not return to the World Series until 1971. By that time, Clemente and Mazeroski were the only members of the 1960 world championship team still remaining with the Pirates.

Forbes Field survives today in bits and pieces. A section of the ivy-covered outfield wall stands beside the University of Pittsburgh Katz Business School. Across the street, inside the main lobby of the Forbes Quadrangle building, home plate from Forbes Field is encased in Plexiglas and set into the floor.[2]

The last game played in Forbes was on July 28, 1970, as Pittsburgh downed the Chicago Cubs, 4–1, to complete a doubleheader sweep. Fittingly, Bill Mazeroski got the last hit by a Pirate—a seventh-inning double—and also recorded the final out in the stadium. The second baseman fielded a ground ball off the bat of Don Kessinger and ran to the bag to force Willie Smith.

The Pirates played their first game in Three Rivers Stadium on July 16, 1970. They moved into their current home, PNC Park, for the start of the 2001 season, with the first official game on April 9 against Cincinnati.

Following are capsule reports of what happened to the members of the 1960 Pittsburgh Pirates.

GENE BAKER—Played nine games with the 1961 Pirates before being released in June. That same year, the Bucs named him the manager of their Batavia farm team, making Baker the first African American manager in organized baseball. He was a coach for the Pirates in 1963 and was later a scout for the team. He died in 1999 at the age of 74.

JOE L. BROWN—Was the Pirates' general manager for 21 years,

1956–1976, and in an interim capacity in 1985. He died in 2010 at the age of 91.

SMOKY BURGESS—Stayed with the Pirates until they waived him in September of 1964. The Chicago White Sox picked him up, and he hit a game-tying, pinch-hit home run in his first time at bat for them. He played for the Chisox through 1967, then worked as a scout and minor league hitting instructor for the Atlanta Braves. He had 145 pinch hits in his career, 16 of them home runs. He was inducted into the Cincinnati Reds Hall of Fame and the North Carolina Sports Hall of Fame. Burgess died in 1991 at the age of 64.

TOM CHENEY—Pitched briefly for the Pirates in 1961 before they traded him to the expansion Washington Senators. He had a couple of pretty good seasons for them (7–9, 3.17; 8–9, 2.71). In 1962, Cheney pitched a 16-inning complete-game victory over Baltimore, striking out 21 batters. Arm trouble ended his career when he was 31. He died in 2001 at the age of 67.

JOE CHRISTOPHER—Was a part-time outfielder for the Pirates in 1961 before the New York Mets took him in the expansion draft. Christopher played with the Mets for four years. His best was 1964 when he played in 154 games and batted .300 with 16 home runs and 76 RBI. He was out of baseball two years later at the age of 30. In retirement, his main interest has been art.

GINO CIMOLI—Was traded to Milwaukee in June of 1961 and went on to play for Kansas City, Baltimore, and California. His best season was 1962 with the Athletics when he played 152 games, batting .275 with 15 triples, 10 home runs, and 71 RBI. His career ended in 1965. Cimoli was 81 when he died in 2011.

ROBERTO CLEMENTE—Played his entire 18-year career with Pirates, batting .317 lifetime with 240 home runs and 3,000 hits. His 3,000th came on his last time at bat in 1972. The following New Year's Eve, Clemente died in a plane crash as he headed a relief mission to Nicaragua. He was 38 years old. He won four batting titles and 12 Gold Glove Awards, and he was named the National League MVP in 1966 when he hit .317 with 29 homers and 119 RBI. He was the MVP of the 1971 World Series as Pittsburgh defeated Baltimore. He had a hit in all 14 World Series games in which he played. His arm has been rated the

Twenty. What Next?

best all-time among outfielders. He had 266 career outfield assists, recording 19 or more four times. Clemente was inducted into the Baseball Hall of Fame in 1973 after a special election.

ELROY FACE—Pitched 15 of his 16 big league seasons with the Pirates, appearing in 848 games, 821 in relief. He had a 104–95 lifetime record with 193 saves and a 3.48 ERA in 1,375 innings. Face pitched in 55 or more games nine years in a row, including 68 twice. He led the National League in saves three times, with a high of 28 in 1962.

BOB FRIEND—Pitched 15 of his 16 major league seasons for the Pirates. He worked 200 or more innings 11 years in a row, averaging 255 innings per season during that time. He won 22 games in 1958 and twice won 18. He also lost 19 twice. Friend always took the ball, averaging 31 starts and making 42 in one year, 38 in two others. Considering some of the teams on which he played, his 3.58 career ERA is far more indicative of the kind of pitcher he was than was his 197–230 record. He was the Bucs' player representative for 10 years and the National League player representative for five. Perhaps more than anyone, Friend was the face of the Pittsburgh Pirates for a decade and a half (1951–1965). He worked nine years as the controller for Allegheny County (of which Pittsburgh is the county seat) and has been a delegate to the National Republican Convention. He was inducted into the Indiana Baseball Hall of Fame. He lives in Pittsburgh.

JOE GIBBON—Started 107 games for Pittsburgh over his first six years in the majors. Traded to San Francisco, he spent three seasons and the early part of a fourth with the Giants before being dealt back to the Bucs. Over two years, Gibbon appeared in 76 games for Pittsburgh, all out of the bullpen, going 5–2 with 14 saves. The left-hander finished up a 13-year career with Cincinnati and Houston. He was later the baseball coach at Clark College in Newton, Mississippi.

FRED GREEN—After being an instrumental part of the Pirates bullpen in 1960, the lefty pitched in only 26 more games in his career. He was finished early in 1963. During the 1960 season, Green hit two home runs, putting the ball in play only twice in his other 15 big league at-bats. He died in 1996 at the age of 63.

DICK GROAT—The 1960 National League MVP played two more years with the Pirates before they traded him to St. Louis. His first season with the Cardinals, 1963, was probably Groat's best in a 14-year major league career. He batted .319, had 43 doubles to lead the league, 11 triples, and six home runs among his 201 hits, driving in 73 runs. He placed second in the MVP voting. He then helped the Cards win the pennant and World Series in 1964. Groat played a full season in Philadelphia and finished out in 1967 with San Francisco, ending with a .286 lifetime batting average and 2,138 hits. He was inducted into the College Basketball Hall of Fame in 2002. He has served as color commentator for radio broadcasts of University of Pittsburgh basketball games since 1979.

HARVEY HADDIX—Pitched for the Pirates through 1963, making 22 starts and winning 10 games in 1961. The little left-hander finished out a 14-year career in Baltimore strictly as a reliever. His lifetime numbers included 136 wins, a 3.63 ERA, and, as one of the better hitting pitchers, a .212 batting average. Haddix's last season was 1965. "The Kitten" coached for the New York Mets, Boston, Cincinnati, and Cleveland, and he was the Bucs' pitching coach when they won the 1979 World Series. He was 68 when he died in 1994.

DON HOAK—Played two more years with the Pirates, hitting a career-high .298 in 1961. He was traded following the 1962 season to the Phillies, who released him in May of 1964. "The Tiger" had a lifetime batting average of .265 over 11 seasons. He did some broadcasting for the Bucs and then managed in their farm system for two years. Hoak died in 1969 at the age of 41.

CLEM LABINE—Pitched in 56 games for the 1961 Pirates, posting a 4–1 record with eight saves and even starting once. He finished the next year, appearing in three games for the New York Mets before being released in May. Labine's 13-year record was 77–56 with 96 saves, 70 of the wins and 83 of the saves coming with the Dodgers of Brooklyn and Los Angeles. He died in 2007 at the age of 80.

VERNON LAW—Pitched his entire 16-year career with the Pirates. After shoulder problems limited him to 59 innings in 1961, he managed a 29–29 record over the next four seasons. In 1965, at the age of 35, he threw 217 innings, 13 complete games, and four shutouts. Law went 17–9 with a 2.15 ERA that was third-lowest in the National League, earning "Comeback Player of the Year" honors. His lifetime record was 162–147 with a 3.77 ERA. "The Deacon" had good hitting numbers for a pitcher

Twenty. What Next?

with a .216 average, 11 home runs, and 90 RBI. His son, Vance, played in the major leagues for 11 years, two with Pittsburgh.

LENNY LEVY—Was a Pirates coach six years, the last in 1963. He died in 1993 at the age of 79.

BILL MAZEROSKI—His life has been defined, to a great extent, by that ninth-inning, game-winning, World Series–deciding home run in 1960. Some have even said that singular feat put him in the Hall of Fame. Baseball purists would argue that defensive superstars deserve to be in Cooperstown, too, and Maz is considered by many to be the best second baseman ever with the glove, unparalleled on the double-play pivot. Playing his entire 17-year career with the Pirates, he drove in more than 80 runs twice and batted .260 lifetime, while almost always hitting eighth in the order. His jersey No. 9 has been retired, a street outside PNC Park, where the Bucs now play, is named Mazeroski Way, and a bronze statue of him stands on that street. He has served as an instructor in spring training with the Pirates over the years.

WILMER "VINEGAR BEND" MIZELL—Pitched 100 innings in 1961, which was a terrible year for him. He threw 54 innings the next season, when the Pirates traded him to the New York Mets. They released him in August, nine days before his 32nd birthday. His nine-year record in the majors was 90–88. Mizell was elected in North Carolina to the United States House of Representatives in 1968 and served seven years. He worked in the commerce and agriculture departments and in veterans affairs under Presidents Gerald Ford, Ronald Reagan, and George Bush. He was the executive director of the President's Council on Physical Fitness and Sports during the Bush administration. He died in 1999 at the age of 68.

DANNY MURTAUGH—Managed the Pirates four different times, totaling 1,115 wins. In 1971, he took the Bucs to the World Series, where they defeated Baltimore in seven games. Murtaugh's No. 40 was retired by Pittsburgh in 1977, the year after he died at the age of 59.

SAM NARRON—Was the Pirates' bullpen coach through 1964. He died in 1996 at the age of 83.

ROCKY NELSON—After reaching the height of his career with his seventh-game homer that helped the Pirates win the 1960 World Series, he struggled the next season, which was his last. The three-time

International League MVP played parts of nine years in the majors with five teams, three of them twice. His lifetime stats included 31 home runs and a .249 batting average. Nelson died in 2006 at the age of 81.

FRANK OCEAK—Was the Pirates' third-base coach in 1960 and 1971. He coached 11 years in the majors. He died in 1983 at the age of 70.

BOB OLDIS—Got five at-bats for the 1961 Pirates and was sold to Philadelphia after the season. In two years with the Phillies, he saw the most action of his seven-year big league career. In 1962, he batted .263 and hit his only home run. A backup catcher who was always strong defensively, Oldis was finished following the 1963 season. He was a coach with the Phils, Montreal, and Minnesota. He began scouting for the Marlins in 2002 and was still doing that in 2014 at the age of 86.

DICK "DUCKY" SCHOFIELD—Served as the Pirates' utility infielder two more years, then as their regular shortstop most of two others, batting .246 both seasons. He was traded to San Francisco and went on to play for the New York Yankees, Los Angeles Dodgers, St. Louis (twice), Boston, and the Milwaukee Brewers. He saw action in the 1968 World Series in which the Cardinals lost to Detroit. Schofield played in more than 1,300 games in a 19-year major league career. His son, Dick, was a fine shortstop who had a 14-year stay in the big leagues. His grandson, Jayson Werth, helped Philadelphia win the 2008 World Series and is now a member of the Washington Nationals.

BOB SKINNER—Played two and a half years for the Pirates after their championship. He bounced back from a terrible 1961 start to finish strong, then continued hitting well the next season, batting .302 with 20 home runs and 75 RBI. Pittsburgh traded him to Cincinnati in May of 1963, and just over a year later, he was dealt to St. Louis. Skinner was a part-time player for the Cardinals. He walked, had a run-scoring single, and doubled in four pinch-hit appearances as St. Louis beat the Yankees in the 1964 World Series. The Cards released him after the 1966 season. In his 12-year career, he batted .277 with 103 homers. He managed Philadelphia for parts of two seasons and was a coach with San Diego, Pittsburgh, the California Angels, and the Atlanta Braves. He was inducted into the San Diego Hall of Champions.

HAL SMITH—Managed three home runs and .223 batting average in a disappointing 1961. Houston picked him in the expansion draft as

Twenty. What Next?

he became an original Houston Colt .45. He caught the first pitch (from Bobby Shantz) ever thrown in a Houston major league game. The regular catcher in the club's first season, he hit 12 home runs and batted .235. Smith played little his final two seasons, finishing a 10-year career with Cincinnati.

DICK STUART—Put up big numbers in 1961, his best season as a Pirate. He batted .301, hit 35 home runs, and drove in 117 runs. After huge dropoffs in all categories the next year, he was traded to Boston. He clouted 42 homers and knocked in 118 runs in 1963, making him the first player to have 30 home runs and 100 RBI in a season in both leagues. He had 33 homers and 114 RBI the following season, and then was traded to Philadelphia. His first year with the Phillies, Stuart slugged 28 home runs and drove in 95 runs. At 32, it was his last productive season. He made stops with the New York Mets, Los Angeles Dodgers, and California Angels before being released early in 1969. In 10 big league seasons, he hit 228 home runs. He died in 2002 at the age of 70.

VIRGIL "FIRE" TRUCKS—Was a Pirates batting practice pitcher and coach four years, the last in 1963. He scouted for the Atlanta Braves and Detroit Tigers, retiring in 1974. He pitched two no-hitters in 1952. Trucks was inducted into the Alabama and Michigan Halls of Fame. He died in 2013 at the age of 95.

BILL VIRDON—Nineteen fifty-five National League Rookie of the Year finished second in the league in batting in 1956. Enjoyed a solid 1961 season, batting .260 with 81 runs and 58 RBI out of the leadoff spot. He won his only Gold Glove Award the next year, and he played consistently well for the Pirates the rest of his career. His last full year was 1965, when he hit .279. After managing two years in the New York Mets' minor league system, Virdon returned to Pittsburgh as a coach in 1968. He also played a little, going to bat three times and getting one hit—a home run. He won 995 games and had a record above .500 in 13 years as a major league manager. His first job was with the Pirates, and he was also the skipper of the New York Yankees, Houston Astros, and Montreal Expos, the longest tenure being eight years with the Astros.

GEORGE "RED" WITT—Appeared in nine games for the Pirates in 1961 and in 13 for the Los Angeles Angels and Houston Colt .45s the next year. He was done at the age of 30, an 11–16 record not coming close to reflecting his once brilliant potential. He died in 2013 at the age of 81.

MICKEY VERNON—Was the Pirates' first-base coach in 1960, then managed the expansion Washington Senators for two years and part of a third. He returned to Pittsburgh as a coach in 1964 and also served on the coaching staffs of the St. Louis Cardinals, Montreal Expos, and New York Yankees. Vernon then worked as a minor league hitting instructor for the Kansas City Royals and the Yankees. The two-time American League batting champion died in 2008 at the age of 90.

Chapter Notes

Introduction

1. David Finoli and Bill Ranier, *The Pittsburgh Pirates Encyclopedia* (Champaign, IL: Sports Publishing, 2003), 3.
2. Ibid.
3. Richard Peterson, *The Pirates Reader* (Pittsburgh: University of Pittsburgh Press, 2003), 166.
4. Ibid., 168.
5. Jim Reisler, *The Best Game Ever* (Cambridge, MA: Carroll & Graf, an imprint of Avalon Publishing Group, 2007), xii.

Chapter 1

1. *Pittsburgh Post-Gazette*, April 12, 1960.
2. Bill Morales, *Farewell to the Last Golden Era* (Jefferson, NC: McFarland, 2011), 27–28.
3. Ibid., 53.
4. Ibid.
5. Dick Groat, interview with the author, February 23, 2007.

Chapter 2

1. Reisler, *The Best Game Ever*, xxvi.
2. Kerry Keene, *1960, The Last Pure Season* (Champaign, IL: Sports Publishing, 2000), ix.
3. Ibid., xii.
4. George Altman, interview with the author, May 30, 2008.
5. Reisler, *The Best Game Ever*, xxviii.
6. Ibid., xxix.
7. Ibid., xxvii.
8. Dick Schofield, interview with the author, April 8, 2014.

Chapter 3

1. Finoli and Ranier, *The Pittsburgh Pirates Encyclopedia*, 312.
2. Dick Groat, interview with the author, February 23, 2007.

Chapter 4

1. *Pittsburgh Post-Gazette*, April 11, 1960.
2. *New York Times*, April 11, 1960.
3. *Pittsburgh Post-Gazette*, March 6, 1960.
4. Ibid., April 12, 1960.
5. Ibid.
6. Ibid., April 8, 1960.
7. Morales, *Farewell to the Last Golden Era*, 53.
8. *Pittsburgh Post-Gazette*, April 11, 1960.
9. Morales, *Farewell to the Last Golden Era*, 62.

Chapter 5

1. Bob Friend, interview with the author, March 9, 2007.
2. Ibid.
3. *Pittsburgh Post-Gazette*, April 27, 1960.

Chapter 6

1. Finoli and Ranier, *The Pittsburgh Pirates Encyclopedia*, 451.
2. Dick Groat, and Bill Surface, *The World Champion Pittsburgh Pirates* (New York: Coward-McCann, 1961), 116.
3. John McCollister, *The Bucs! The Story of the Pittsburgh Pirates* (Lenexa, KS: Addax Publishing Group, 1998), 192.
4. Peterson, *The Pirates Reader*, 255.
5. Danny Peary, *We Played the Game* (New York: Hyperion, 1994), 365.
6. Dick Groat and Frank Dascenzo, *I Hit and Ran* (Durham: Moore Publishing, 1978), 57.
7. Perry, *We Played the Game*, 470.
8. *New York Times*, September 26, 1960, 43
9. Ibid.
10. Ibid.
11. Peterson, *The Pirates Reader*, 182.
12. Bob Friend, interview with the author, March 9, 2007.
13. Dick Groat, interview with the author, February 23, 2007.
14. *New York Times*, May 7, 1960.
15. *Pittsburgh Post-Gazette*, May 19, 1960.

Chapter 7

1. *Pittsburgh Post-Gazette*, May 23, 1960.
2. Ibid., April 26, 1960.
3. Ibid., April 30, 1960.
4. John T. Bird, *Twin Killing: The Bill Mazeroski Story* (Birmingham, AL: Esmerelda Press, 1995), 96.
5. *Pittsburgh Post-Gazette*, May 28, 1960.
6. Ibid., May 29, 1960.
7. Rick Cushing, *1960 Pittsburgh Piraes—Day by Day: A Special Season, an Extraordinary World Series* (Pittsburgh, 2010), pp. 124–125.
8. Groat and Dascenzo, *I Hit and Ran*, 61.
9. Ibid., 58.
10. Bob Friend, interview with the author, March 9, 2007.

Chapter 8

1. Groat and Surface, *The World Champion Pittsburgh Pirates*, 147.
2. Ibid., 148.
3. Bird, *Twin Killing*, 254.
4. Groat and Dascenzo, *I Hit and Ran*, 40.
5. Perry, *We Played the Game*, 293–294.
6. Bird, *Twin Killing*, 287.
7. Ibid., 8–9.
8. Ibid., 33–34.
9. Ibid., 16–17.
10. Finoli and Ranier, *The Pittsburgh Pirates Encyclopedia*, 276–77.
11. Groat and Surface, *The World Champion Pittsburgh Pirates*, 150.
12. Finoli and Ranier, *The Pittsburgh Pirates Encyclopedia*, 292.
13. Peary, *We Played the Game*, 473.
14. Bird, *Twin Killing*, 274.
15. Groat and Surface, *The World Champion Pittsburgh Pirates*, 121.
16. Groat and Dascenzo, *I Hit and Ran*, 46.
17. Ibid.
18. Ibid.
19. Groat and Surface, *The World Champion Pittsburgh Pirates*, 121.
20. Ibid.
21. Groat and Dascenzo, *I Hit and Ran*, 55.
22. Ibid., 58.
23. Dick Groat, interview with the author, February 23, 2007.
24. Dick Groat, interview with the author, February 23, 2007.

Chapter 9

1. Burt Solomon, *The Baseball Timeline*, in association with Major League Baseball (New York: DK Publishing, 2001), 582.
2. Ibid.
3. *Pittsburgh Post-Gazette*, June 19, 1960.
4. Dick Groat, interview with the author, February 23, 2007.

5. Bob Friend, interview with the author, March 9, 2007.
6. *Pittsburgh Post-Gazette*, July 26, 1960.
7. Ibid., June 28, 1960.
8. Ibid.

Chapter 10

1. Bob Friend, interview with the author, March 9, 2007.
2. Ibid.
3. Ibid.
4. Ibid.
5. *Pittsburgh Post-Gazette*, September 12, 1960.
6. Ibid.
7. Bob Friend, interview with the author, March 9, 2007.
8. Ibid.
9. Groat and Surface, *The World Champion Pittsburgh Pirates*, 133.
10. Bird, *Twin Killing*, 82–83.
11. *Pittsburgh Post-Gazette*, September 13, 1960.
12. Finoli and Ranier, *The Pittsburgh Pirates Encyclopedia,* 286.
13. Bird, *Twin Killing*, 83.
14. *Pittsburgh Post-Gazette*, September 10, 1960.
15. David Maraniss, *Clemente, The Passion and Grace of Baseball's Last Hero* (New York: Simon & Schuster, 2006), 111.
16. *Pittsburgh Post-Gazette*, September 11, 1960.
17. Bird, *Twin Killing*, 95.
18. *Pittsburgh Post-Gazette*, September 13, 1960.
19. *New York Times*, February 23, 1999.
20. Ibid.
21. Bird, *Twin Killing*, 104.
22. Mariness, *Clemente*, 114.
23. Bird, *Twin Killing*, 104–105.

Chapter 11

1. Thad Mumau, *When the Grass Turns Green* (Boone, NC: Parkway 2010), 125.
2. Ibid., 126.

3. Bruce Markusen, *Roberto Clemente: The Great One* (Champaign, IL: Sports Publishing, 2001), 9.
4. Ibid., 10.
5. Mariness, *Clemente*, 44.
6. Ibid.
7. Markusen, *Roberto Clemente The Great One*, 28.
8. Roberto Clemente, interview with the author, August 1, 1970.
9. Ibid.
10. Idib.
11. Ibid.
12. Bob Friend, interview with the author, March 9, 2007.
13. *Pittsburgh Post-Gazette*, September 13, 1960.

Chapter 12

1. *Pittsburgh Post-Gazette*, July 8, 1960.
2. *New York Times*, July 11, 1960.
3. *Pittsburgh Post-Gazette,* July 17, 1960.
4. *New York Times*, July 10, 1960.
5. *Pittsburgh Post-Gazette*, July 18, 1960.
6. Reisler, *The Best Game Ever*, 121.
7. *New York Times*, July 19, 1.
8. Ibid., July 13, 41.

Chapter 13

1. Solomon, *The Baseball Timeline*, 583.
2. Ibid.
3. Mariness, *Clemente*, 95.
4. *Pittsburgh Post-Gazette*, August 11, 1960.
5. Dick Schofield, interview with the author, April 8, 2014.
6. Bob Friend, interview with the author, March 9, 2007.
7. Dick Schofield, interview with the author, April 8, 2014.
8. *Pittsburgh Post-Gazette*, September 8, 1960.
9. Ibid.
10. Ibid.

11. Ibid.
12. Solomon, *The Baseball Timeline*, 585.
13. *Pittsburgh Post-Gazette*, September 19, 1960.
14. *New York Times*, September 19, 1960.
15. Groat and Surface, *The World Champion Pittsburgh Pirates*, 101
16. Ibid.
17. *Pittsburgh Post-Gazette*, September 26, 1960.
18. Ibid., *October 1, 1960*.
19. Ibid.

Chapter 14

1. Dick Schofield, interview with the author, April 8, 2014.
2. Dick Groat, interview with the author, February 23, 2007.

Chapter 15

1. *Pittsburgh Post-Gazette*, September 18, 1960.
2. Groat and Surface, *The World Champion Pittsburgh Pirates*, 128.
3. *Pittsburgh Post-Gazette*, September 12, 1960.
4. Ibid.
5. Dick Groat, interview with the author, February 23, 2007.
6. Finoli and Ranier, *The Pittsburgh Pirates Encyclopedia*, 478.

Chapter 16

1. *Pittsburgh Post-Gazette, October 3, 1960.*
2. Reisler, *The Best Game Ever*, 11
3. Mariness, *Clemente*, 111.
4. *Pittsburgh Post-Gazette*, October 4, 1960.

Chapter 17

1. Morales, *Farewell to the Last Golden Era*, 166.

2. Mariness, *Clemente*, 109.
3. Ibid., 111.
4. *New York Times*, October 6, 1960.
5. Mariness, *Clemente*, 114.
6. *New York Times*, October 6, 1960.
7. *Pittsburgh Post-Gazette*, October 6, 1960.
8. Dick Groat, interview with the author, February 23, 2007.
9. *Pittsburgh Post-Gazette*, October 6, 1960.
10. Ibid.
11. Ibid.
12. Mariness, *Clemente*, 117.
13. *New York Times*, October 7, 1960.
14. Mariness, *Clemente*, 116.
15. *New York Times*, October 7, 1960.
16. Mariness, *Clemente*, 119
17. *Pittsburgh Post-Gazette*, October 10, 1960.
18. Ibid.
19. *New York Times*, October 10, 1960.
20. Ibid.
21. Ibid.
22. Ibid.
23. *Pittsburgh Post-Gazette*, October 10, 1960.
24. Ibid.
25. *New York Times*, October 11, 1960.
26. Ibid., October 12, 1960.
27. Ibid., October 13, 1960.
28. Mariness, *Clemente*, 124.
29. *New York Times*, October 13, 1960.

Chapter 18

1. *New York Times*, October 14, 1960.
2. Bobby Richardson with David Thomas, *Impact Player, a Memoir* (Carol Stream, IL: Tyndale House, 2012), 103–104.
3. *New York Times*, October 14, 1960.

Chapter 19

1. Roberto Clemente, interview with the author, August 1, 1970.
2. Perry, *We Played the Game*, 470.
3. Dick Groat, interview with the author, February 23, 2007.

4. Dick Schofield, interview with the author, April 8, 2014.
5. Bob Friend, interview with the author, March 9, 2007.
6. *Pittsburgh Post-Gazette,* September 12, 1960.
7. Bob Friend, interview with the author, March 9, 2007.
8. Dick Schofield, interview with the author, April 8, 2014.

Chapter 20

1. *New York Times*, October 19, 1960.
2. Peterson, *The Pirates Reader,* p. 209.

Bibliography

Periodicals
New York Times, 1960
Pittsburgh Post-Gazette, 1960

Books
Bird, John T. *Twin Killing: The Bill Mazeroski Story*. Birmingham, AL: Esmerelda Press, 1995.

Cushing, Rick. *1960 Pittsburgh Pirates—Day by Day: A Special Season, an Extraordinary World Series*. Pittsburgh, 2010.

Finoli, David, and Bill Ranier. *The Pittsburgh Pirates Encyclopedia*. Champaign, IL: Sports Publishing, 2003.

Groat, Dick, and Frank Dascenzo. *I Hit and Ran*. Durham: Moore, 1978.

Groat, Dick, and Bill Surface. *The World Champion Pittsburgh Pirates*. New York: Coward-McCann, 1961.

Keene, Kerry. *1960, The Last Pure Season*. Champaign, IL: Sports Publishing, 2000.

Maraniss, David. *Clemente, The Passion and Grace of Baseball's Last Hero*. New York: Simon & Schuster, 2006.

Markusen, Bruce. *Roberto Clemente: The Great One*. Champaign, IL: Sports Publishing, 2001.

McCollister, John. *The Bucs! The Story of the Pittsburgh Pirates*. Lenexa, KS: Addax, 1998.

Morales, Bill. *Farewell to the Last Golden Era*. Jefferson, NC: McFarland, 2011.

Mumau, Thad. *When the Grass Turns Green*. Boone, NC: Parkway, 2010.

Peary, Danny. *We Played the Game*. New York: Hyperion, 1994.

Peterson, Richard. *The Pirates Reader*. Pittsburgh: University of Pittsburgh Press, 2003.

Reisler, Jim. *The Best Game Ever*. Cambridge, MA: Carroll & Graf, an imprint of Avalon Publishing Group, 2007.

Richardson, Bobby, with David Thomas. *Impact Player: A Memoir*. Carol Stream, IL: Tyndale House, 2012.

Solomon, Burt. *The Baseball Timeline*, in association with Major League Baseball. New York: DK Publishing, 2001.

Index

Aaron, Hank 15, 23–25, 39, 44, 90, 104, 112, 114, 121, 143
Abrams, Al 40, 56, 62, 89
Acker, Tom 158
Adcock, Joe 44, 97–98, 112, 114, 121, 138
Ali, Muhammad (Cassius Clay) 20
Allen, Mel 167
Alley, Gene 74–75
Alston, Walter 49, 84, 113–114, 149
Altman, George 24–25
Amoros, Sandy 149
Anderson, Bob 43
Antonelli, Johnny 59
Aparicio, Luis 144
Arroyo, Luis 167–168, 188
Ashburn, Richie 132, 159

Bailey, Ed 45, 48, 90, 116
Baker, Gene 31, 40, 84, 140–141, 151–152, 178–179, 211
Ball Four 119
Banks, Ernie 23–25, 82, 90, 114, 138, 143, 204
Barger, Jack 12
Barone, Dick 40
Baumann, Frank 144
Bauta, Ed 32, 39, 63
Bavasi, Buzzie 107
Beatles 20
Bell, Gus 45, 48, 90
Bench, Johnny 14, 157
Benock, Benny 170
Berra, Yogi 14, 21, 114, 162–163, 167, 171–173, 176–177, 180, 183, 185, 190, 195–196, 198, 199
Bierbauer, Lou 5
Blackburn, Ron 38, 40
Blanchard, John 184, 190, 193–194, 196

Blasingame, Don 83, 126
Boggess, Dusty 183
Borkowski, Bob 158
Bouchee, Ed 82
Boudreau, Lou 54, 87
Bouton, Jim 119
Boyer, Clete 84, 167, 171, 173–174, 193, 196
Boyer, Ken 15, 56, 90, 204
Bragan, Bobby 51–52, 78
Brecheen, Harry 97
Bressoud, Ed 83
Brewer, Jim 123, 126
Brock, Lou 24
Broglio, Ernie 128, 132, 137, 143
Brosnan, Jim 87, 118–119, 139
Brown, Joe L. 8, 28, 30–35, 40, 47, 51, 62–63, 76, 136, 150, 211–212
Bruton, Billy 135
Buhl, Bob 112, 117, 122–123, 135, 141–142
Bunning, Jim 144
Burdette, Lew 20, 44, 47, 97, 112–114, 117, 120, 123, 135–136, 138, 141, 145
Burgess, Smoky 11, 32–33, 35, 37, 40–41, 44–45, 47–48, 58, 65–67, 83–84, 89–90, 114, 117, 136, 141, 149, 151, 153, 156–159, 166, 171–172, 177–179, 183, 188, 193–194, 197, 200, 202, 204–207, 210, 212
Burgess, Tom 40
Burwell, Bill 95
Busch, Gussie 28
Busch Stadium 83, 131–132

Campanella, Roy 14, 23–24, 26, 60
Campanis, Al 105, 107
Candlestick Park 2, 83, 132–133
Cardwell, Don 20, 47, 55, 62

225

Index

Carey, Andy 184
Carey, Max 5, 6, 168
Cepeda, Orlando 15, 24, 58–59, 90, 118, 127
Cerv, Bob 180–184, 187, 189
Cheney, Tom 33, 38–39, 90, 116, 120, 180, 190, 203, 212
Christopher, Joe 30, 40, 55, 66, 113, 127, 136, 151, 178, 189, 212
Cimoli, Gino 9, 11, 33, 37, 40–41, 43–44, 555, 58, 65, 67, 84, 127, 129, 137, 148–149, 163, 166, 174, 178–179, 181, 183, 188, 196, 212
Clarke, Fred 50, 129
Clemente, Melchor 106
Clemente, Roberto 2, 7, 11–12, 14–15, 23–25, 29–30, 35, 37, 39–40, 43–45, 47–48, 54–56, 59, 61, 65–68, 73, 81, 83–84, 88, 90–91, 104–110, 113–114, 117, 122, 126–128, 130–137, 140–141, 151, 166, 171–175, 177, 181, 183–184, 186, 188–189, 194, 197, 199–200, 202, 204–206, 210–213
Cleveland Stadium 84
Coates, Jim 165, 172, 174, 196–197
Coker, Jim 64
Colavito, Rocky 28, 32
Combs, Earle 6, 14
Comiskey Park 84
Concepcion, Dave 14
Conley, Gene 47, 62–63, 72, 116
Connie Mack Stadium 139
Continental League 120, 125–126
County Stadium 2, 43, 97, 165
Cox, Glenn 106
Crandall, Del 90, 114, 136
Cronin, Joe 171
Crosby, Bing 94–95
Crosetti, Frankie 183–184, 192
Crosley Field 48, 115–116, 158
Crowe, George 89, 159
Cunningham, Joe 56
Curry, Tony 131
Cuyler, Kiki 5, 6, 168

Daley, Arthur 36, 52–54, 119, 179, 200
Daniels, Bennie 37–39, 41, 48, 57, 61–62, 85, 90, 204
Dark, Al 77–78
Dean, Dizzy 98, 188
Del Greco, Bobby 31, 64–65

DeMaestri, Joe 34–35, 184, 196–197
Demeter, Don 61
Dickson, Murry 139
DiMaggio, Joe 23
Ditmar, Art 165, 171–172, 187–188
Dominican Republic 20, 76
Dotterer, Dutch 66
Douglas, Whammy 32–33
Dressen, Charlie 49, 113, 117
Drysdale, Don 21, 43, 61, 113, 143
Duren, Ryne 168, 174–175, 189
Durocher, Leo 49, 85
Dykes, Jimmy 28

Eastwood, Clint 16
Ebbets Field 26, 165
Eckman, Charlie 71
Elliott, Bob 6
Elston, Don 156
Erskine, Carl 92
Estrada, Chuck 144

Face, Elroy 2, 7, 11–12, 30, 35, 37–38, 40, 44, 50–51, 53–54, 58–59, 64–66, 77, 82, 84, 85–88, 99–102, 114, 116–117, 121–123, 126–127, 131–134, 136–137, 139–140, 143, 166, 171, 175–176, 182, 184–189, 195–196, 199, 202–203, 205–206, 210, 213
Farrell, Dick ("Turk") 47, 65
Feezle, Stan 92–93
Fenway Park 140
Fisher, Jack 140
Flood, Curt 149
Foiles, Hank 33–35, 66
Fondy, Dee 31
Forbes Field 1–2, 7, 32, 40, 44–46, 56, 58–59, 61, 63, 81, 89–90, 117, 128–130, 141, 144, 167, 169–171, 175, 177, 192, 211
Ford, Whitey 14, 163–165, 180–182, 189–191, 193
Fornieles, Mike 88
Foster, George 14
Fox, Howie 158
Fox, Nellie 21
Francis, Earl 39–40, 90, 118, 123, 204, 210
Freese, Gene 31
Frick, Ford 120
Friend, Bob 2, 7, 11–12, 15–16, 30, 37, 38, 41, 43, 45, 47, 53, 55–57, 59, 61, 64,

226

Index

67–68, 78, 80, 82–83, 87–88, 91–94, 96, 111, 114–115, 117, 121–122, 125, 127–129, 132, 137–140, 143, 164–165, 177–179, 190, 197, 202–203, 206–207, 210, 213
Furillo, Carl 60, 149

Galbreath, John 7
Garagiola, Joe 6
Gehrig, Lou ("Iron Horse") 6, 14
Geronimo, Cesar 14
Gibbon, Joe 30, 37, 39, 41, 47, 102–103, 135–136, 178, 180, 203, 210, 213
Gibson, Bob 24–25, 86, 122, 128, 130
Giel, Paul 38–40, 46, 115–116, 203
Giles, Warren 120
Gillette 167
Gilliam, Junior 97
Ginsberg, Joe 150
Gorbous, Glen 158
Gordon, Joe 28
Gray, Dick 34
Grba, Eli 190
Green, Fred 11, 30, 38, 46, 54, 58, 65–66, 82, 102, 121, 123, 178, 181, 203, 213
Greenberg, Hank 7
Greengrass, Jim 158
Greenwade, Tom 110
Griffey, Ken 14
Griffey, Ken, Jr. 127
Grimm, Charlie 54
Groat, Dick 2, 7, 11–12, 16–18, 21–22, 26, 29, 34–35, 37, 41, 43–45, 48, 51, 53–56, 58, 65–67, 69, 71–74, 76–80, 83, 86, 88, 90, 92, 112–117, 120, 126–128, 130, 132–138, 140–143, 145–148, 159, 166, 171–172, 175–176, 178, 186, 188–189, 193–194, 196, 198, 200, 202, 204–207, 210, 213–214
Gross, Don 38

Haak, Howie 38, 107–108, 151
Haas, Eddie 114
Hacker, Warren 156
Haddix, Harvey ("Kitten") 11, 32–33, 35, 37–38, 46–47, 54, 58, 64–65, 67, 82–83, 88, 96–97, 114, 121, 125, 128, 130, 133, 137, 139–140, 148, 151, 159, 164–165, 187–188, 197–198, 203, 214
Hall, Dick 33
Hamey, Roy 30

Hamlin, Ken 33
Haney, Fred 123
Hansen, Ron 114
Hardy, Carroll 138
Hawkins, Wynn 84
Hemus, Solly 55, 127–128
Hendrix, Claude 140
Henry, Bill 45, 87, 115
Herman, Babe 94–95
Hernon, Jack 62, 133–134
Hitchcock, Alfred 20
Hoak, Don ("Tiger") 11, 16, 32–33, 35, 37, 41, 43–46, 56, 58, 65, 67, 84, 90, 112–116, 118, 123, 129, 132–135, 139–140, 143, 153, 155–156, 163, 171–172, 174, 176, 178–179, 182–183, 186–190, 193–194, 196, 200, 202–203, 205, 210, 214
Hobbie, Glenn 141
Hodges, Gil 14–15, 60, 92
Holtzman, Jerome 87–88
Home Run Derby 25
Hook, Jay 66, 118
Hopp, Johnny 30
Howard, Elston 14, 166–167, 175, 177, 179–181, 188, 190, 193
Howard, Frank 61–62, 113
Hutchinson, Fred 66, 115, 119–120

Jablonski, Ray 156
Jackson, Alvin 38–39
Jackson, Larry 43
Jackson, Randy 156
Javier, Julian 34, 40, 63–64
Jones, Sam ("Toothpick") 43, 83, 126, 158
Jones, Willie ("Puddin' Head") 139
Jordan, Niles 158

Kasko, Eddie 48
KDKA (radio station) 1, 159
Keene, Kerry 21–22
Kennedy, John F. 20
Kessinger, Don 211
Khrushchev, Nikita 192
Killebrew, Harmon 25, 34
Kiner, Ralph 6, 7
Kirkland, Willie 15, 54
Kline, Ron 33–35, 41, 53, 56
Kluszewski, Ted 154
Koenig, Mark 6, 14
Koppe, Joe 64

227

Index

Koufax, Sandy 21, 23, 61, 85, 132
Kravitz, Danny 40, 47, 55, 66
Kubek, Tony 14, 167, 171–172, 174–177, 180–181, 183, 185, 187–188, 190, 193, 195–196, 200
Kubrick, Stanley 153
Kuenn, Harvey 28
Kuhn, Bowie 104

Labine, Clem 34, 88, 102, 130–131, 133, 135, 140, 156, 163, 178, 180–181, 190, 203, 214
Landrith, Hobie 58
Lane, Frank 28, 31–32, 99
Larker, Norm 60, 121, 132–133, 137–138, 140, 143
Larsen, Don 150, 193
Law, Vernon ("Deacon") 2, 8, 11, 16, 30, 37–38, 44, 46–48, 54, 56–57, 65, 81–84, 86, 89, 94–96, 113–114, 116–117, 121–122, 125–128, 131–134, 137, 139–140, 142, 158, 164–165, 171–174, 182–184, 186, 193–196, 199, 202–206, 210, 214
Lazzeri, Tony 6, 14
Lee, Bob 40
Lee, Harper 20
Lemon, Jim 117
Levy, Lenny 215
Lewis, Buddy 98
Loes, Billy 58
Logan, Johnny 90, 138
Long, Dale 31, 127, 168, 173, 178, 186, 197, 199
The Long Season 119
Lopez, Al 113
Lopez, Hector 167, 171, 175, 188–189, 195
Lynch, Jerry 26, 116
Lyons, Al 30

Maas, Duke 174
Mack, Connie 49
Macon, Max 106
Mahaffey, Art 133
Malkmus, Bobby 138
Malzone, Frank 114
Mantle, Mickey 13–14, 21, 23, 25, 111, 114, 118, 144, 162–163, 167, 171, 175, 177–180, 182–183, 185, 188, 190, 195, 197–199

Marichal, Juan 20, 24–25, 122
Maris, Roger 14, 28, 34–35, 114, 138, 144, 162, 167, 171, 173, 175, 177–178, 180–181, 183, 185, 187–190, 193, 195–197
Martin, Billy 116, 126
Mathews, Eddie 15, 43, 90, 112, 114, 136, 141
Mathews, Fred 100
Mattingly, Don 127
Mauch, Gene 46
Mays, Willie 15, 23–25, 54, 58, 90, 104, 108, 111, 114, 117, 122, 126, 133, 138, 140, 173, 204
Mazeroski, Bill 2, 3, 8, 11–16, 18, 29, 34–35, 37, 40–41, 43–45, 48, 51, 54–56, 65, 67, 69, 70, 72–80, 82, 84, 90, 92, 113, 115–118, 132–133, 136–137, 139, 141, 143, 146, 148, 171, 173–179, 183–184, 188–189, 194, 198, 200–203, 206, 210, 211, 215
McCormick, Mike 137, 143
McCovey, Willie 15, 24–25, 54, 58–59, 118
McDaniel, Lindy 88, 204
McDevitt, Danny 84
McDougald, Gil 163, 167, 174–175, 177, 180–181, 184, 186–188, 197–198
McGraw, John 49
McLish, Cal 43–44, 66, 120, 131
McMillan, Roy 90
Mejias, Roman 55, 151
Memorial Coliseum 84
Meusel, Bob 6, 14
Meyer, Russ 156
Mitchell, Henry 40
Mizell, Wilmer ("Vinegar Bend") 11, 34–35, 63–66, 82–83, 88, 98–99, 121, 123, 125–127, 133, 135–137, 139–140, 143, 148, 164–165, 180–181, 203, 210, 215
Moon, Wally 33
Morgan, Joe 14, 24
Moryn, Walt 82, 156
Murtaugh, Danny 7, 11, 13, 30, 35, 37–39, 41, 44, 48–54, 59–60, 64, 67, 78, 82, 84, 90, 96, 112–113, 116–117, 120, 123, 125–126, 128–131, 143, 147, 154, 165–167, 173, 175, 179, 182, 184–190, 193, 194–195, 197, 205, 210, 215
Musial, Stan ("The Man") 15, 21, 23, 28, 36, 51, 86, 104, 117, 128, 132, 149, 178

Index

Narron, Sam 215
Neal, Charlie 90, 113
Nelson, Rocky 11, 32, 37, 114–115, 128, 130, 133–134, 143, 150–151, 163, 178, 194, 196, 198, 210, 215
New York Times 36, 52–54, 119, 179, 200
Newcombe, Don 23–24, 45, 119–120
1960: The Last Pure Season 21
Nixon, Richard 20

O'Brien, Eddie 31
O'Brien, Johnny 31
Oceak, Frank 116, 216
O'Dell, Billy 58, 122, 133
Oldis, Bob 33–34, 40, 58, 114, 142, 151, 216
Olivo, Diomedes 38, 40
O'Toole, Jim 139
Owens, Jim 46, 62, 64

Pafko, Andy 149
Page, Joe 101
Palmquist, Ed 132
Pellagrini, Eddie 158
Pendleton, Jim 32
The Pennant Race 119
Perez, Tony 14
Perry, Jim 144
Piche, Ron 136
Pinson, Vada 36, 45, 90, 118, 139
Pittsburgh Pirates Encylopedia 50
Pittsburgh Post-Gazette 12–13, 32, 40, 56, 62, 89, 118, 129, 133, 139, 141–142, 164, 169, 176
Pittsburgh Press 32, 67
Pizzaro, Juan 122
Plays, Stan 158
PNC Park 211
Podres, Johnny 61, 113
Polo Grounds 78
Post, Wally 65, 97, 115–116
Powers, John 32–33, 66
Pramesa, Johnny 158
Prince, Bob ("Gunner") 2, 18, 105, 110–111, 146, 157, 160–161, 167, 200
Psycho 20
Purkey, Bob 81, 115

Quinn, Joh 47, 62

Raydon, Curt 37, 39–40
Reese, Pee Wee 14, 60

Richards, Paul 167
Richardson, Bobby 14, 165, 167, 171–172, 174–186, 188, 190–191, 193, 195, 197, 199, 205
Rickey, Branch 6, 8, 12, 29–30, 35, 70–72, 78, 93–94, 100, 107–108
Ridzik, Steve 158
Rigney, Bill 85–86, 89
Roberts, Robin 21, 43, 65, 117, 130
Robinson, Brook 23
Robinson, Frank 23–24, 45, 116, 118
Robinson, Jackie 7, 14, 23, 50, 60
Roe, Preacher 26
Rose, Pete 14, 74
Roseboro, John 61, 90
Runnels, Pete 114, 143
Russell, Bill 116
Russell, Jim 30
Ruth, Babe 6, 14, 28, 104, 182
Ryan, Connie 158

Salkeld, Bill 30
Sanchez, Raul 45
Sanford, Jack 89
Sawatski, Carl 56, 86
Sawyer, Eddie 46
Schenley Park 61, 174
Schmidt, Bob 122
Schoendienst, Red 28
Schofield, Dick ("Ducky") 11, 27, 31, 37, 47, 75, 115, 129–130, 135–137, 139–140, 143, 145–148, 207–208, 210, 216
Scott, Mark 25
Secory, Frank 65–66
Sellers, Peter 153
Seminick, Andy 158
Sewell, Rip 139
Shantz, Bobby 178, 184, 195–196
Sheehan, Tom 85, 89
Sherry, Larry 84, 113
Simmons, Curt 46, 86
Singleton, Elmer 156
Sisler, Dick 158
Skinner, Bob ("Dogie") 2, 7, 11–12, 16, 29, 35, 37, 39–41, 43–48, 55, 58–59, 64–67, 82, 83, 90, 92, 111, 113–118, 122, 130, 132, 135, 137, 140, 146, 166, 171–174, 179, 194–196, 202–203, 206, 208, 210, 216
Skowron, Bill ("Moose") 14, 114, 162–

Index

163, 167, 171, 173, 180–181, 183–186, 188, 190, 194–196, 198
Slaughter, Enos 110
Smith, Frank 156
Smith, Hal R. 150
Smith, Hal W. 11, 33–35, 37, 40–41, 44–46, 48, 54, 59, 65, 67, 84, 90, 121, 132, 149–151, 159, 166, 168, 181, 193, 197, 199–200, 202, 208, 210, 216–217
Smith, Phenomenal 5
Snider, Duke 14–15, 21, 60, 111, 149, 178
Spahn, Warren 20–21, 43–44, 65, 112–113, 117–121–123, 132, 136, 138, 141, 143
Spencer, Daryl 86
Spink, J.G. Taylor 87
Sport Magazine 36, 90
The Sporting News 87–88, 131, 201
Stafford, Bill 187–188, 192, 194
Stargell, Willie 24
Stengel, Casey 49, 84, 142, 164, 167, 172–173, 177–180, 184, 186–187, 189, 192–194, 196–197, 210
Stevens, John 183
Stevens, R.C. 40
Stoneham, Horace 86
Stuart, Dick 11, 29, 37, 43–45, 47, 55–56, 58, 67, 82–85, 89–90, 113, 118, 131, 135, 137, 139, 141–143, 153–155, 160, 166, 171–172, 181, 183, 186, 188, 194, 198, 201, 210, 217
Sukeforth, Clyde 51, 107–108
Surkont, Max 168

Tasby, Willie 84
Tebbetts, Birdie 156
Terry, Ralph 142, 165, 183–184, 197–198
Thomas, Frank 32
Three Rivers Stadium 211
To Kill a Mockingbird 20
Total Baseball 75
Traynor, Pie 5, 6, 154, 168
Trucks, Virgil 217
Turley, Bob 42, 150, 163, 165, 177–179, 189, 192–194

Umbricht, Jim 37–39, 41, 44, 54, 57, 61–62, 65, 84, 90, 204
Usher, Bob 158

Vaughan, Arky 6, 143
Veach, Peek-A-Boo 5
Veeck, Bill 84
Vernon, Mickey 133, 136, 218
Virdon, Bill ("Quail") 11–12, 16, 26, 31, 34–35, 37, 39–41, 45, 52, 54, 66–67, 72, 78, 83, 90, 92, 110–111, 115–116, 120, 122, 126, 128–131, 140–141, 148, 166, 168, 171–178, 181–183, 185–186, 188, 190, 194, 196, 199–200, 202, 206, 217

Wagner, Honus 5, 6, 143
Wagner, Leon 149
Walls, Lee 31
Waner, Lloyd ("Little Poison") 6
Waner, Paul ("Big Poison") 5
Watt, Bob 106
Wayne, John 61
Welker, Herman 94–95
WGN radio station 141
Whelan, Danny 143, 165
Whisenhunt, Pete 156
White, Bill 128, 149
Wieand, Ted 45
Wilhelm, Hoyt 100
Willey, Carlton 114
Williams, Stan 84, 113, 137
Williams, Ted ("The Kid"; "The Splendid Splinter") 20–21, 23, 84, 104, 117, 131, 138, 140, 148
Wills, Maury 15, 24, 143
Witt, George ("Red") 12, 30, 37, 40–41, 47, 54, 123, 126, 178, 180, 203, 217
Woods, Jim 140
Woods, Jim ("Possum") 2, 161
Wrigley Field 54–55, 82, 122–123, 126, 131, 154, 158

Yastrzemski, Carl 23, 138